D0984204

BUSINESS
SECRETS
FROM THE
BIBLE

BUSINESS SECRETS FROM THE BIBLE

SPIRITUAL SUCCESS STRATEGIES *for* FINANCIAL ABUNDANCE

RABBI DANIEL LAPIN

WILEY

Published by John Wiley & Sons, Inc., Hoboken, New Jersey.
Published simultaneously in Canada.

Library of Congress Cataloging-in-Publication Data:

Lapin, Daniel (Daniel E.)
    Business secrets from the bible : spiritual success strategies *for* financial abundance /
  Rabbi Daniel Lapin.
        pages   cm
    Includes bibliographical references and index.
    ISBN 978-1-118-74910-4 (cloth); ISBN 978-1-118-74920-3 (ePDF);
    ISBN 978-1-118-74914-2 (ePub)
        1. Business—Religious aspects—Judaism.   2. Success—Religious aspects—
Judaism.   3. Wealth—Religious aspects—Judaism.   I. Title.
HF5388.L36   2014
658—dc23

                                                                              2013049991

Printed in the United States of America.
10 9 8 7 6 5 4 3 2 1

TO SUSAN
"Enjoy life with the wife you love all the
days of your fleeting life."
(Ecclesiastes 9:9)

Contents

Introduction

You might be wondering, Why *Business Secrets* from the Bible? Why not *Tennis Secrets* from the Bible, or *Car Racing Secrets* from the Bible, or *Beauty and Makeup Tips* from the Bible? One can find pretty much whatever one seeks within the pages of that mysterious and majestic volume that has had so much influence on the story of civilization. Over the years, many have projected onto its pages their own visions, fears, and hopes and have subsequently seen it reflect back confirmation of their convictions. Unfortunately, this has led to all kinds of misguided and invalid projections upon the Bible. The Bible can tell us much, but we cannot impose whatever we feel like upon it. The original meaning of the Bible must be preserved, even as we attempt to interpret the Bible.

But how to know the difference? Let ancient Jewish wisdom be your guide.

Meticulous meanings, diligent intergenerational transmission, and specifics laid out in the Oral Torah have helped preserve the original meanings. There is magic in what I call the Lord's language—Hebrew. Teachers of the Torah must impart a deep adherence and responsibility for original meaning on the next generation of faithful students of the

Torah. Teachers should faithfully transmit to their students exactly what they learned from their own teachers. This has been the case for generations. Thus, within the authentic chain of transmission, there has been very little distortion and almost no imposition of personal agendas.

Fortunately, you don't have to take my word for this or for any other axiomatic propositions you will encounter in this book. I will ask you to unshackle yourself from the dreadful intellectual prison of "expert-itis" and allow room for your own powers of observation and deductive reasoning. Stop worrying about whether any expert has already published what I am about to disclose.

If many of this book's propositions were already widely published, you'd be wasting your time reading my repetitive account. Instead, you will gain enormous value from many of the premises presented and espoused within this book. You may wonder if they are in fact true. This is allowed—again, use your own powers of observation and reasoning. Reflect upon what you read here, perform diligent research, and arrive at your own conclusion. Don't surrender your discernment to others, regardless of how qualified they may be. Remember, nobody cares as much about your money as you do.

I invite you to evaluate the ideas espoused in this book for yourself, because I expect some degree of resistance. You may be skeptical of, or even disturbed by, the biblical origins of some of the ideas contained herein.

For some—particularly those who are not Jewish or Christian, or perhaps not even religious—your initial instinct may be to reject this material because of its deistic or religious source. I have come to expect this, too. Many have been trained and schooled by the educational bureaucrats and propaganda professors of the academy to accept as true only that which originates from the academically anointed. Do not misunderstand me: I have the greatest of respect for authentic scholarship. But I also have disdain for the scam scholarship and bogus education masquerading as truth that is so common on American campuses these days. I have a sneaking suspicion that any course of university study that needs the word "studies" after it is most likely a waste of students' time and their parents' money. Have you ever heard of "physics studies," "mathematics studies," or "computer science studies"? No, of course not—because those are real fields. I reject the political correctness, bigotry, and prejudice that have taken an undue place in our secular-only education system.

And yet, I witness prejudice within academia against all things nonsecular. Most universities today have adopted a blind and baseless hostility toward anything biblical. This is just plain ignorant. It certainly is not education. Teaching students to utterly ignore a text so preeminent as the Bible, a text that has shaped the outlook and beliefs of countless generations of very wise and accomplished people over two millennia, is doing a colossal disservice to young people.

Perhaps you do not believe in the Bible. I want to be clear that I do not intend to exclude you. I very much still welcome you to read this book and evaluate it on its own merits. I am confident that, if you approach this work with an intellectual openness, you will find value. Even if you are not currently religious, certainly you would not consider it immaterial that billions of people do believe in the truth of the Bible. As such, certainly you would not deny that the book has had a lasting and nearly unimaginable effect upon our history and our present lives. For example, billions of people date their letters, documents, and checks with the year in this format: AD 2014. They may leave out the AD and perhaps even be oblivious to the fact that AD is an acronym for *anno Domini*, which translates to "in the year of the Lord." Whether or not someone is ignorant of the influence of Christianity and religion upon something so basic as how we measure the passage of years does not change the fact that it is a religious effect and, in a way, a daily religious observance. It does not change the fact that for very many people, we remind ourselves of our religious convictions and heritage each and every time we write a date. You ignore us at your own peril. These are the same religious people with whom you will interact in your personal and professional life as customers, vendors, fellow travelers, and so on. Surely, even as an atheist, you would want insight into how believers approach the world, numerous as we are.

For instance, I consider it important to understand the following words: "The fear of the Lord is the beginning of wisdom" (Psalms 111:10). It is sheer folly to try to attain wisdom while ignoring Him. Whether or not you believe in God, just too many people do believe in Him for you to ignore His influence in the world. In this book, we will focus on the Jewish people, my coreligionists, the people of Israel who have pored lovingly over the pages of the Bible and who have put into practice its teachings with conspicuous success.

We will focus only on those areas of the human experience that emerge organically and truthfully from the Bible—here and only here is where we will find those "secrets" of the Bible, its hidden teachings. Could someone attempt to derive principles of victory on the tennis court from Scripture? I don't doubt it, but the result would lack credibility and possess the thin unsatisfying consistency of improperly strained spinach soup. The same would go for car racing, cosmetology, and television production—the Bible has nothing specific to tell us about these subjects.

However, *business secrets* from the Bible is quite different, and that is what this book will focus on exploring.

Before I tell you why business is different, I should mention a few other topics for which invaluable information can be found in the Bible. One would be military secrets of the Bible. Why? Just think of the famous British army officer Major-General Orde Wingate, who trained the yet-to-be-founded State of Israel's army, the Haganah, during the 1930s. Wingate, a military genius, was a devoutly religious Christian, who based his strategies and tactics on the exploits of Gideon, Samson, and other biblical warriors. He would stage his attacks on Arab forces at sites of ancient biblical victories and to this day is honored in Israel as having been instrumental in its founding. Unlike the aforementioned subjects upon which the Bible does not comment directly, here we can see the clear influence that Scripture has had upon military tactics as well as the appearance of military tactics within the Bible itself. There is no stretching or distortion of the original meaning of the Scripture here.

Similarly, it would be quite plausible to study the Bible for insight into male/female relationships and marriage, the ordinary pains and problems that are an inescapable part of living, and, of course, business.

But we'd find no credible guidance in the Tanach on tennis, the culinary arts, or staging theatrical productions. What is the difference? It's that some things are a universal part of the human experience, while other things belong only to a certain time or perhaps a certain place. The game of tennis played at Wimbledon today is quite different from the tennis played by Louis X of France in the thirteenth century or from the game played by King Henry VIII in England's Hampton Court Palace 200 years later.

This does not mean that the Bible cannot be relative to your life as a person who plays tennis, of course. That ordinary, hardworking citizens now have the leisure time to regularly play a game formerly restricted to monarchs is revolutionary. This is a cultural shift upon which the Bible might be able to give us insight. Scripture certainly offers us information on how to use our time effectively and on the proper role of leisure, which is perhaps relevant to the tennis player as a human, but Scripture does not give specifics on how to best play a game of leisure, tennis included. So look not to the Bible for guidance on how to play tennis, but perhaps you might look to Scripture for guidance on the role of games of leisure, such as tennis, in your life. Do you see the distinction? Scripture seriously addresses the role of entertainment in human affairs and the biblical secrets that pertain to it, but not the *specifics* of theater, movies, circuses, or video games.

Similarly, Scripture devotes considerable space to information on male/female relationships because they have always been a part of human life in every location. The prospect of space travel has aficionados debating how these relationships would function under otherworldly conditions; these are valid discussions (though somewhat esoteric and of limited current relevance) upon which the Bible may provide truth, because the discussions are about classic male/female relationships within a new "alien" context rather than about the context itself. It is the timeless importance of male/female relationships, not the context in which they occur, that makes them a matter of Scripture.

Thus we'd correctly assume that while God might well not offer us details of lawn maintenance, carburetor rebuilding, and pottery making, He would provide us with the biblical secrets that apply to war and conflict, family relationships, transport, birth and death, farming, and, yes, money.

Which brings us to business. What is business? Simply put, business is that most effective process of specialization and exchange by means of which humans can wrest a living from an often reluctant Earth. Business is the way we interact with each other and our environment. It is thus a timeless lynchpin of civilization.

Of course, each of us could declare ourselves independent of all other people and live in isolation on a remote piece of land. We could grow our own wheat and corn. We could grow fruit and vegetables and raise chickens, goats, sheep, and cattle. We could spin and weave fabrics from wool and cotton and sew our own clothing. All of this is true and, to a degree, possible even today. Some weary urban dwellers yearn for this sort of existence, which they fondly imagine to be idyllic. But this is pure nostalgia. Almost everyone who has tried their hand at such a life has discovered it to be grueling and punishing, offering very little quality of life.

Such nostalgia makes a mockery of those who are truly trapped in such a life. True subsistence farmers and hand-to-mouth peasants typically cannot escape such a life quickly enough. In developing countries, such individuals gladly flee the grueling existence of trying to eke out a living and a life from a small plot of land as soon as they can. They flock to cities where they can sew clothing or stitch shoes. Not that the life in those hot and crowded factories is delightful—it isn't—but trading their specialized skill of sewing and stitching gives them a far superior lifestyle to the alternative of stitching, sewing, planting, milking, threshing, harvesting, milling, baking, churning, and making everything else the solitary human needs to survive. In a true subsistence life, one must do almost everything by oneself. Specialization allows these individuals to throw off the shackles of the subsistence lifestyle, and business allows them to ply their trade for profit.

Most humans, when given the chance, have discovered that life is easier and more pleasant when we abandon complete independence for specialization and exchange. Homesteading is terribly inefficient when compared to a system of specialization and exchange. If Frederick grew wheat and Gerald grew corn; if Harry grew fruit and Irwin grew vegetables; if Julia raised chickens and goats while Kirk kept cows; if Lewis turned cotton into fabric and Michael did so with wool, and Norma sewed those fabrics into clothing and then Frederick, Gerald, Harry, Irwin, Julia, Kirk, Lewis, and Michael all met once a week to exchange these goods with one another, astonishingly, all would have more of all these things with far less time, not to mention energy, expended on acquiring them. This is the power of specialization and exchange. In the late eighteenth century,

Scottish philosopher and economist Adam Smith, who was a believing Christian, popularized this understanding of the efficiencies of a specialized market economy, but Jews had already known this for millennia.

This is why you will almost never find Jews tinkering with their cars in their driveways on weekend afternoons. In the Jewish neighborhoods of most cities, you'll almost never find Jews mowing their lawns. Why? Because we understand the power of specialization. If I pay my incredibly competent mechanic to maintain my BMW automobile and if I pay the ambitious youngster down the block to mow my lawn, I thereby purchase valuable hours in which to practice and perfect my own craft or trade. Each of us accomplishes our task far more quickly than we could do individually, because we have acquired proficiency at our particular task and are able to apply efficiency by not spreading ourselves thin. By hiring them, I have more time and attention to devote to becoming better at my own trade, and I will certainly earn more money working in my own specialized trade than I will trying to save a dollar by spending my time tinkering with my car rather than paying a proper mechanic. The difference adds to my wealth. It adds to the mechanic's wealth, too. Everyone wins.

God Wants Each of Us to Be Obsessively Preoccupied with the Needs and Desires of His Other Children

As long as we all grow our own wheat and corn, and stitch our own clothes, and churn our own butter, and make our own shoes, we need nobody else. We aren't even thinking of anyone else. We're only thinking of how to find enough time in the day to grow vegetables, feed the goats, shear the sheep, and shoe the horses. This is no way to live if you don't have to, and in the modern world, we do not have to.

By contrast, when Frederick, Gerald, Harry, and friends all specialize, they are able to focus on how to better serve one another, and in doing so, they will gain more in return. The good Lord incentivizes us to increase our dependency upon each other by offering the blessing of financial abundance for those of us who comply. In other words, we each win more of a living with less effort when we specialize and trade. This process is called business.

I've already told you what business is, but not what the definition of *a business* is. This need not be made more complicated than it is. Some define a business as any organization or individual engaged in commercial, industrial, or professional activities. Others define a business as any organization involved in the trade of goods or services to consumers. While these definitions are not wrong, they are overly precise. The truth is simply that a business is any person or group of people who have customers. If you have someone willing to pay you voluntarily for the work you do, products you produce, or service you provide, then you're in business.

Everyone who works for compensation can be considered "in business." If City Transit pays you for driving a bus, you're not an employee—you're in business. Admittedly you're in business with only one customer—City Transit—but you're in business nonetheless. If you knit scarves for fun and agree to make a few for your friends in exchange for a few dollars for your time, guess what, you are in the fashion/clothing business.

The difference between the bus driver and the person who knits scarves in this example is that the bus driver makes more, in part because they have specialized. If the person who knits scarves quits her part-time retail and food service jobs to focus on growing her business, she too might make more money by specializing. By specializing in a trade, rather than doing a little of everything, she can enjoy better efficiency and more disposable income, rather than spreading herself thin. If she goes into her own business, she will find that her customers become valuable human beings to her and she will desire to please them.

Are you beginning to see why specialization and exchange are the foundations for God's plan for human economic interaction? If you care about your customers as people—if you like, appreciate, and desire to serve them—you will be rewarded. However, if you prefer to spurn others in favor of making yourself utterly independent of all other humans, your life will be considerably less pleasant. There's a reason almost no one still homesteads in the developed world. Thomas Hobbes, the seventeenth-century British political philosopher and author of *Leviathan*, who was almost certainly a Bible-believing

Puritan, once wrote that when we are alone, "the life of man [is] solitary, poor, nasty, brutish, and short."

We all sometimes think we just want to get away from everyone else. We may daydream about some calamity sweeping away everyone in the world except ourselves. We think, finally, we will be able to get a parking space downtown. There will be no traffic on the freeway. At last you'll be able to watch television without fighting with your family over who gets the remote.

This is silly daydreaming, though. Imagine if it actually happened! What if everyone did disappear? Who would be operating the television station? That remote won't do you much good if there is nothing to broadcast, no news anchors, no TV actors. What good is that parking space downtown if there is nowhere to work? And with nobody operating gas stations or oil refineries, parking will be the least of your problems! Good luck trying to capture a wild horse or donkey once you have used up all the gas in your tank! Time for dinner? Feel like a restaurant meal? Out of luck—no cooks, no wait staff. In the grocery stores, food is rotting on the shelves. At home, your heat and electricity have gone out because no one is running the utility company.

The truth is that without other people, your life becomes even worse than that of the most impoverished third-world subsistence-level peasants—at least they have one another to depend on!

The Jewish people have always known the power of specialization. But where did they learn it? From the Bible, of course! Jews have always understood specialization, as it is described in both Genesis and Deuteronomy. In chapter 49 of Genesis, verses 1 to 28, the elderly Jacob blesses his 12 sons. He could simply have gathered them and said these few words: "I am about to be gathered to my people, I bless you all with everything good. May God take care of you always, and please bury me in the Cave of Machpelah, which my grandfather Abraham prepared. Good-bye." But that's not what happened. Instead, there are 28 verses to record the distinct and separate blessings that he gave to each son.

Similarly, in Deuteronomy 33, before ascending the mountain to be shown the Land of Israel before his death, Moses spent 29 verses blessing the individual tribes. Again, he could easily have issued one comprehensive blessing to the entire children of Israel and promptly taken his leave.

The idea behind both Jacob's blessing and that of Moses was unity with diversity. Each tribe was to have its own unique niche in the rich tapestry of a durable nation. Each tribe was to have its own specialty and to become dependent upon their brethren for everything else. If one thinks about it, isn't this what all parents would like to ensure for their children? Some way of guaranteeing that they would all have remained united, each as concerned with the welfare of his siblings as with his own? The same is true for our Father in Heaven. In desiring to unify His children, He created a world that rewarded those who specialized in some area of creative work and then traded their efforts for everything else.

Compare the outlook of the solitary survivalist with that of the business professional. The former views other people as competitors and threats. By contrast, the business professional's life is intricately linked to many other people. He has to be concerned with providing goods or services at sufficient quality and at an attractive price in order to attract and serve his customers. He has to be concerned with his employees and associates because only if they are happy and fulfilled will his enterprise prosper. Finally, he needs to be concerned with his vendors who supply him with the raw material of his production, because without them he is incapable of operating. Now whom do you think God prefers: the lonesome isolationist whose slogan is "I need nobody," or the business professional active within a complex matrix of connectivity in which he is preoccupied with making life better for so many of God's other children?

An Infinite God Created Us in His Image with Infinite Imagination, Potential, Creative Power, and Desires.

Though God placed Adam in the Garden of Eden in which all was provided, He nonetheless insisted that Adam was to work (Genesis 2:15). Adam could have lived an idyllic and idle life drinking from the bountiful rivers of Eden and plucking luscious fruit as he desired from all but two trees. We shall soon see that, while a balanced life is necessary, God's plan is for man to strive to achieve more. Ambition is a good thing. We all were created to desire as much as possible, but we also wish to expend only the least possible effort. Discontentment and unhappiness are wrong, but this in no way contradicts our legitimate desire for more.

Most of us have had the experience of being teenagers and thinking, "If only I could lay my hands on three hundred dollars, I'd be so happy." As we get older, three hundred dollars quickly is no longer so unattainable for most, but we are still discontent because now we want more. The target has moved. The target, it seems, is always moving.

This may seem like greed and taken to excess, it can be a bad thing. But it is actually a powerful motivator, and drives us to do God's work, the work of living that we all depend on each other to do.

Imagine what would happen if tonight at midnight, all other humans decided that they already had enough of everything they need and no longer needed to work. From now on, they decide, they will stay home. Picture your own life in this scenario. You get up the next morning unaware that all of your fellow citizens have abandoned all ambition and are sleeping in forever. There goes your day! Good luck trying to get milk for your morning coffee: The dairy farmer and the delivery-truck driver are home in bed rather than producing and supplying fresh milk to your grocery store. It won't much matter, of course, because the grocery store will be shut down—the manager who ordinarily works the morning shift is also still at home contentedly asleep. The same goes for getting gasoline for your car, gas or electricity to cook your meals, or a new suit of clothing. The economy and all it provides has come to a screeching halt. Your fellow man's innate desire for more is what makes it possible for your own life to function as smoothly as it does. Likewise, your decision to work makes life easier for your fellow man.

As a student, I once spent a long but rewarding summer selling fine English bone china door-to-door in Europe. After a rigorous and immensely valuable training period, all of us rookie trainee sales professionals were gathered together and the manager announced that we were each to choose our preferred compensation plan. Choice A was that we received a guaranteed base salary, or draw, of $250 a week in advance against our sales and 10 percent commission on all sales. Choice B provided zero base salary or draw, but we would receive a 40 percent commission on all sales.

I did not know what to do. Not knowing how effective I would be at selling, I figured I could at least count upon a few thousand dollars if I took Choice A. This was reassuring. I was about to sign up for Choice A when all of a sudden I had an epiphany. If I turned out to be unsuccessful at selling, why would they continue to pay me $250 a week merely for trying? And if I did find myself successful at selling, why would I want to earn only a small commission of 10 percent? I thought this through again and I could think of no reason why the company would keep paying me if I failed to sell. They might pay me for a few weeks but would then surely terminate me. On the other hand, if I developed any aptitude for sales, I could do far better with Plan B. I worried about the "sure" $1,000 a month I was perhaps giving up, but surely it was not really guaranteed if I did poorly, so I went with Plan B.

We had to write our choice on slips of paper along with our names and pass them to the front where the manager's assistant quickly divided them into two piles, which I assumed to be a tall pile of the As and a much smaller pile of Bs. Picking up the larger pile of papers, he asked everyone whose name he called out to go into the next room. That was the last I ever saw of many of my former fellow trainees.

To the rest of us, he spoke warmly and congratulated us on successfully completing our training. He welcomed us into the company and explained that he wanted only ambitious men and women who yearned for unlimited potential working for him. He wanted people interested in infinite possibilities. Anyone seeking the security of a minimal $1,000 a month was not nearly as interesting to him as those of us who had ambition for considerably more. And considerably more was exactly what I did earn that summer.

It is the exciting possibility of the infinite that drives medical research to come up with life-enhancing and life-extending drugs and devices. It is the exciting possibility of the infinite that drives all technological advances. It is the exciting possibility of the infinite that drives the business professional to find ever better ways of serving more customers more effectively. It is what drives progress in the world and is surely God's will.

On some subconscious level, we humans are always trying to emulate God. One reason that television so fascinates us is that it allows us to enjoy a taste of God's omnipresence. While God can be everywhere at once, the nearest we can achieve that is to be able to sit in our living rooms and observe the activities of our fellow human beings half a planet away. Television grants us the illusion of almost godly power.

This is also true with regard to air travel. Travel by ocean liner is far more comfortable and less expensive than by jet. Yet by the 1960s, most transatlantic ocean liner services were being discontinued. Why would people forsake a leisurely, comfortable, economical three-day journey from New York to Southampton in favor of being squeezed into a long aluminum cylinder and being hurtled across continents within only a few jet-lag hours? Again, one explanation is our deep desire to try and overcome human limitations of space and time just as God does.

God created us with an urge for the infinite. We need to embrace it and never surrender to the seditious and spurious summons of contentment cowering in the sanctuary of security. Accepting our desire for the infinite doesn't condemn us to misery and unhappiness. On the contrary, rejecting contentment doesn't mean being unhappy. In a green and lush meadow on a sunny afternoon, a cow can be content. A human should never be content. Happy—yes, always. But content? Never!

Humans Alone Possess the Ability to Transform Themselves

The reality of animals is that they are what they are, and will always be so. A cat, a cow, a camel, or a kangaroo will always be a cat, a cow, a camel, or a kangaroo. But a homeless person can transform himself into a published author and successful motivational speaker. This is just what Richard LeMieux did. As he describes in his personal odyssey, *Breakfast at Sally's: One Homeless Man's Inspirational Journey*, he went from sleeping in his car and eating at the Salvation Army (Sally's) to an eventual middle-class lifestyle. An aimless teenager can get a grip on her life and become an accomplished academic, professional, or businesswoman. An immigrant can arrive in a new land with nothing but the clothes on his back and ultimately achieve greatness without ever having to feel imprisoned by the promise of permanent poverty.

In his book *The Wealth Choice: Success Secrets of Black Millionaires*, courageous author and motivational speaker Dennis Kimbro insists that wealth has little to do with birth, luck, or circumstance, but everything to do with choice, commitment to change, discipline, self-improvement, and hard work. I could not agree more. His sentiment echoes this

Jewish theme: There is no shame attached to starting out poor, but remaining that way is a different story.

I have known Jewish men who didn't have a fraction of what most others have going, and yet these men have prospered beyond anyone's wildest dreams. This is clearly not a case of "where you come from" or of "what you've got." It's a case of a deep visceral commitment to change.

In every industry, you see Jewish men who have made indelible marks on history and the economy. There's a man named William Konar who lives near Rochester, New York. Have you heard of CVS Pharmacy? He started that and owned most of it, and as you may have guessed, did pretty well for himself. There was Nathan Shapell, who was one of California's largest homebuilders. There was Jack Tramiel who, way back in the dawn of the computer age, founded Commodore Computers, which he grew into a substantial company. And how about Fred Kort, who invented those little bouncy rubber balls that every kid in the world seemed to have a few years back? Or how about the bubble machine and the stuff that makes soap bubbles? Fred Kort made those, too. He marketed these and other toys under the Los Angeles Toy Company. There was Felix Zandman, who started Vishay Intertechnology, a major electronics firm supplying the computer and aerospace industries.

These are not people who became internationally known billionaires. But they are people who have each given away millions of dollars to charity. They have all made serious money.

But there's something else that unites these people, something harrowing and nightmarish. They were all Holocaust refugees. William Konar was 12 years old when his family was uprooted from their small Polish village and carted off to the Auschwitz death camp. The last time he saw his mother and siblings was in July 1942, shortly before they were murdered by the Nazis. He witnessed more horrors than any adult, let alone a child, should ever have to endure, before arriving in the United States on a refugee boat in 1946. He was a 16-year-old orphan. He ended up in a foster home in Rochester, which, as a result, now boasts the William and Sheila Konar Center for Digestive and Liver Diseases in the city's Strong Memorial Hospital.

Nathan Shapell fled from the Germans and lived in hiding until he was finally captured and brought to the Auschwitz concentration camp in the summer of 1943. He was a teenager and, like all other inmates, destined for death. His arm was tattooed with a registration number by the meticulously bureaucratic Nazis. He bore that number, 134138, quite clearly on his forearm until the day he died in Beverly Hills in 2007. When the war ended, he was a shattered refugee and spent a few years as a DP, a displaced person, as they called it back then. He arrived in the United States in the early 1950s, and by starting from scratch by building a few houses at a time, eventually became a real estate tycoon.

In April 1945, Jack Tramiel, the emaciated and beaten 16-year-old lone survivor of his entire family from Lodz, Poland, was liberated from Auschwitz by American forces. He found part-time work with the U.S. Army in Poland and eventually made his way to New York, where he worked as a janitor for a Fifth Avenue lamp store. He joined the Army, which is where he learned to repair office machines. Upon his discharge several years later, he bought old and broken typewriters, which he repaired and sold. By the 1960s and 1970s, he was moving from office machines to computers, and he is now part of the history of the personal computer. Over the years, Tramiel and his wife, Helen (herself a survivor of the notorious Bergen-Belsen concentration camp), have given away vast sums of money.

Fred Kort was one of only nine survivors of the hundreds of thousands of Jews who were exterminated at Treblinka concentration camp. He lost his entire immediate family and 60 relatives there before arriving in the United States, penniless and destitute. He took a job at the Bendix Company and eventually began making toys. This is how he got into the toy business, where he later made his fortune.

Felix Zandman survived in a tiny hole cut in the ground beneath a peasant's hut. He lived there for several years, foraging for food in the nighttime. One of the few Jews of Grodno who survived the war, he was caught and enslaved in a Nazi factory, where he witnessed the massacre of family members. After being freed by Allied forces, he immigrated to America.

All of these men survived the unimaginable. They arrived as young refugees with scarred souls and broken bodies, but they knew one fundamental Jewish principle: The way I am today has nothing to do with what I'll be tomorrow.

The Jews knew this secret when few others did. For centuries in Britain, the socioeconomic class into which you were born was where you lived and died. In Europe, peasant girls never married princes regardless of what the fairy tales would have you believe. The situation was no different in most of Asia and all of Africa. The early Greeks saw destiny as a function of birth; Plato and Aristotle believed that some were born to rule while others were born to be ruled. The Romans also lacked any mechanism for anyone to rise in rank socially or economically.

These beliefs stunt people emotionally and intellectually. If you don't know and believe that human beings have the power, unique within nature, to utterly transform themselves, then you are fatally handicapped. How did Jews know and believe that change, growth, and transformation are the natural legacy of humans? From the Bible, of course, where there is account after account of people becoming better, kinder, stronger, more effective, more powerful, more successful people than they were before.

The Bible is full of such transformations. Consider Abraham, the first Hebrew. Wait! Before looking at Abraham, let's find out what the word *Hebrew* means. The original Hebrew word for *Hebrew* is *Ivri*, which means "one who crosses over." In other words, his badge of pride, his very identification means his willingness and ability to transform himself from someone who stands on one side of a matter into someone entirely different who takes quite a different approach. This classic term for Israelites or Jews, *Hebrew* identifies the children of Abraham chiefly as possessing this characteristic to recognize that their destiny is not engraved in stone.

Now on to Abraham.

And God said to Abram, "Leave your country, your family, and your father's house, to a land that I will show you." (Genesis 12:1)

Ancient Jewish wisdom posits a very important question here: why did God choose to issue his famous command, "Leave your

country . . ." to Abraham rather than to anyone else? There is nothing in previous passages to suggest the special suitability of Abraham.
We're told almost nothing of his life, certainly not anything that would
explain his lofty qualities. Why, then, did God choose Abraham? The
answer is that God did *not* choose Abraham. The command was offered
to everyone, but only Abraham responded. Abraham thus chose himself.

God continues to offer this command to each one of us today,
if only we will take heed. The command is not intended exclusively
for Abraham to have departed his homeland and family, although for
Abraham it did mean just that. And so it means just that to each of us.
Each of us is invited by God to depart from our comfortable situations
to which we've become accustomed, but it is up to us to take heed of
this invitation.

You can see, here and elsewhere, the Torah is not just a historic
account of long-forgotten people and anachronistic events, but it is also
a handbook to life. It is the foundation of ancient Jewish wisdom. Yes,
everyone in Abraham's generation heard God's call to reinvent himself or herself and redirect their footsteps, but only Abraham seized
upon the challenge. Similarly, each of us today has the opportunity to
clearly hear God's clarion call: "Leave your country, your family, and
your father's house, to a land that I will show you." Each of us has the
opportunity to seize the challenge. Move into a new zone in which
you can fully fulfill the potential God planted into you. You might not
yet know the destination, but rest assured God will show it to you,
though He will not do so until after you have commenced the odyssey.

We see this vitally important directive to do things a little differently today from how we did them yesterday not just in Genesis, but
also in Exodus, where a similar message is offered to us.

And an angel of God appeared to him [Moses] in a flame of
fire from inside a bush; and he looked, and the bush burned
with fire, but the bush was not consumed. And Moses said, "I
will now turn aside to see this great sight, why the bush is not
burnt." (Exodus 3:2–3)

Again the question posed by ancient Jewish wisdom here is, why
Moses? There is nothing in the earlier narrative that suggests anything

particularly outstanding about him, either. He was just a man. So what was special? I will tell you: his choice to listen to God. Hundreds of people went by the burning bush that morning and nobody else stopped to look. Nobody else was perplexed enough to ask why the bush wasn't being consumed by the fire. Moses alone was transfixed by an event that appeared to contradict his vision of normality. This mindfulness and openness towards God is what opened up Moses' life, and it is what can open up our own life as well. If we can be open to an alternative vision of normality, our lives can develop in amazingly unexpected ways.

I implore you to be open to the monumental significance of what you're reading now. Just think for a moment about what is your most important external organ for purposes of increasing your ability to generate income. Well, unless you're a swimsuit model, wouldn't you agree that it is your mouth—your ability to speak and communicate effectively?

This is one of the great things about business. You can be tall or short, male or female, black or white, splendidly hirsute or bald, it all makes very little difference. Your business success will depend upon how well you can communicate and how well you understand *what* to communicate.

Of all the handicaps Moses could have been inflicted with, he suffered from the one condition most likely to diminish his chances of success:

> And Moses said to the Lord, "O my Lord, I am not eloquent,
> neither yesterday nor the day before, nor since you have spoken
> to your servant; I am slow of speech, and of a slow tongue."
> (Exodus 4:10)

You may not know this, but Moses had a speech impediment! He really did. God accepted this as true. God didn't respond to Moses impatiently by saying, "Oh, come on, Moses. You speak perfectly well, stop making excuses!" No, instead God said, "Look, if you accept this commission and do something that is as different from being a mere shepherd than you can ever imagine, if you go ahead and transform your destiny, I as He who gives man the power of speech, will ensure that you will be able to communicate more than adequately."

Sure enough, Moses goes ahead and rescues the Hebrews from Egypt, leads them through the desert for 40 years, teaches them the Law that God gave him on Sinai, and speaks out the entire text of Deuteronomy during a month of nonstop talking, and during all this we never again hear of Moses' speech impediment. As you can see, often the obstacles we see obstructing our progress vanish once we accept God's invitation to resculpt our lives.

Nobody is saying change is easy. The Bible also provides examples of those who were simply incapable of bringing about change in their lives. For example, in chapter 19 of the first book of Kings, we encounter Elijah. God wants him to transform himself from a zealous prophet constantly criticizing Israel into a gentler prophet who guides Israel. God shows him spectacular pyrotechnic signs and soft, quiet ones, yet Elijah's response remains the same: He shows no ability to change his path, style, or life. Finally, God recognizes that Elijah is incapable of developing himself into the kind of person who could successfully fulfill his destiny, so God tells him to appoint Elisha as the new prophet who will replace him.

Often, remaining just where you are and just who you are isn't really an option. It is true that animals possess no ability to change, but humans often have no alternative but to change and grow. The alternative is not remaining where we are. Often, reluctance to transform ourselves condemns us to slide backwards.

Sometimes the change is painful, which accounts for the reluctance most people feel towards change. For example, few changes are more painful than terminating a marriage. And as anyone who has loved and lost knows, losing a loved one is indeed trying. But if you are in the wrong relationship, you must endure ending it if you are ever to move on and unite with the right person. I'm not advocating divorce as the easy solution to marital difficulties, I assure you, but if marriage can serve as a metaphor for the most productive human partnership, then its breakup can also teach us something. It is, after all, one of the hardest changes to make.

My wife and I often nursed young congregants through the heartbreak of a relationship coming to an end. Indeed, we often encouraged and hastened the good-bye, assuring our tormented friend that only by suffering the tears of breakup now could the joys of tomorrow arrive.

Henry Ford's Model T automobile first arrived in 1908. By 1914, a quarter million autos were being built each year. This was truly terrible for people who had spent years in the horse-wagon business. In the year 1900, about 110,000 people were employed building or repairing carriages and harnesses. Nearly 250,000 blacksmiths lived and worked in America that year fitting shoes on countless horses. And thousands more earned a living by sweeping tons of horse manure off city streets.

But the coming of the first mass-produced automobile meant that jobs in the horse-driven transport business quickly vanished. The end of the horse-drawn era was tough on many, but those who simply couldn't divorce themselves from the past deprived themselves of the blessings that were rolling down the new highways. There were soon far more automobiles than there had ever been horses and carriages, and along with the cascade of cars, came not thousands, but millions of new jobs. All those wagon builders, harness makers, wheel makers, horseshoe smiths, and manure street sweepers who were capable and accepting of change now had exciting new possibilities at their disposal.

The divorce that allows two people in a doomed marriage to rebuild new lives, the breakup of an empire that allows the newly sovereign nations to thrive, the demolition of a building that has fallen into disrepair so that a new building may rise in its place, the smashing of an atom releasing unimaginable amounts of energy and freeing humans from drudgery—all of these things share a common thread. Every act of breaking, changing, or separating, as painful as it always is, can launch us into something new that carries us further down the path of our own development as individuals, as a nation, and as the human family of God's children.

The Universe Was Created for Connection

R olling a 50-gallon drum of water downhill is far easier than lugging it uphill. The reason for this asymmetry is a powerful force in nature called gravity. Preventing a parked car from rolling downhill takes far less work than throwing on the same emergency brake to bring a fast-moving car to a standstill. This is due to another powerful force in nature—inertia. Now you may certainly choose to try rolling the heavy drum of water uphill. You can even try to stop a moving car with a weak parking brake instead of the power-assisted foot brake. You're free to attempt whatever you want; just know that fighting forces larger than yourself is likely to end in failure.

Perhaps instead you may choose to use a winch to haul the barrel up the hill. Perhaps you engage the foot brake to stop your car instead of futilely yanking on the hand brake. You will probably be far more likely to succeed. But a wise and experienced bystander could have confidently predicted these very outcomes without having to test out lesser tactics. The lesson is this: Success is always more likely when you are swimming with the current rather than against it.

Needless to say, there are times when we must emulate the indefatigable salmon that relentlessly fights its way upstream. In matters of principle and honor, we often must fight our way upstream. However, when it comes to finding the best way to serve our fellow humans and earn their trust, going with the stream is nearly always more effective and efficient. Trying to overcome the spiritual laws of reality is just as futile as fighting the physical laws of nature.

Connecting with other people makes for a better life—this is a law that is inextricable from the natural world. Trying to achieve happiness and fulfillment while remaining isolated from others is as futile as all other attempts to defy nature's laws. God clearly wants us to connect with one another. He wants us each to be obsessively preoccupied with serving one another. He wants us to provide for one another's needs and desires. Cynics may denounce monetary motivations as greed, but this is false thinking. The virtue of service is in no way compromised or diminished by the monetary reward received for doing so.

Just consider the case of poor "Godfrey," who is beset by seemingly insurmountable problems. Godfrey is in desperate need of a leg up. He needs some money to get himself out of a fix and start himself off on some successful path. Now we introduce him to two different people. One is a struggling good man who at considerable self-sacrifice has come up with $100 to give to Godfrey. He loves all needy people and is genuinely happy to have less this month if his $100 can help Godfrey escape his painful predicament.

The other would-be benefactor is a prosperous financier who is offering gifts of $1,000 to needy folks like our Godfrey. What is more, the prosperous financier has worked out some complicated tax loophole by means of which, not only will his gift not cost him $1,000, but he will actually receive $1,100 for every $1,000 he distributes. Lastly, we must sadly report that unlike our first benefactor who loves the needy, our affluent philanthropist could hardly care less.

Godfrey asks you for advice. Should he accept the $100 from the kind, compassionate, and caring donor, or should he go for the $1,000 from the second man who will benefit from the transaction? Surely you would not hesitate to recommend that he accept the larger gift. Now, looking at the circumstances from the other angle, which donor is doing more good? Yes, of course I accept that the former might be a better human being, though not being God, I cannot be sure of this. However, my question concerned which benefactor is doing more good. I hope that as humans with no ability to peer into the hearts of other people, we can agree that the man who is making the sum of $1,000 available is, strictly speaking, doing more good.

It is hard to dispute that he who helps more people is doing more good than he who helps only a few. Though of course I mean no disrespect to the venerable and beatified Mother Teresa of Calcutta, I do ask myself this: Who did more good for more people—Mother Teresa or Bill Gates, founder of Microsoft and the Bill and Melinda Gates Fund? I am assuming that most people who have purchased Microsoft products did so because those products enhanced their lives in some way. Either Microsoft products make their lives more productive or somehow more satisfying or they would not have made the purchase. It can safely be said that Bill Gates improved the lives of tens of millions of people even *before* he started giving away large sums through his charitable foundation.

How many people's lives were helped by Mother Teresa? Between those who found solace in her hospices and other institutions, those she cured, and those whose poverty she eased, what might the total be? I don't know the exact number, but whether it be a thousand or a million, or even slightly more, the fact remains that Bill Gates, to name just one conspicuously prominent business professional, has done more good for mankind than Mother Teresa, and this can be measured quantitatively.

Why then, do so few religious people sing his praises compared to Mother Teresa? Certainly there is no talk of beatifying Bill. But why not? He has done so much good!

People have adopted the mistaken view that benefiting from the good one does somehow diminishes the virtue of your good deeds. And certainly Bill Gates, perhaps the richest man on earth, has benefited enormously from his good work. But why should this diminish the virtue of his deeds in the eyes of his fellow man? I can assure you this is not how God views the situation. To Him, win-win situations are the best all around. The measure of doing good for people should naturally be how much good you do for other people, not some other concern. The goal is to try to do as much good as you can for as many other people as possible. And if you also benefit from doing good, well, that is icing on the cake. It allows one to earn a living and continue doing more good. It is self-perpetuating.

From time to time, individuals who have enjoyed spectacular financial success have consulted me on the best way to commence a career in philanthropy. While many of us think we'd enjoy the problem of how to distribute $5 million to charitable causes, the reality is that much work is required to distribute money philanthropically, and the results, because they are not driven by the hand of the market, are often imperfect.

Imagine that you had only one week in which to distribute $5 million. How would you go about doing so without harming the very people you hoped to help? Just think of what happens to the lives of most people who win fabulous sums of money in state lotteries. Suddenly receiving a large sum of money you did not have to work for doesn't necessarily improve your life. It undoubtedly provides a period of intoxicated disbelief in which all seems possible. The evidence, however, suggests that for most people, a lottery windfall turns into a curse within a short period of time. People tend to squander the money on their worst vices. Knowing this, is it wise to give away money for free? Perhaps not. So what would you do if you had only a week in which to choose how to give away $5 million?

To put this into perspective, in order to maintain its charitable foundation status, the Ford Foundation must distribute an average of more than $1 million per day. The Bill and Melinda Gates Foundation must distribute more than $3 million per day. No wonder these organizations and others like them employ hundreds of highly trained professionals. And even so, their giving often creates considerable controversy. Giving away money is no simple matter.

Today's philanthropists are recognizing that giving away money is not always, or even usually, the best use of resources. Take, for example, Pierre Omidyar, who founded the online-auction website eBay. Omidyar stepped down from his role as chief executive officer of eBay in order to spend his billions of dollars by trying to make the world a better place. But rather than form a normal foundation supporting only nonprofits, Omidyar has chosen to give to organizations doing good and useful work, whether they are nonprofit or for-profit groups.

This new form of philanthropy, which eschews traditional philanthropic giving in favor of investing in companies doing real good, is known as "impact investing." So far the results have been spectacular. Omidyar and others are showing that by supporting the market and investing in those businesses that are doing good work, rather than throwing money at inefficient philanthropic bureaucracies, philanthropists can more effectively serve their fellow man.

This is why when people ask me how they should best use their money to create a greater good for mankind, my usual response is to recommend that they put that money back into the source that created the treasure in the first place—their talent for business. They should reinvest in their own skills and expand or start a new business. This way, they benefit the employees who will be employed in the enterprise. They also benefit the suppliers of raw material, office goods, furniture, tools, and anyone else who provides the goods and services necessary to the success of a profitable company. These people are very grateful to have a new customer in you and they will benefit from the exchange. Last but not least, this reinvestment in business will benefit all of the customers who will purchase the goods or services you provide. Your customers' lives are obviously enhanced by your goods and or services, or else why would they make the company profitable by purchasing them?

I am sorry to report that very few of the entrepreneurs to whom I have given such counsel have followed it. I am also sorry to have to tell you that I am not surprised. Their explanations are usually the same. "We want to be acknowledged for doing good," they proclaim, and few of their friends and associates will praise them for doing good if "all" they are doing is making more money. What they do not realize is that making money is far from "all" they are doing for the world. That is not all they are doing—they are creating valuable and useful goods and services. Granted, they are making more money in the process, but how exactly does that diminish the good they are doing for their employees, their vendors, and their customers?

The answer is that it does not.

I cannot stress this point sufficiently. Regardless of whether or not you subsequently give away to charity any of the money you make (and God does want you to do so), the very act of creating wealth in a free and transparent market in which nobody is forced at the point of a gun to purchase your goods, services, labor, or skills, is, *in itself*, virtuous.

Wealth is God's way of incentivizing you to do exactly what He wants you to do, which is to care obsessively about satisfying the needs and desires of His other children. Should you live your life either ignoring others or else filled with disdain towards them, the likelihood of you prospering is very low.

Why would God want us to be so committed to connection? Most parents would be thrilled to see their children utterly devoted to one another's welfare. A husband and wife become one in the conceiving of those children, and they see the unity of the family as a reflection of their own unity. Our Father in heaven is no different. To God, all of us humans are His children and our unity echoes His own. Furthermore, to God, the entire world becomes a mirror of His unity by connecting, joining, and bonding.

For this reason, though the good Lord created 92 elements, we use very few of them just as they are. For instance, among those elements is iron. Yet, other than cast-iron pans and lawn ornaments, we make very little out of pure iron. We must blend it with carbon, another element, to make steel. Throw in a few more elements and we get stainless steel, useful for everything from cutlery to surgical instruments and beyond. We breathe air, a mixture of two elements, oxygen and nitrogen. We drink water, a compound made of hydrogen and oxygen. We enjoy furniture made of wood, a complicated blend of several elements, and we use plastic extensively, which is a complicated hydrocarbon blend. The elements themselves seem to be God's eloquent call for connection within nature. It is as if He is saying there are 92 basic substances, but to get anything really useful, you're going to have to learn to connect and bond them to one another. It is true that the periodic table today lists 20 or 30 additional elements, but these all have to be synthesized in the laboratory, and few last much more than a few seconds before breaking down through nuclear reaction into one of the basic elements. These "new" elements themselves require the hand and manipulation of man to bring them together.

In 1886, scientists invented a new electrolytic process that would become the basis for all aluminum production today. This process allowed for aluminum to be combined with other elements, such as iron, silicon, zinc, copper, and magnesium, which yields useful alloys. Prior to this, aluminum was quite useless, but now we use these alloys to create materials that are used in airplanes, corrosion-free materials for use in building bridges and boats, and many other products. Aluminum was thought useless for so long. And it is, until we combine it with other elements to create materials of value.

This is true of most other elements as well. Very little is made from the approximately 92 basic substances that God created as the building blocks of creation. Man has had to learn to combine the elements God gave us in order to make them more useful. There are countless products that make your life easier, healthier, longer, more comfortable, and more enjoyable and almost none are made from pure elements. Elements include things like iron, carbon, hydrogen, oxygen, sodium, gold, copper, chlorine, and many others. When was the last time you picked any of these up from the store? Most of the things we actually need and use are made of wood, plastic, steel, glass, alloys, and other complex elemental compounds. Even water and air are made up of multiple elements.

God is giving us a message here. He is telling us to combine things in order to produce utility and value. This is the basis of manufacturing and invention. There has never been a better way to sell milk and eggs than by combining them into ice cream. Meat has been around for quite a while, as has bread, but someone made a fortune putting them together and calling it a sandwich. Rubber is collected from the latex sap of rubber trees but it wasn't much good for making wheels until we learned to blend rubber with sulfur in a process called vulcanization. Presto—we have tires. I could go on and on. Unless you are in the business of selling helium for balloons or gold bullion, chances are you make or sell something that requires combining elements and ideas.

To be a successful entrepreneur, useful to millions of people, and able to get rich, you don't need to invent anything new. You just need to think of yet another useful way to blend, mix, combine, or connect two or more existing things. God intended for us to find ways to bond, combine, and connect.

Let me give you one example. Cement is strong enough to carry a very heavy load. It becomes even stronger when aggregates like sand and crushed rock are added to form concrete. But even concrete still crumbles quite easily when pulled on. This is because concrete is strong in compression but weak in tension. Concrete isn't terribly useful in real-world construction because of that weakness of tension—it does not bend, but breaks.

Concrete is used in construction though. How? Engineers learned to combine steel and concrete to make steel-reinforced concrete. Steel is strong in tension, though weak in compression. Concrete is the opposite. Combine them and you get a material strong enough to hold up a skyscraper but flexible enough to sway without breaking. Steel and concrete compensate for each other's weakness.

Steel and cement were literally made to complement each other. This is no coincidence, for no such thing exists in God's creation. Not convinced? Consider this: Concrete and steel have identical coefficients of expansion. This means that, when heated or cooled, they expand and shrink at the exact same rate. In the jungle or the Arctic or anywhere in between, steel-reinforced concrete holds up for generations because both materials expand and contract in unison. If they did not have exactly the same expansion and contraction rate, they would warp and break over time. These two materials don't just go together—they seem made to be combined. And indeed they were. God intended humans to continue His act of creation by connecting steel and concrete and He made it possible by giving them the exact same expansion characteristics.

There can hardly be a more compelling indication that connections are integral to creation. In striving to connect with others, we are riding nature's wave of intent.

Letters, syllables, and sounds join into words that join into sentences in order to create communication. Notes, beats, and rhythms leap into harmony with one another to make music. "It is not good for man to be alone," God said early in Genesis. This is far more of a sweeping divine pronouncement than merely a precursor to Adam meeting Eve. After all, though very busy people living frenetic lives can be forgiven for suspecting that solitary confinement is a reward, the truth is that it is a torture. We humans simply do not thrive alone.

People have been known to take leave of their senses when alone for too long. Regardless of how overwhelmed we sometimes feel when surrounded by throngs of people, connections don't ultimately drive us crazy. Being alone, on the other hand, very much can and does.

Some young people in the West used to feel drawn to escape to quiet ashrams high in the remote Himalayas and sequester themselves in solitude in order to find themselves. This is generally counterproductive. The truth is that in order to find oneself most effectively, the best circumstances are in close contact with other people. It might be in proximity to a loving family or within the embrace of a positive work environment. Whatever the case, our best mental balance can be found when connected to others in our day-to-day lives.

The connectivity principle is built into the world. Living successfully requires that you be attuned to the manifestations of this principle. You want to internalize this principle into your worldview so that you may raise your connectivity quotient. The connectivity principle is built into the world and firmly implanted in God's blueprint for reality, the Bible.

The Torah cannot be sliced and diced, and neither can life. You may not pick and choose which verses you want to abide by. They are all essential. For instance, you cannot keep the rules forbidding incest, which you find distasteful, while tossing out the rules about honesty in business because you would rather make some easy money by cheating the system. It doesn't work that way. The Torah is a package deal. There is a continuity to the Torah and the book is one comprehensive entity that cannot be subdivided. You do not get to keep the parts you like and extirpate the passages you find difficult to live by.

A proper Torah scroll is generally written in 248 columns and every single column must start with the letter *vav*, the sixth letter in the Hebrew alphabet. This letter is imbued with special meaning because it serves as the ultimate connector letter that bridges other words and letters. *Vav* serves a similar function to the English conjunction "and." Conjunctions are connector words, such as *but, with, and, therefore*, and other similar words. One of these conjunctions following a phrase signals that another phrase is to follow and that both will be connected in some way.

Starting every column of the Torah with a *vav* may sound difficult, but in fact it is not. About 65 percent of all verses in the Torah begin with the *vav*, with the word "and." This is to indicate the connectivity built into the book and that the Torah is of one piece. It is one long unbreakable story.

Not every section of the Tanach has the same number of verses that start with a *vav*. The frequency of this is about 65 percent of the verses in the Five Books of Moses. Once you move onto the Prophets and the other books of the Tanach, such as Ecclesiastes, Esther, and Daniel, the proportion of verses that begin with *vav* (or "and" in English) drops to about 40 percent. This is because some of these books can stand alone. You can read Joshua without reading Jonah. You can read Chronicles without reading Kings. But you cannot read Genesis without reading Exodus, Leviticus, Numbers, and Deuteronomy.

There is one conspicuous exception to this trend of decreasing appearance of the *vav*. The Book of Ruth has about 90 percent of its verses starting with the letter *vav*. Yes, 90 percent! Why does the Book of Ruth alone seem to disrupt the pattern? The clue appears when the Book of Ruth is read during synagogue. The Book of Ruth is read on Shavuot, the feast of Pentecost, 50 days after Passover. Pentecost or Shavuot falls on the sixth day of Sivan, the day on which the Torah was given to Moses on Mount Sinai. In a breathtaking display of synchronicity, the book that is read on the day of receiving the Torah best encapsulates the connectivity characteristic by starting the vast majority of verses with "and," with the *vav*.

The Book of Ruth is replete with instances of spiritual connectedness. It reveals an utterly disconnected Elimelech. We do not know much at all about his father, family, or other connections. He seems not to care about those connections since he abandoned them to the famine and moved to Moab. But by the end of the book, we see many connections highlighted. Powerful father-son connections that link King David through many generations all the way back to his great-great-great-grandfather, Judah. Ruth will never abandon her mother-in-law, Naomi, come what may. Boaz does not abandon his distant relative Ruth. All of this is highlighted by the lyrical repetition of the *vav*—and, and, and, and. . . .

Naturally it makes sense to read the Book of Ruth, which is all about connection, on the day that the ultimate Book of Connectivity was given to humanity. This day has become a symbol for connectedness. It might surprise you to know that the telegraph—that instrument that would beget the telephone, radio, television, and the Internet, in a long lineage of increased human interconnectedness—was introduced on May 24, 1844, when Samuel Morse turned on his new invention, the electric telegraph, and tapped a few words from the Book of Numbers (23:23), "What Hath God Wrought," from the Capitol in Washington, DC, to Baltimore.

There is a biblical significance to this date. May 24, 1844, fell out in the Hebrew calendar exactly on the Feast of Pentecost, the sixth day of the month of Sivan, in the Hebrew year 5604, the holy day of Shavuot. Of course! When else would have made so much sense. The biggest moment in human connection would occur on the day when God gave us the book that is the key to human connection—the Torah. You could rightly say that the Torah is the Book of Connectivity and that it proves that you and I, and all children of God, were indeed created for connectivity.

Making Money Is a Spiritual Activity

A

ll human activities can be located somewhere along a spectrum that is anchored on one end by spirituality and on the other by physicality. Praying is near the spiritual end; reading and writing, composing music, and making tools are its neighbors. As the source of both great sensual pleasure and also of all new life, sex might be somewhere near mid-spectrum, while eating and all other bodily functions belong over toward the physical end.

So where do commercial transactions fit? When a man exchanges coins in his pocket for goods he desires, is he performing a physical act or a spiritual one?

One way of identifying a spiritual act is by determining whether a chimpanzee would understand the action. When I return home from work and slump into a comfortable armchair, my pet primate undoubtedly sympathizes. As I move to the dinner table and begin eating, he certainly knows what is going on. When I open a newspaper, however, and hold it motionless before my face for 20 minutes, he becomes quite confused.

Another criterion for the spiritual is whether the action can be replicated by a machine. If a human soul is indispensable for a certain process, that process is at least partially spiritual. Only a human soul can compose music that inspires men to march to war or brings a lump to the throat. No machine exhibits loyalty or can even test whether an individual possesses that quality. We therefore know loyalty to be another spiritual characteristic.

These tests suggest that a business transaction is more spiritual than physical. A chimpanzee would not have the slightest idea of what is transpiring between proprietor and customer at a store counter. No machines exist that can independently affect transactions, nor can they predict whether a customer will buy something or for how much. Economic exchange takes place only after two thinking human beings will the exchange into existence. The process is spiritual.

It is important to analyze actions because we human beings are always slightly uneasy with pursuits that lack spiritual overtones completely. When necessary, we superimpose spirituality just to avoid being exclusively physical because it makes us feel uncomfortably animal-like. We apply ceremony and ritual to our actions that are also animalistic.

Only people read books or listen to music; hence these activities require no associated ritual. On the other hand, all living creatures eat, defecate, engage in sexual activity, give birth, and die. If we do not confer a uniquely human ritual upon these functions, we reduce the distinction between humans and creatures in the animal kingdom. Therefore, we celebrate the birth of a child, often by a naming ceremony—no animal does this. We prefer to serve food in dishes on a tablecloth rather than straight out of the can, although doing so does not enhance the physical or nutritional qualities. We even say a grace or a benediction before eating, and according to ancient Jewish wisdom, afterward as well.

After encountering an attractive potential partner, psychologically healthy people tend not to proceed directly to physical intimacy. An engagement announcement followed by a marriage ceremony serves to accentuate that all-important distinction: marriage. No animal announces its intention to mate and then defers gratification for three months while it calmly prepares its wedding and future home.

Burials traditionally are similarly full of ritual. After a long and good life, the mortal remains of old Aunt Agatha are not simply left out in the alley for the city to pick up on Tuesday. There is mourning, and a burial ceremony, followed perhaps by annual visits to the cemetery.

The more physical the activity, the more awkwardness and subconscious embarrassment surround it, the more we need ritual to give our lives purpose and spiritual meaning.

Nudism is practiced with a certain bravado in order to conceal the underlying tension. Famous photographer Richard Avedon shattered a barrier by capturing images of people as they ate. Frozen in the act of chewing, humans resemble apes rather than angels. Similarly, we express a normal and healthy reticence about bathroom activities. In fact, it is the bathroom that is often the most adorned and decorated room in the house. At the moment of urination and defecation, when we are perhaps at our most animal-like appearance, we take deep comfort in reflecting upon the little soaps cast in the shape of seashells and upon the monogrammed hand towels and the other crafts of man with which we adorn our restrooms. They remind me that although I am doing in private what most animals do in public, it would be a mistake to think of myself as an animal. No animal decorates the room in which he relieves himself. I am a human being and I exult in my specialness.

On the other hand, as purely spiritual occupations, reading and art evoke no discomfort. We need no act of ritual here to dress up that which is already so spiritual.

Our entire approach to manners is based on this aspect of biblical tradition. Any male born in the English-speaking world before 1980 probably had a mother or grandmother who, following some egregious breach of manners on his part, would ask him, "What are you doing? What is the matter with you? Were you raised on a farm?"

This wasn't a slur on farmers; in fact, my mother was a farmer's daughter. It was a suggestion that your behavior was reminiscent of the barnyard and therefore unacceptable among humans. When your mother told you, just as mine told me, not to comb my hair in public, she was in essence reminding us that we are not animals. Baboons groom themselves in public; humans do not. How many times did your father object to you making animal noises at the dinner table? Mine did so frequently, always explaining that people must not let their bodies sound like animals. Even allowing our bodies to emit involuntary animal sounds is a source of embarrassment, as well it should be.

Emphasis on manners is the way civilized members of a Judeo-Christian society remind one another that our entire culture is founded on the conviction that we are not merely animals, but that we are so much more. We are unique creatures touched by the finger of God. Forgetting this dooms our society to descend into an abyss of animalism, economic failure, and ultimately barbarism.

Economic activity is another way in which we satisfyingly distance ourselves from the animal kingdom and draw closer to God. Revealing his own brand of genius in *Paradise Lost*, John Milton etched the Bible's indelible centrality into man's literary consciousness. He reflected everyone's subconscious awareness that the opening chapters of the Bible focus on the eternal tug of war for man's soul between the angels and the apes. There is a titanic struggle between the divine aspirations of a person's nobility and his basest indulgences. Whom would Adam obey, God or the serpent personification of the animal kingdom? After thousands of years of human history, the lingering memory of that tussle still resonates in the human soul. All heirs to the Judeo-Christian tradition feel the need to distinguish themselves from animals and to unequivocally demonstrate who won that primeval conflict. Seizing another's property by force is animalistic and a victory for the serpent; purchasing that property voluntarily for a price negotiated with the seller finds favor in God's eyes.

That relationship between currency and God's favor springs from the Bible and the Hebrew language itself, in which the word for God's favor is *cheyn*. This word, really meaning God's plan for human economic interaction, is not only the etymological origin for the English words *coin* and *gain* but also for the Chinese word for coin, *ch'ien*, and similar words in many other languages. The word *cheyn* also serves as the root of the Hebrew word for store or shop, as well as for a market-based economy. A store or market is a place for people to interact and make voluntary exchanges, leaving both parties happier and better off than they were before.

Even Ayn Rand observed that when extracting specific performance from people, the only alternative to a gun is money. No wonder then that God smiles upon the marketplace! Freedom from tyranny is a necessary precondition for both worship and trade, and money paves the way for this freedom.

One of the Hebrew words for a business professional is *ohmein*, which means *man of faith*, and shares the same root with the liturgical *amen*. With no verifiable information that he will be successful in selling his wares, the merchant nonetheless purchases inventory. He then delights in selling out his entire inventory, even vital commodities like food or clothing, in exchange for little metal discs. Instead of despairing about how he will now feed and clothe his children, he has complete faith that whenever he wishes, there will be someone who will gladly sell him food or anything else he may need for those very metal discs. It is that faith that converts metal discs and printed paper into money. This faith gives currency value. Were he to trade on the basis of doubt and suspicion, he would contract no business at all. It is chiefly his faith that makes possible his profits.

It is therefore not surprising that economics used to be a field of study that belonged within the realm of religion and theology. Adam Smith, as well as many other eighteenth-century economists, were religious philosophers first, economists only second. Smith wrote his book *Theory of Moral Sentiments* before he wrote the more well-known *Wealth of Nations*. When the great universities moved the study of economics from their religious departments to their science departments, they were actually driving a wedge between capitalism and the moral arguments and spiritual dimensions that underpin its validity. Faith is the fuel that drives both commerce and religion, despite what academia would have you believe.

It is difficult for a successful business professional to remain self-centered. It is precisely a preoccupation with the needs of others that characterizes the entrepreneur. Concern for customers is the hallmark of a business professional. This is where the phrase "the customer is always right" comes from—from business professionals putting the customer before himself.

The business professional also must value his employees as well, for they are his most valuable asset. He must attend to their welfare. Recognizing them as spiritual beings with their own divine aspirations, he must not only endeavor to compensate them fairly but also help them find transcendent meaning in their work. Ancient Jewish wisdom prohibits an employer from instructing his worker to perform meaningless work. For example, he may not hire the worker to dig a hole one day, fill it the next, and thereafter repeatedly dig and refill it. This prohibition applies no matter how generous the pay may be, because it leaves the worker with no sense of accomplishment, and therefore, no sense of the value of his contribution. The business professional whose own selfish wants and needs constantly fill his mind is doomed. Thus, both business and religion discourage selfish and narcissistic behavior. Thankfully, there is synergy between business and religion because, as we have discussed, business transactions are spiritual actions.

Knowing that a close relationship exists between God and the marketplace helps us in three crucial areas. First, this fact helps to explain why atheism and business are not natural allies. One would have supposed that a philosophy of secular humanism, recognizing no authority sanctioning all behavior, would be naturally drawn to the world of money and power. One would have expected the political left to excuse what it calls the "greed" of capitalism and to recognize it as nothing other than Darwinian law applied to the life of modern man. Yet, this is not possible; something as truly spiritual as commerce simply cannot coexist with socialism. The atheist himself recognizes that, to be true to his credo, he must reject the free market because of its godliness.

Secondly, belief in the relationship between God and the marketplace helps us integrate our career into our greater life so that we need not regard those daily eight or ten hours a day that we spend at work as a faintly distasteful and isolated part of life. "Business is business" cannot serve as a convenient explanation for moral departures in the marketplace, because business is really tied to life by overall spiritual awareness. Immorality in business is as repugnant as immorality in marriage. Business success is actually secondary to our private relationship with God. It is precisely that relationship that makes sense of everything else.

Finally, recognizing the congruence between work and spiritual reality, the business professional is all the better able to sell himself and his product. His work is creative and therefore a legitimate way of emulating God and his infinite creativity. Anyone with a sneaking conviction that socialism has a point—that man and his abilities are as finite as the economic pie and that he who brings that pie to the market and slices it for customers exploits both the baker and the public—is forever handicapped as a business professional. Nobody throws himself wholeheartedly into an endeavor he secretly considers demeaning and unworthy. The difference between the animal instinct of a squirrel gathering nuts and the inherent nobility of a human being earning a living becomes clear when you perceive economic enterprise in its correct position, at the spiritual end of the spectrum.

Everything Important and Joyful You Have Achieved Has Been in Partnership with at Least One Other Person

The power of partnership true for both individual industries and whole industries. Consider the pharmaceutical industry. New drugs must go through extensive clinical trials in which they are tested on thousands of people before they ever go to market. Drug companies do not test medicines on a single patient and say, "It worked! Start up the factory, roll out the machines!" Thousands of people work on trial drugs before they can go to market. This is not limited to medicine, but is also true in every business. All products have to be tested by the public before they can go to market. Business professionals depend upon their colleagues and their customers to make money.

It is this community process by which people make money. What businesses make their money in is less important to success than the principles that get them there. Larry Ellison, who is Jewish, by the way, became enormously wealthy by starting Oracle in Redwood City, California, but that doesn't mean that you should move to Northern California's Bay Area to try your hand at designing and selling software for customer relations management, as he did. Of course not, unless that just happens to be your business, industry, and desired market. It probably isn't, and it definitely need not be! What we need to know are the specific biblical secrets that made him so successful, not what his business was or what it did. These principles have worked effectively not just for one person but for vast numbers of people across time and space. We also need to know that the principles worked yesterday. This is why we call them permanent, of course, because they transcend time. They will work today and they'll work tomorrow.

Every time I study or teach the Torah, that crucible of ancient Jewish wisdom, I see myself as one engaging in a multigenerational symposium. When helping my son study, I will often explain a complex passage of Scripture by relating to my son that which my father taught me before. It is as if my father is now also at the table with us. When we invoke the insights of Rabbi Moses Maimonides of the twelfth century and the teachings of Rabbi Akiva of 2,000 years ago, those sages and many others begin to fill our room as well. Their company warmly reassures us that the knowledge we are gaining has been time-tested again and again. Now I pass some of this knowledge on to you. It is a testament to the power of the tools presented in this book that they have worked for countless individuals in every age, every place, and any circumstance. Do not worry: These people were and are just like you, and the principles will work for you too, if you allow them.

Consider your best moments and greatest accomplishments. Have they not always been the product of participation or cooperation with at least one other person? Of course they have! Your most memorable moments, your most significant achievements, your most joyful and jubilant experiences occur when other people have been there to assist and take part in them. This is a matter of fact. Without others to share our joy, where is there any place for joy? There is not.

The myths about lonely artists creating magnificent and unforgettable classical masterpieces alone in their attic studio are just that— myths. The isolated human can create a masterpiece about as well as he can create a baby, which is to say, not at all.

The biblical depiction of Adam and Eve is much more than a description of humanity's start on earth. In the perspective of ancient Jewish wisdom, the Bible is not a history book. The Bible is an instruction manual.

It provides a blueprint for successful living on this planet. The Bible instructs us on business and money because these activities are essential to successful living. Success in business is an end in and of itself, but that aside, how can one support any activity without making a living for oneself? Clearly, you cannot! All creation must include the act of making money, making a living.

The Bible is the ultimate guide to creativity. It allows us to ask the question: What is the ultimate creation of which humans are capable? The beginning of Genesis gives us our answer.

The ultimate act of creativity that any human being could be involved in is the creation of a baby. We know this, right? That baby could start a scientific revolution. After all, I don't know who they were, but I think you'll agree that there was a certain man and a certain woman who were the parents of Albert Einstein. There was a certain man and a certain woman who were the parents of Henry Ford and of James Watt and of Marconi and Edison and thousands and thousands of other scientific innovators and medical minds. People who changed the world. It's possible your baby might grow up to have a baby who discovers the cure to a terrible disease. Clearly, there is little we can do that is more creative than bringing a baby into the world and raising that baby to become a happy and successful human being.

There are, of course, many other acts of creativity. We can paint a beautiful piece of art. We can write a novel. We can discover a miracle drug. We can invent something. If you were to ask me, I would say that the best act of creativity is creating a business, because this allows us to enhance the lives of untold customers, employees, shareholders— the good done reverberates through the economy and world. All of the many acts of creativity that a person may engage in can be modeled after that ultimate act of creation as outlined in the Bible: the creation of a baby. We can use this ultimate act of creation as a metaphor for all of creativity and, by extrapolating from the advice given in the Bible, apply the same wisdom about creating a baby to all other acts of creation.

The Bible tells us that there are three things needed for an ultimate act of creativity.

First, it requires at least two people. Oftentimes, creativity requires far more, as in the case of business, but always at least two people are needed.

Secondly, the two people need to be different from one another. Just as mother and father must be different in order to create a child, so must any two creators be. Imagine yourself trying to create something with yourself—you would agree on everything! There would be no mingling of minds, no give and take. That's not a very good way to be creative because a creator needs somebody who won't just agree with them all of the time. This is the reason for Genesis 2:18—a helpmate *opposite* him. What is the value of a wife who always agrees with her husband? Now I certainly don't want to be publicly humiliated by my wife, but I do value her input. Whether I have succeeded or failed at something, I value her honest feedback. Similarly, imagine trying to start a business with a clone. What could you learn from each other? What have you to offer each other? Nothing. Working with a clone just makes no sense. There can be no creativity.

Male and female partners, mother and father—these are a metaphor for giver and receiver. When sitting down with a partner to discuss a business proposal, the listener assumes the role of the female, regardless of the person's true gender, and the talker is the male, again, regardless of true gender. The "male" puts out a "seed" of an idea and hopes for a conception. (Jewish wisdom bears out this idea, and even in English, we speak of "conceiving" of a plan or idea.) At this point, the "female" must respond, and there is an exchange of male and female roles, and if all works out, after much give and take, we may see a conception—a viable idea born into fruition. It may take days, weeks, months, perhaps nine months, as with the ultimate act of creativity. That is the model provided by the Bible in the story of Adam and Eve. The story of Adam and Eve is a model for the act of creativity, and one of the greatest acts of creativity is entrepreneurship, building a business.

The third thing that the Bible tells us about the act of creation, with the creation of a child as our model, is that—and I am not being coy or suggestive here—creating anything is one of the most exciting and pleasurable things that people can do.

Creating anything, whether it is a novel, work of art, invention, or a small business, is both fun and rewarding. This creation involves interacting with others in creative pursuits that we find immensely satisfying. You cannot do this by yourself.

Perhaps you are again thinking of the myth of the "solitary artist" working all by himself to create a masterpiece. But does he really work alone? Who provided his food while he painted? Who provided with him with paint in the first place? Where did the canvas come from? As you can see, nobody creates anything alone. It is not possible.

Imagine if you were the last person on earth. You may think you would be the richest person ever; the whole world would be your oyster. Just think, you would own all of the real estate; everything on Earth would be yours. Every nation, and every nation that ever was, would belong to you. Or maybe your aspirations are humbler and you are again thinking of that perfect parking spot downtown and having the remote all to yourself.

Do you remember the red/blue election maps the networks showed in 2000? They showed how blue states like California, Colorado, and New York voted Democratic while red states like Texas and Oklahoma voted Republican. Let's examine how America's three-thousand-plus counties voted. The county map shows that large swaths of California, Colorado, and New York are red Republican.

Obvious question: If such large parts of California, Colorado, and New York are red, how come the states went blue? The answer is equally obvious. The population concentration in California is in Los Angeles and San Francisco. In Colorado, much of the state is conservative but the cities voted liberal and most people in Colorado live in Denver, Boulder, Fort Collins, and Pueblo. Similarly, New York City and its environs house most of the inhabitants of the Empire State and cities tend to vote more Democratic.

The fact is that more and more Americans are abandoning rural neighborhoods and moving into cities. In only the ten years that separated the 2000 census from the 2010 census, the percentage of Americans that moved from living rurally to the cities was two percent. That is more than five million people in only ten years. That means that more than a half million Americans are moving into cities each year. And this trend has been evident since the founding of America and is happening just as reliably in most other countries.

People just plainly come to recognize that their most vital interests are best served by living in close proximity to others. While rural living is often synonymous with poverty, proximity to other people promotes prosperity.

Our true wealth is other people.

You must start loving other people and giving them the respect they deserve. They are your everything. Love them. Respect them. Value them. Every single one of them. No matter how irritating or inconsequential a person may seem, you need them. People, collectively, are your wealth. This is why our ability to make money depends on how well we connect and communicate with others.

Later in this book, we're going to help you learn to become more fluent, articulate, and persuasive in order to better connect, communicate, collaborate, and *create* with other people.

Have you ever wondered why bread is sacramental in all of the faiths that are based on the Bible of the God of Abraham, Isaac, and Jacob? A sacred sacrament involving bread is common to many churches, not just Judaism and Christianity, though certainly all flavors of those. I have my regular Sabbath table at which my wife prepares two special Sabbath breads, and nothing starts until we make a blessing over the bread. What is so special about bread, you may ask?

The answer can be found in the beginning of Genesis, when Adam and Eve sinned by eating the fruit of the tree in the Garden of Eden. They were upset, they prayed, they atoned for their sin. Finally God said, "By the sweat of your brow, you will eat bread." This is often erroneously believed to be part of their punishment for eating the forbidden fruit. This is false. The punishment was eviction from the Garden of Eden and the ushering of death into the world.

Eating bread is no punishment. Bread is delicious! "By the sweat of your brow, you shall eat bread." This is God's mercy. Adam and Eve have sinned, and they are now being shown mercy. God is telling them from now onwards they will eat that which they have worked for by the sweat of their brows. He does this because he knows they will find satisfaction in reaping what they have sowed. They will better savor that bread which they have earned. God invents a food that only human beings are going to eat—bread.

Bread is an incredible food because it takes cooperation between people. Someone must farm the wheat. Someone must grind the wheat into flower. Someone must bake the flour into bread. Here we see cooperation among at least three separate disciplines, usually three different people. (In modern times, it also requires agricultural workers, an industry to build the farm equipment, trucks and truckers to haul the bread, and vendors to market it.) All of these people cooperate and the result is a delicious, crusty, warm loaf of bread.

Prior to bread, whenever Adam or Eve felt hungry, they simply reached up for the nearest plum or apple and ate whatever was on hand. But from here on out, they would have to plan in advance in order to make bread. When you are hungry for bread is not the time to start planting wheat for flour—that must be done in advance. Making bread requires faith when you put wheat seeds in the ground that the crop will grow. Flour must be made into dough. That must then be baked. Cooperation and time are needed to create anything of true human value—that is the lesson of bread, and it's absolutely essential.

There is more, however, to the ritual. After making the blessing on the bread over my table, I sprinkle the bread with salt, and not because it tastes good or because salt is a nutrient for the body. The Bible is not a handbook for our bodies. God assumes that human beings will develop medical science and medical science will tell us what our bodies need. If the salt in the sacrament was for health reasons, we might also sprinkle a little potassium and iron filings over our bread and put them on the offering as well! Of course we do not do that.

We sprinkle salt over the bread because in the book of Leviticus, chapter 2, verse 13, it reads, "You shall salt every meal offering with salt. You must not stop the salt of your God's covenant from upon your offerings. On every offering you must offer salt."

The salt creates a little environment of holiness, a mini-temple at our dinner table. In the sacramental moment, salt has a very important role to play. The salt is nothing other than a capturing of a primeval human memory that the sacrifices in the temple in Jerusalem used salt.

This, of course, begs the question: why salt? Why not iron or potassium? The answer is that salt is special and metaphorical. Salt is the combination of two elements: sodium and chlorine. It takes an atom of each to make a molecule of salt. One of these atoms is a positive ion and the other a negative ion, causing them to join together to form salt. It may interest you to know that, prior to joining, sodium is terribly toxic and chlorine is poisonous. But together, they become something the body needs and craves. They become something good.

And so it is with people.

The message here is that you can take two separate human beings who may be no good, useless, or even toxic alone, but when you merge them together, they become more than the sum of their parts. This merger may be a marriage, or it could be a business partnership. This is what salt in the temple reminds us: that when you bring people together, the result is something so much more creative, so much more powerful than individuals could ever do or be alone.

Have you ever stopped to wonder why so many expressions for money involve bread? Will you lend me some *bread*? Got any *dough*? Many languages engage in this metaphorical association, not just Hebrew, because there is a primeval recollection of bread's capacity for bringing people together to bring about creativity and wealth. It reminds us that, in emulation of God's ability to create the universe, we too have the collective power of creation. We create babies. We create art. We create inventions, medicine, and bread. And, yes, of course, we create business enterprises. Just remember that the creativity, this wealth, is only possible when we join together. Collaboration requires at least two people working together, at least two people who are not identical. And while it brings about joy and gratification, the third tenet, creation, requires a deferment of gratification.

If you understand that creativity requires you to join with others, it should be obvious that other people are the key to your success. You must begin to look at them with love. You can express that love by looking for ways to serve and do favors and treat others with respect and love. This can be as simple as smiling and silently admitting your love for others to yourself. Try this: Before job interviews, phone conversations, business meetings, or any other interaction with another human being, put a smile on your face and tell yourself that you really love this other person. Realize that, were you in their shoes, you may be less gracious than they are. You must show authentic warmth to others, even if they do not visibly reciprocate. Force yourself to do this, if need be. Over time, it will become natural and feel and be genuine. Over time, your words and actions penetrate your soul and your soul believes and adopts them. Don't be discouraged by negative thoughts that may arise unbidden in your mind. You may feel like you should not say or do things that do not feel true in your heart, but such thoughts are destructive and violate biblical secrets of ancient Jewish wisdom.

There are many instances in which we should and must say things we don't believe, both to ourselves and to others. Consider a friend who asks for your advice about a new suit only after they have purchased it and removed the tags. Though you might well believe the suit to be a sartorial disaster, they can no longer return it and your advice is moot. In these cases, God wants us to respond only with warm enthusiasm so that we may add to their joy of their new possession. Obviously, if they ask your opinion prior to purchase, your honest assessment is probably being solicited and you should probably offer it. But if they are simply seeking affirmation of their choice, why would you criticize them for it?

Focus on Other People's Needs and Desires, and You Will Never, Ever Be Short of What You Yourself Desire and Need

Does God want you to be rich?

Let me ask you this instead: Does God want men and women to enjoy physical intimacy? People are sometimes made uncomfortable by this question, but I ask it to draw a parallel. I cannot tell you with any certainty that your pleasure is one of God's top concerns. But what I do know is that God wants men and women to live together as couples in the exclusive and holy covenant of marriage. It should not surprise us that a loving and gracious God would reward couples that follow His will with the greatest sensual pleasure available to humans. Similarly, I cannot assure you that God wants you to be rich. However, this I can tell you: God does want us to be obsessively preoccupied with one another's needs and wants, and if a good and loving God should reward those who follow his wishes with the incredible blessing of wealth, why should that surprise us either? It should not.

There is only one way to make money: finding out what other people want or need and then providing those things to as many of our fellow humans as possible. This is the only way to earn money, no matter your occupation. In order to do this effectively, you need to establish meaningful connections with your customers. This is no accident: God has designed money to be an instrument that both rewards and motivates us to do His will.

Earning a living requires *making* money, not *taking* money. We literally bring money into existence by making another human being happier. As long as you haven't robbed, defrauded, or coerced someone into giving you money, then I know that every dollar in your pocket was made by making people happy enough to reward you with their money. Maybe it was a boss, a customer, a client, maybe even a relative who gave you the money; I don't know. But I do know that they did so willingly because of what you did to earn it.

Have you ever wondered how so many companies can afford to offer money-back guarantees? Shouldn't they be worried that people will return the merchandise and want their money back? Some might, but by far the majority of shoppers are happier after purchasing a wanted or needed product or service. If we wanted our money more than the product or service, we wouldn't have made the purchase in the first place. Willful transactions are proof that you have created happiness by fulfilling someone's wants or needs.

Making money is not something we do when we think God is not watching. Making money is not the result of an occupation that we reluctantly undertake just to pay the bills. Making money is not an unworthy and selfish activity, and you need not be ashamed of engaging in the making of money. On the contrary, making money—when done in an honest manner in an open and transparent marketplace—is dignified and moral and the consequence of carrying out God's will. In other words: money is the consequence of working, not the goal. Profit comes from connecting with God's other children and serving them. We were in fact, created for this very purpose—to connect with one another.

I am the kind of person who talks to the people seated next to me when flying. Conversation invariably turns to what we each do for a living. I have trained myself no longer to think of it as making a living, but as serving humanity. I ask people, "How do you serve humanity?" When I ask this, people don't tell me about their occupation. They don't tell me they sell insurance, teach classes, or broker real estate deals. Instead, they tell me about the work they do at the soup kitchen, their pro bono clients, or the time they spend at the animal shelter.

While I commend their compassion, I explain to them that supplying other people with goods and services for pay and profit is no less an act of serving humanity than their volunteerism. Chances are the work they do for profit does more total good than the few hours they spend volunteering. The reward for a service rendered does not corrupt the service itself. Money is what comes to us when we focus on serving all God's other children. To think of your occupation and work as only "making a living" suggests that you are only interested in what you get out of work. There is nothing wrong with wanting to make money, but make serving (the process of making money) your goal. If you consider your work to be a calling, your way of serving humanity, then you both make money and serve. This is the correct way to approach work. Work is your calling. Align your work with your values, align your values with your work, and you will see the innate purpose and worth of all compensated work.

The money is what happens as a result. It is your reward. But the reward does not negate the value or sanctity of the work. In fact, the money you make substantiates the fact that you have done good for others. Making money proves to yourself and others that you are serving God's other children. To serve them, you must first get to know them. You must understand their wants and needs. You must earn their favor and trust. This is what making money is all about.

Have you ever wondered why a worship service is called a *service*? The phrase uses the same construction as another phrase: *customer service*. This is no accident. Consider what goes on at the shoe store. When you sit down at a shoe store to try on a shoe, a salesperson goes down on one knee in front of you and takes your shoe off for you. And what if you do not like the new shoe and instead want to try a pair of fancy sneakers that are the hot new item this year? No problem, the salesperson says, as he or she runs off to find it for you.

The customer service you see here is not that dissimilar to what happens at worship service. People are again down on their knees. This is one of the reasons that the Hebrew word for blessing is the same as the word for knee: *berech*. Hebrew uses the same word because going down on your knees is a way of serving. It should not be considered a menial or degrading gesture. It is one I take joy in because I know I am serving another one of God's children. This is no different than the service given by a salesperson who understands that the customer needs new sneakers. The salesperson understands that he fulfills this desire. This is beautiful harmony. The salesperson is happy to serve God by making His other children happy, and the customer is happy to walk out of the store with the perfect new sneakers on her feet. These feelings are inherently rewarding, but our good and loving God and our fellow man provide us with further rewards in the form of a salary or a commission or both.

When I was 16, I got my first car, which I remember as clearly as if it were yesterday. I had saved my money for years and spent all of it on this one purchase. I was in love with this car the first time I drove it. I had one hand on the stick shift and the other arm hanging out the open window. I was in heaven. But then the car began to make a horrible grinding noise, and my heart sank. I went home to tell my father that there was something seriously wrong with my car and I wasn't sure what. My father referred me to Sam Goldberg, a member of my congregation who runs an auto repair shop. So I drove to see Sam Goldberg at his shop. I only vaguely remembered seeing Sam in synagogue. I told him that my father had recommended him to me. Sam opened up the hood and asked me to start the engine and give it some gas. Sam let out a long, low whistle that descended in pitch, indicating a problem. My heart sank again . . . I knew there was something significant wrong and that it was going to be expensive. That whistle meant lots of money. And I realized that I didn't have lots of money because I'd spent all my money on the car. So I became very unhappy.

Sam told me to sit still and took my car out back to the shop to look at it more. I tried reading magazines while I waited, but I was too distracted wondering how I would deal with this. Finally, Sam brought the car back around, only now the grinding was gone. It was as if he put in a whole new engine. I'd never heard a car sound so good. It sounded better than my mom's sewing machine. It was smooth. It was softly musical. It was beautiful.

Only now I was torn. I was happy the car was fixed but scared to get the bill, for which I had no money. Sam handed me the keys and told me I was good to go. When I asked him how much it was, he said, "No charge." I must have looked pretty confused. He explained that my father had done him a huge favor he could not repay. I explained to him that the car was mine, not my father's.

And he said something to me that I've never forgotten: "When you get older and have your own children, you will discover that the best thing somebody can do for you is to do something for your kids."

So this person repaid his debt to my father by doing something for me. When someone does something for your children, it is just as good or even better than if they had done it for you. Don't believe me? Consider the opposite. Would you rather someone do something horrible to you or to your children? Most would say, of course, do it to me instead! But this works both ways, and most people would rather see goodwill and favors showered upon their children than themselves.

If this is all true, and I assure you it is, now consider our Father in Heaven. Think about how He feels when you do something to please His other children. I believe He smiles upon those who smile on His other children. So we must all be kind and serve one another. Loving other people is the key to both spiritual happiness and wealth. Do not forget this: By loving and serving others, you are turning the key to unlock wealth and happiness.

You must surround yourself with other people if you want to make money and be happy. This is why people flock to cities. If you were going to open a jewelry store, where would you open it? Most cities have many jewelry stores, and they are often located in the same part of town. This is very common. Often you will see furniture stores or clothing stores all clustered in the same part of town. But why? How can all of these stores compete with each other with so much competition? Perhaps to avoid competition, you could go across town, or way out into the country where there are fewer jewelry stores. Better yet, what if you opened a jewelry store in Death Valley, California, where there are no jewelry stores for hundreds of miles! No competition! You'd make a killing, right?

Of course not.

The place you should put your jewelry store is right next door to the other jewelry stores. You will benefit from your competition.

Everyone who wants to buy engagement rings or jewelry knows exactly where to go to get it—that same area. Some of them will shop at your competitors, but you know what? Some of them will come to your store as well. You will do better if you cluster your store with all the other similar stores. This clustering is not the result of city government saying that all jewelry stores must be on the same road; no, it happens by itself, because God rewards with wealth those of us who get together and connect with other people. This is why you see such distinct business districts in every town and city.

Business begets more business. The winemaking industry in Napa Valley, just north of San Francisco, spurred an entire subindustry of hundreds of smaller companies that supply the vineyards and the winemakers with everything they need at prices and service levels they could never expect to receive if they were alone and isolated. Likewise, high-tech areas always sprout up in clusters; proximity breeds the connectivity and constant cross-pollination of ideas. This is why tech companies flock to Silicon Valley. It is why the publishing and finance industries are based in Manhattan.

One of the reasons for Israel's extraordinary economic success is that the nation is small and compact. This keeps the entire nation well connected. People know each other. Knowing everybody and being known by everybody is the ultimate recipe for success, though this is, of course, impossible. You cannot know everyone. But you can dramatically increase the number of people who know you, the number of people who like you, and the number of people who trust you simply by remaining in proximity to them and being a good neighbor.

One of the bestselling books of the past few years is Malcolm Gladwell's *The Tipping Point*, in which Gladwell writes that a person's financial success is directly correlated to the number of people they know. This is not arguable. It's not up for debate. It is not opinion. It is quantifiable fact: The more people you know, the more they like and trust you, the better you are going to do in life and business. Cynics may argue that people with money have others flock to them, and not necessarily because they are friends. This is true, but not the driving factor. People with many friends often make their friends first and their money later. Successful people have all worked on developing relationships first. Then the wealth followed, just as it can and it will for you.

I want you now to consider Cain, the first child of Adam and Eve. Remember, when we speak of the Bible, we're not talking about a history book here. We're not talking about some obsolete account of some long-forgotten people in some anachronistic circumstance. We're looking to the Bible as a blueprint of how to live. Ancient Jewish wisdom tells us that every name in Scripture has a specific meaning; there are no casual names anywhere in the Bible. Cain's name means "acquisition," which refers to a desperate eagerness to accumulate stuff. This was the entire essence of Cain's identity.

In the book of Genesis (4:8), Cain says to his brother Abel . . . nothing. Cain says nothing to him. It is unclear in the Scripture what he said, but we are told, "And Cain spoke to Abel." But what they spoke about is not reported. The weather? Not likely. Nothing in Scripture is irrelevant. Nothing in Scripture is accidental. Nothing in Scripture tells us anything that we could have known by ourselves. We know Cain spoke to Abel, but we do not see what he said. Why?

The Bible doesn't have to tell us what he said because ancient Jewish wisdom fills in the story for us. If we are willing to "read between the lines," we can figure out the mystery. We know that Adam and Eve are getting old and they're going to die. And Cain gets hold of Abel and here's what he says to him, "Hey, Dad's going to be on his way soon. Mother's going to be on her way. That means we inherit the earth. And so I just want to establish with you that since I'm the oldest son, I will be getting everything, and you may live wherever you like but you have to pay me rent." Abel says back in return, "Cain, no, I don't think you understand. It's not going to be like that. As a matter of fact, we're going to be splitting it in two."

Cain says, "No, I don't go for your division."

How does Cain, whose name literally means acquisition and whose only one purpose in life is taking from others, react to this refusal? He kills his brother, of course. This is his natural choice because other people are the obstacle to his wealth. Right? No. Cain has it exactly backwards. Cain's folly is that he thinks that the fewer other people who exist in the world, the better off he will be. He thinks that if he can get rid of everybody else, then he will have everything to himself. Abel wants half of what is his, and Cain's response is, *This Abel has got to go.*

God then punishes Cain in a way that makes him appreciate and understand the error of his ways. He finally understands. People do not detract from your life; they enrich it.

Cain then has a baby. He calls the baby Enoch, or Hanach in Hebrew, which means "now educated." The birth of his child shows us that Cain has caught on; he now understands. Before, he thought that having other people around was counter to his own interests, but he now understands that more people are good for him. And because the Bible is our blueprint, we should now be educated. We should now understand that other people enrich our lives, not detract from it.

The very next thing Cain does is build a city, which is surprising when you consider that, at this point, there are only about five human beings on the planet. So why would he need a city? This question misses the point. The Bible is showing us here that cities are good for people. Cities produce people. People flock to cities because it is a place where everyone can live better with less effort. You can extract a living from the often-reluctant earth more easily in a city than in remote isolation.

In 2007, *Scientific American* published an article detailing what would happen to New York City and all other cities if all humans were to vanish from the earth. Over the course of only decades, cities crumble without human maintenance. Abandoned cities become overrun by nature. Skyscrapers topple and bridges collapse into the water. Mountains, rivers, and deserts do not need people. But cities do. And we need cities. There is a special relationship here, but it is less between city and man than between man and man. Man needs cities because they allow people to be in proximity so that they can communicate, collaborate, and create.

Traditional Jewish surnames indicate a person's profession. If you are a Goldberg, it means one of your ancestors worked in the gold industry. If you are a Wasserman, you have an ancestor who worked in the water industry. In those days, there was no piped water; water came to homes in a barrel on the back of a wagon. The waterman (or *wasserman*, in German) would come down the street with a bell, signaling people to bring out their jugs and other water containers to be filled with water. Are you a Silverman? Someone in your family worked in silver. Drucker? My late friend, the management guru Peter Drucker, must have come from a family of printers, for drucker means printer in German.

Why did they have these surnames? Because it was a label that identified how someone could serve his fellow man. I think that today we should all walk around with such labels, perhaps printed on the front and back of our shirts. We could all use big labels saying, "I can help you and this is how. Here is what I can do!" We should all walk around with these labels because we should be desperately eager to try and serve other human beings. Of course, we do not need to wear such labels or adopt such names because modern marketing and advertising allows us to effectively advertise our services. Still, such surnames provide reminders that we should always do so. Everyone can serve someone. There's nobody who can do everything for everybody, but we all have our niche and our role to play. You may as well let others know how you can serve them.

Notice that the focus here is not on how to make more money, but how to better and more frequently serve more human beings. You should not ask yourself how best to get rich, but rather, what do people around me need done? How can I fill their needs or their desires? How can I improve their lives? And then you've just got to notify them of your ability to do that. Focus on service, and wealth will follow. How can I improve a lot of other people's lives? That's the big question. The money follows . . . you don't have to worry about that, it will take care of itself.

Become a People Person

What psychologists call the intelligence quotient (IQ) is just an attempt to quantify human intelligence. The problem with this is that intelligence is hard to pin down and define. Measured IQ is poorly correlated with happiness, health, and wealth. There is even some evidence that people with a very high IQ tend to be less successful at making money. Highly intelligent people gravitate towards academia more than the general population. Almost any financial planner will tell you that few demographics are, generally speaking, as bad with money as university professors.

There are exceptions, of course. Bill Gates, founder of Microsoft, and Warren Buffett of Berkshire Hathaway are both exceptionally brilliant businessmen and they both happen to have super-high IQs. But they are in the minority. Most people with high IQs are not outstandingly successful, either financially or socially. Many people with very high intelligence do not have a lot of friends because they have trouble befriending people they consider less intelligent than themselves. Furthermore, people are often uncomfortable around someone who seems to be too smart for their own good. Extremely intelligent people can come across as aloof and not completely forthright. They are not necessarily dishonest; there is simply a big cognitive gap between them and the average person, and this can be alienating to the general population.

While a high intelligence quotient (IQ) is poor at predicting success in life, a high connectivity quotient (CQ) is very positively correlated with success. Your CQ is a measure of your ability to establish connections. People with a high CQ are likely to have many friends and large professional and social networks, which definitely will make you happier, healthier, and, yes, wealthier. These things, and also faith, depend upon your ability to make connections. This is confirmed by Scripture when God declared: "It is not good for man to be alone." This is as true for you as it was for Adam. The fewer people you are involved with, the more disconnected you are, and the less healthy, happy, and wealthy you will be.

In 1971, Dr. Moriyama, Dr. Krueger, and Dr. Stamler published *Cardiovascular Disease in the United States*, an authoritative study of the correlation between marriage and mortality. The study found that, even when controlling for all other factors, annual mortality of single people is three to five times higher than that of their married counterparts. Other studies published by esteemed medical journals, such as *The Lancet* and the *New England Journal of Medicine*, have shown that military camaraderie and civilian friendships both positively affect measured health. We could hardly ask for a clearer message: God doesn't want humans to live alone.

Dr. Irving Janis, author of *Air, War, and Emotional Stress*, described the positive impact of military camaraderie on the medical outcomes of wounded soldiers. The Medical Department of the United States Army has reported that a soldier's willingness and ability to endure the severe stress of combat was primarily dependent on how close a soldier feels to the rest of his unit. We can thus see that friendship aids not only health, but also happiness. Princeton professor and Nobel laureate Daniel Kahneman did research into what he called "hedonic psychology"—the study of what gives people pleasure and happiness. Dr. Kahneman found that having strong friendships with many people is one of the primary factors positively affecting our sense of satisfaction and happiness.

If close relationships and friendships can make such a difference in your health and happiness, imagine what those relationships and friendships can help you achieve in your business. Every major economic expansion in history arose from some dramatic breakthrough in our ability to connect with one another. The expansion of railways in the early 1800s was followed by an enormous explosion of wealth. The invention of the telegraph, telephone, radio, and television all led to booms in prosperity. The advent of the Internet ushered in an age of wealth such as had never been seen before. Not surprisingly, social networking websites are now growing at astonishing rates, because, again, they make it easier for us to connect.

God created a world in which the economy rewards human interconnectedness. Why? Because that is the entire purpose of the economy: to encourage and cultivate human connections. We were made by Him to be connected. You ignore this truth at your own personal and professional risk.

We have already established that anyone who works is technically in business, whether they are a bus driver or barista, coffee shop owner or CEO. Secretaries should, even as hourly employees, consider themselves in business. Because they are. They are in the business of providing secretarial services, even if at that moment, they might only have one customer, their employer. This is not a matter of semantics, but an important distinction that requires you to change the way you think. The company that writes your paycheck every two weeks is not your employer; they are your customer. Adopt this mind-set and everything changes. You are free from the daily grind—free to grow your business and serve your customers, your fellow man.

One time, while visiting a church in Dallas, I imparted this lesson to a thoughtful audience. Afterward, a woman, a single mother who worked as a checker at a supermarket, came up to me and told me she was trying to apply this biblical business secret to her life. "I work very hard, but I just am having a hard time wrapping my head around it." She said that she always thought of the people in line as her customers. How could her employer be a customer too, she wanted to know. I invited her to the hotel where I was staying to have a cup of coffee with my wife and me so that we could discuss this principle in detail.

What it boils down to is this: People feel an obligation to their customers that they do not feel to their employer. So often we forget that our employer is our customer. Remember, everyone is in business, even if their one and only customer is their boss. Successful employees treat and value their bosses the same way successful shopkeepers treat the people who patronize their establishments. One feels a sense of ownership over and obligation toward their customers. When you realize that your boss is really your customer, you will have an easier time treating him or her with due deference.

A good analogy is the difference in the way we treat rental cars and our own cars. You never take a rental car to a car wash. You take it back dirty. What do you care? It doesn't belong to you! I am not saying this is the way we *should* think, but it is the way we *do* think. It is the same way with work. When things are busy at your job and your employer needs help, many people just want to go home and let someone else worry about it. But if you owned the shop at which you worked, you would never treat a customer this way. Imagine I am trying to build a small business, say, as a roofer, and I am about to go home for the day and the phone rings—it is a potential customer. He says, "Hey, Lapin, you're a roofer, right? I met you at Synagogue the other day and I heard somebody say you were in roofing." He tells me his roof just started leaking through the ceiling and he is scared of damage. If he's my customer, how do I react? I say I will be there right away and drop everything because somebody needs me.

It is not just doctors who do that, but all successful business professionals. Everybody in business does and should. Some people may thinly veil their own laziness or misplaced priorities by dressing them up in misplaced morals. They may say that the business professional should seek "work/life balance" . . . by which they mean, let the customer suffer. You should be with family, they may say. They ask if you really want your epitaph to read: "He spent another day at work."

Don't buy into this spoiled way of thinking. Precious few independently wealthy people live in such easy luxury that they can afford not to worry about business. And even if you can, you should not, because such idleness is not God's plan for you.

So we should not shame parents for working long hours to take care of their children. Taking care of business is the most important way that we show them our love. Taking a child to a ballgame is important, but business is more important because it is the foundation of wealth upon which all else in life must be built. That does not mean you pursue wealth to the exclusion of everything else. Balance is good and necessary. It doesn't mean you ignore your kids. It doesn't mean you never see them. But you must also support them, and you must be a role model. Do you really want to instill in your child the idea that it is okay to abandon a customer in need just so you can be there when your kid hits a home run? Of course not. You want your children to see you putting the needs of another human being before your own personal wants. Life requires this kind of balancing act of your personal and professional lives, and you do not want your kids seeing you putting your personal self before your professional self. We want our children to be happy, yes, but first and foremost we want to instill in them proper values. There are times when you put your own wants aside for the sake of a customer precisely because doing so is in the best interests of your child, both financially and morally. You want to teach your kids the importance of taking responsibility for and ownership of their customers.

This is what I explained to the single mother in Dallas when we were having coffee at my hotel. And slowly she began to understand. She began to see that the people in her line were not just customers, they were the customers of her customer—her employer. "And I have to take care of all the customers of my customers," she said, "because that is my job and my duty to my main customer, who is my employer." I told her I couldn't have said that better myself.

It may interest you to know what became of her. This realization completely changed her life. She no longer saw herself as an hourly employee, but as someone running her own business and taking care of the people whom she cares for and wishes to serve.

Six months later, I was invited back to the same church to speak. Sure enough, she was sitting in the audience, but this time she was dressed quite differently. I'm not a master of women's fashion, by any means, but I can tell the difference between a dress that comes from Kmart or Sears and a dress that comes from a higher-end clothing store. The last time we saw her, she was wearing one of Sears's specials; now she had on a high-fashion outfit. We sat down with her again after the service. She told me a story that brought much joy to my heart.

"I started doing everything you taught me," she said. "And for the first time in my life, I actually started enjoying work. Before then, my head was always down on the cash register, pushing things past the scanner. Now I began to look at customers and smile and engage them. I treated them like real people, as I wanted to be treated."

And this was how she was "discovered." By engaging people. Her line at the supermarket had become the longest because regulars wanted to say hello to her as they checked out. One day a person came in whom she had never seen before and asked when she got off work. At first, she thought he was hitting on her and she spurned the advance.

"You misunderstand me," he said. "I don't want to date you. I want to hire you."

He gave her a business card from his real estate company. She didn't understand but agreed to meet later at a local coffee shop. There he offered her a job. He needed someone to work the front desk and serve as the face of first contact with potential clients. He had been watching how she treated people in the checkout line and decided she was perfect for the job. He offered her a salary and benefits that far surpassed the minimum wage she was making as a checker. This has completely turned around both her life and the life of the child she supports.

And how did she accomplish this? By chasing wealth? No, not exactly, though she seized upon an opportunity at hand. But that opportunity was only at hand because she first put in the effort to communicate and collaborate effectively with the customers already around her.

The lesson here is important for all people in business. It is relevant to entrepreneurs and incipient entrepreneurs. It is relevant to those who are frustrated with where they are working and want to start their own business. It is relevant to employees simply seeking better employment. Even the unemployed should take note. All of these people need to understand this one thing: However many people you know now, you will always need to know more. You want to connect with as many people as possible to increase your chances of meeting the right people who will change your personal and professional life.

But you cannot just stand there waiting. You must work to be seen. And that requires making changes to yourself as necessary. To succeed at making money, it is not enough to only learn new techniques and skills. Those things are important, but they are not enough. You must become a new person who is open to the world and all of its possibilities. Doing so is like being reborn. You cannot fake this—lack of it is more easily spotted in business than almost any other endeavor. This is because business requires us to interact with so many people. Your customers and partners will want to know and see that a coherent and genuine structure of integrity rules your life. To succeed in making money in business, you will need many people who know, like, and trust you. Even for those not in what is traditionally thought of as business, this still holds true. Consider a researcher who works alone in a laboratory. That researcher will perform much better if he begins to see himself as someone in business, producing research for his customers—the laboratory, the pharmaceutical industry, and sick people everywhere.

I understand that this does not come naturally for everyone. Some people find that cheerful bonhomie and gregarious camaraderie are just not their strengths. Plenty of people just don't see themselves as a people person. They may have issues with shyness, social anxiety, or self-confidence and they find it hard to talk to new people. What do you do if you are that person?

The answer is this: If you're that person, you have to learn to change. There is no other way to succeed in business.

Before you say you can't, let me promise you that you can. One of the main things that separates humans from the animal kingdom is our ability to induce change in ourselves. Is it easy? Not always. Is it possible? Definitely.

Jews have always understood the importance of and mechanisms for change, because we see change as the root of human fulfillment. By contrast, the feeling of stagnation is one of the worst feelings a human can feel. Birthdays, New Year's Day, and any other annual marker can make us feel depressed because it reminds us that another year has gone by, and if we feel that nothing has changed, then we feel we are going nowhere. It is not enough to tread water, to stand still; we must constantly grow to feel happy and healthy.

Growth produces human happiness, but growth never comes without pain. There is an American saying: no pain, no gain. This is a clunky but very true sentiment. Growing requires us to do things that we are unaccustomed to, which hurts because it is difficult. So growth is difficult, but when achieved, the result is joy and happiness.

I remind you of this if you are one of those who claims not to be a people person. You may not believe this, as I have my own radio and TV show and lecture regularly, but I am a naturally shy person. So I do sympathize and understand how you feel. But you can change.

There is no magic pill that will make the discomfort of experiencing new company and overcoming shyness any easier, but I can promise you that you do have it in you to change. How do I know? Because you are a human being. You are not a beaver. You are not a camel. You are not an otter. You are not any other animal. You're a human being. While this fact doesn't mean change is easy, it does, according to the Bible, mean that change is possible.

You're going to have to overcome your shyness. It will be difficult and possibly painful at first, but it will get easier with time, and eventually—and this is what is meant by true change—your new habits will become innate. You will realize that other people are nice and interesting and there was no reason to have been nervous in the first place. But before you get there, you must leave the place you're at and move to a new one. You must accept the journey. It is a great journey, and at its end lies your new destiny. You will eventually find a place where you are no longer held back by yourself and you are now able to meet and befriend new people. You will make new friends and more people will know you, more people will like you, and more people will trust you. You will build a network that will allow you to achieve great things, personally and professionally.

While the Internet has been revolutionary in connecting us online, be wary of online friends. Online friends can give us a false feeling of interconnectedness. People on social media sites, such as Facebook and Twitter, often boast about having thousands of "friends." These so-called "friends" that we make or declare online are not equivalent to real friendships that we make and maintain through face-to-face interaction. Just because some celebrity accepts your friend request on a social media site does not mean they are really a friend. Generally speaking, if someone won't take your personal phone call, they do not belong on your special list of authentic connections.

Scripture reveals the enormous importance of face-to-face connection by highlighting the special relationship between God and Moses. Scripture is replete with references to Moses and God speaking face to face, such as Exodus (33:11): "And the Lord spoke to Moses face to face, as a man speaks to his friend." Do you see that language? Friends speak face to face in order to nurture their friendship.

The Hebrew word for "face" is *PaNiM*, which is similar to the word for "inside," which is *PeNiM*. These are actually the same word with the same spelling; they simply have a slightly different pronunciation. The Lord is trying to reveal a connection between these two words. The face reveals what is going on inside of us by providing a window into our souls. God gave our faces over fifty muscles because control of the face is the key to effective communication and human connection. People can sense when your interest in them is insincere based on what your face reveals.

I was once introduced to a candidate in a presidential primary who went on to win his campaign for the presidency of the United States. His countenance was animated and intense, but somewhat mechanical. His eyes darted around the room while he talked. I could tell that his interest in me was feigned. It was as though he was looking for a more rewarding guest upon whom to lavish his attention. He was busy and I do not blame him. But I do think it goes to show that we can all tell when someone feigns interest in us.

The thing to take from this anecdote is that interest and sincerity are not easily faked. You need to be sincerely interested in the person with whom you are speaking to avoid offending them. You also must learn to make your face reveal the sincere warmth and interest that turns strangers into friends. Making your face more expressive is a skill that can be practiced. Some of us are cursed with lazy faces that do not show a deepness of expression, which can make you come off as muted, cold, or disinterested. But practice can remedy this. Have you ever carefully studied actors practicing their craft? Note how good actors are careful to emote clearly and distinctly. You may not be able to be as emotive as a world-class actor, but anyone can make improvements through practice.

We can train our facial expressions in the same way we can train our voices. Stand in front of a mirror and smile. What does your smile say about you? Do you have a ready smile? Or does your smile look more like a threatening grimace? Move your face around until you can smile the way you want—warmly and sincerely. A camera can also be useful so that you can compare different facial poses. Now try to show surprise. Now concern. Practice a gamut of expressions. Do this for a few minutes a day and you will see improvement. It will make your face nicer to behold and much easier for others to interpret.

Try to look animated when it is your turn to speak. The human eye is attracted to movement. People will converse in a far more focused fashion with you if you have an animated face. Learn to focus intently on whoever is speaking to you. Give them your full attention. Don't just act interested—be interested. Use your face to convey that interest while the other person speaks. When others are speaking, you should be listening. Appear focused. Do this well, and you will find that your face will bring you fortune. It need not be a pretty face, or a young and fresh face. None of that matters.

What matters is expression and focus. Use emotive expression to make it easier for others to focus on you when you speak; when it is the other person's turn to speak, give them the same focused, undivided attention. Your face is the window into your soul. Use it properly.

When seeking out new people, be open to others who are different from you in some ways. You do not want all of your friends and associates to be your clones. You can't share and trade anything with someone who is your clone. The more different you are, the more you will be able to benefit from one another. Differences allow us to trade and exchange knowledge and wisdom. Differences allow us to do business; for if we had nothing to learn and receive from one another, what would there be to exchange? Nothing. The only reason we can do business is because we are different. So celebrate that difference.

This is why it is so glorious to be human. Animals do not have this power of exchange because they are all identical. Dogs do not engage in exchange because all dogs are the same. All dogs like a good bone. Therefore, a bone is of the same value to each of two dogs, and they will not, for example, trade it for a bag of carrots, or tools, or currency. They have nothing to trade. Humans, on the other hand, may barter with one another. A human may realize that he needs a pair of shoes, but does not need the entire field of wheat he has grown. So he may trade wheat to a cobbler so that he can have new or mended shoes. This may seem like a small matter, that humans beings are all unique and different—it is so fundamental you have maybe not stopped to consider it. But the fact is that our differences are what allow for exchange and commerce and collaboration.

No two humans are identical, not even identical twins. How do I know? Science proves it. Consider fingerprints, which police officers use to identify one person from another. They can do this because all human beings have different, unique fingerprints. Even identical twins, who have the exact same DNA, have different fingerprints. Even though they have the exact same genetic material with which they are born, identical twins still grow up to have different fingerprints.

How can this be? Modern science has no answer, but we can infer the answer from ancient Jewish wisdom. The answer is that fingerprints are not biological, they are spiritual. In my mind, fingerprints are not just your handprints but also the prints of your soul. They are one way in which God puts a mark of uniqueness upon you. Note that God did not put this mark of my uniqueness on my elbow, which I might use for jabbing people, nor on my fist, which I might use for punching people, nor on my foot, with which I can kick others. He put this mark on my fingers. And why? Because my fingers are what I use for creating, constructing, making, and doing.

Fingerprints are not the only difference, nor are they the most important; they are just one of the most physically undeniable, and a spiritual metaphor for the power of exchanging the work we do. But we are unique in many other ways as well. We have our own skills, talents, abilities, and ideas. This is why business is so important—because it allows us to exchange that which is different between you and me. I can do things you can't do. You can do things I cannot do. But we can trade and thus enjoy each other's bounty.

In this way, we are able to help one another as we help ourselves.

We Love the People Whom We Help More Than We Love Those Who Help Us

Ancient Jewish wisdom makes a point that my following example illustrates. A judge was once waiting for a bus in the rain when another man walked up, soaking wet because he did not have an umbrella. The judge asks the man if he would like to stand next to him under the umbrella. The man thankfully accepts the shelter with the judge, and when the bus comes, they both climb aboard and get off at different stops. The next day the judge goes to work at the court. The first case he sees that day is between two people. One is a stranger, but the other is the fellow whom the judge invited to stand under the umbrella. The judge gets up from his bench and recuses himself, saying he cannot sit on this case because he had offered this man shelter from the rain the day before. The judge who was being reassigned to the case said that he did not understand the first judge's reasoning: "I don't understand. Had he let you under his umbrella, I would understand you recusing yourself, because you might treat him favorably for the favor he did you. But why does it matter that you offered him an umbrella?"

This second judge did not understand this biblical business secret or he would not have said this. Doing a favor for somebody else causes you to love him or her more. The first judge was well aware of this principle of ancient Jewish wisdom and understood that it would be wrong not to recuse himself because he would show favor to the man whom he had helped and, as a result, now felt closer to and invested in. Because he may have been subconsciously biased toward the man he helped, it was right of him to recuse himself. Because the truth is, we love those whom we help even more than those who help us.

Consider the parent–child model for more insight into this principle. Who should love whom more, parent or child? Parents do much—and in the early years, everything—for their children. So shouldn't children love their parents more than parents love their children? This seems to be true. We would not even be here were it not for our parents. We would not be successful had they not raised us, clothed us, put a roof over our heads. We would not have been able to play soccer, or football, or go to ballet rehearsal, or anything else when we were young were they not there to drive us to practice or rehearsal. We would not have an education were it not for their care and support; nor would we have good jobs. Think about how much you owe your parents for room and board, dental work, nice vacations, your college education—for anything they ever did for you. It adds up to an incalculable figure.

And yet all around the world, there are thousands and thousands of therapists who make a very good living listening to people complaining about how their parents destroyed their lives. This is a refrain repeated again and again. Now I don't know about you, but in my family, if anybody can claim that their lives were "destroyed," it would be my wife and me, not our kids. My wife and I had a happy-go-lucky existence pursuing hobbies like sailing when we were younger. But when our first child was born, suddenly our lives weren't our own anymore.

I would not, of course, say that my children wrecked my life, because they did not. My life would be far less rich without my children, and I love them and consider them a blessing, but they sure did change our lifestyle! And so my point is this: If anybody has the right to tell a therapist their life was ruined, it is the parents, not the children. The parents are the ones who make all of the sacrifices. And yet,

I know quite a few therapists who do pretty well listening to people complaining about their parents.

A few years ago, I checked the Los Angeles County records to see how many cases there had been of parents evicting their children for not paying rent. It was an experiment I was running to confirm something I feared to be true. I couldn't find one case. I then did a search for cases of children evicting their parents. We found 11 cases, all of them in a short span of time, a four-year period. The record specialists allowed me to look through the transcripts of the court proceedings and filings where these landlords were trying to get a judge to evict their parent. In one case, the judge flat out accused the plaintiff of being a disgusting human being for throwing his father out of an apartment. The son responded by saying, "Your honor, you've got to understand, he hasn't been paying rent for the past three months!"

What did he expect the judge to say? "Oh, okay, now I understand why you want to throw your dad out on the street! Well, if he's late on the rent, by all means!" The judge was right: The plaintiff was being a disgusting, ungrateful human being.

So as you can see, the love of children for their parents isn't nearly as great as the love of parents for their children. This illustrates the truth of this biblical business secret: that we most love those for whom we do things for, far more than we love those who do things for us. We love most those in whom we invest.

The painful truth is that most people feel resentful when we are the recipients of benevolence from others. Consider those who receive government handouts. You might expect citizens who are on public welfare and the government dole to be the most patriotic citizens out there. You might expect them to be thankful and full of love for others who have given them so much. But in fact, those citizens who receive regular weekly or monthly payments at the expense of other taxpayers are, across all societies and people, generally quite resentful and negative.

As human beings, we find it difficult to be grateful when we receive things for free, which is why expressions of gratitude are seen as morally prestigious. This is because expressing gratitude goes against our nature. Our natural instinct is to feel some level of discomfort about people doing things for us. One reason why so many children are often ambivalent about their parents is precisely because they owe them so much. On the other hand, parents have been doing nothing but giving to their children for years, which instills a sense of deep commitment to their children.

So, perhaps paradoxically, parents can engender love in their children by doing less for them. Children will love their parents more if the parents give them more responsibility and also have the children do things for the parents as well. This is one principle behind the Fifth Commandment. God tells children to honor their father and mother because doing so allows children to discharge their debt and thereby feel less resentful towards their parents. Sharing in household chores are but one very important way to honor your parents. Households in which parents have their children help with chores are more harmonious than households that employ servants to do this work. When children do household chores, they feel like an important and contributing part of the family. They become more invested in the family and love their parents and siblings more. Those who help us love us more than we love them, so it is important that everyone in the family help and serve other family members in order to keep the bonds of family strong.

This principle does, of course, transcend family dynamics. It also applies to business relationships. We must be ever vigilant to help our fellow man as much as we can. You may find that you often begrudge people who have done many things for you if you have not helped them in return. Why? Because these people remind us of our own inadequacies. It takes great character strength and much goodness to love those who benefit us. However, there is a way to make this easier to do: Simply pay back favors. Also, pay them forward to others. Do not let yourself be a burden on your fellow man.

If every one of us is always seeking opportunities to do favors for others, we need not feel bad when people do favors for us. This is the best way to build your personal and professional network: Seek out new friends by doing favors and allowing others to do favors for you. God looks favorably upon such behavior for it is His plan for human and economic interaction: building relationships between others and ourselves by doing things for one another. If you begin to implement this strategy and technique today, it will pay infinite dividends in your personal and professional life.

The very first verse of the Bible, Genesis (1:1), reads: "In the beginning, God created heaven and earth." From the very first verse of Scripture, we see that heaven and earth, the spiritual and the physical, are linked. A principle that is true for heaven is also true for the earth, and vice versa. For instance, a pile of uranium needs to be a certain size for a nuclear reaction to take place. This is what is known as critical mass. Critical mass applies not only to physical objects, though. On the spiritual level, a group of people gets a certain magical energy when it reaches a certain size.

As we have seen, bonding is how the physical world works. Bonding is also crucial to the spiritual world. Just as aluminum works best when bonded with other metals, so too do human beings perform best when bonded to other humans. Living life without spiritual connections is just as drab, brutal, and impossible as living life without physical connections. We need other people just as much as we need water, air, and food. We must increase our connectivity to really thrive.

Consider, how many different patterns can a single coin make when flipped? Two, right? It can land either heads or tails. Now, how about if we toss two coins simultaneously. Those two coins can produce four combinations: H-T, T-H, T-T, or H-H. It is fairly easy to see that if we added another coin to make three coins tossed together, we'd arrive at a total of eight different ways those three coins could fall. Now, what if instead of coins we used dice, each offering six options? Thus, two dice thrown simultaneously could land in 36 different possible arrangements and three dice would produce 216 possibilities. The more possibilities each unit has, the greater the consequence of throwing a few together.

Think of humans now, each with our own infinite list of possibilities and ideas. Throw us together and the number of possible outcomes is almost limitless. Connectivity and constant crosspollination drive the progress made by tech companies clustered in Silicon Valley or Boston's Route 128 high-tech corridor. These clusters exist because proximity promotes interconnectedness. One explanation for Israel's extraordinary economic success is that the entire nation is so small and well interconnected that, as the citizenry say, "Everyone knows everyone here."

I have a strange thought experiment for you: How many ways can you think of to ruin your life? How many different ways are there for you to make your existence worse? There are innumerable ways. You could rob a bank. You could purposefully crash your car. You could imperil your marriage by committing adultery. You could yell at your boss, treat your children unfairly, and stop doing your fair share of the household chores. There are as many ways to mess up your life as there are stars in the sky.

But how many different ways are there to improve your life? What kinds of things can you do right now that would dramatically improve your life? It's harder, isn't it? What you are observing is the law of moral entropy, a principle of ancient Jewish wisdom. It is much easier to be destructive than constructive. Becoming overweight is much easier than losing weight. Knocking down a beautiful house is much easier than constructing one. But there are things you can do to improve your life and one of the most important is this: increase your interconnectedness.

Increasing your interconnectedness is the primary way of increasing your income. Spending time and energy building social connections is a vital step towards financial prosperity. There are simple strategies you can adopt today that I absolutely guarantee will help you build wealth and improve your life. Increase the number of people in your life. Make new acquaintances. Develop your existing acquaintances into full-fledged friendships. Deepen your relationship with existing friends. In other words: devote some time each day to expanding and building upon your connections.

In order to know that you are improving an area of your life, you must be able to measure that improvement. You cannot effectively undertake a weight-loss program without a scale with which to measure progress. Making money and budgeting requires keeping financial records. Likewise, you will never improve your connectivity if you cannot measure it. You must track your connections.

Make a list of all of the people you know well enough to telephone out of the blue. You probably have innumerable Facebook contacts and numbers saved to your phone, but you are only allowed to include people who would accept a phone call or call back if you left a message. Online-only friends don't count, unless you are housebound.

Over the course of the next month, add new names to the list as you actively seek out new friends. Do this each month to keep a record of your progress. This monthly tally will allow you to gauge how well you are making new friends.

Making new friends is not something you do once and then forget about. Like hygiene and exercise, expanding your social network is an ongoing process. It requires maintenance and sustained effort, just like weight loss or any other healthy activity. You don't coast along on that wonderful meal you ate four years ago. Neither do you coast along on the friends you made back in kindergarten, high school, or college. Those friendships must be maintained and new ones forged. The act of meeting new people and converting them into friends is an ongoing effort, but it will contribute to your health and wealth.

Life Isn't About What You Know—It's About Who You Are

Society has adopted the mistaken belief that knowledge can solve all problems. We are led to believe that young schoolgirls become pregnant because they lack sex education or that criminals commit crimes because they don't get a good education. The government mandates that the dangers of smoking be printed in great big letters on packs of cigarettes under the faulty notion that if people just knew the dangers of smoking, no one would smoke. When immoral doctors are charged with molesting patients, we bemoan the fact that they did not receive more continuing education courses on ethics, as if this would have prevented their evil deeds. This country has an obesity epidemic because of our failure to exercise and follow a healthy diet, but if you were to listen to the media or the Department of Health, you would think the problem is just that people don't know any better, that they don't know about nutrition and health.

On the face of it, all of these assertions and assumptions are patently false. The dangers of smoking, overeating, and lack of exercise are well documented and understood by most. These are not failures of knowledge; they are failures of behavior. They are moral failures.

Even when we have perfect knowledge of the problems that we face, that knowledge does not relieve us of the problems without our own commitment to actions that can change our situations and ourselves. Knowledge alone is not the answer to anything. Knowledge will not make better choices for us.

Imagine for a moment that we did have perfect knowledge of a societal ill. We know, for example, that alcohol and certain psychotropic drugs have the potential to create dangerous chemical dependencies and addictions that can ruin one's life. We know this is reliable information borne out as fact by countless scientific studies. Knowing this, what if we were to launch a public information campaign? Suppose we gather funds and disseminate these facts about addiction by using billboards, television commercials, speaking tours at high schools and college campuses, and other means, sparing no expense when it comes to marketing. Perhaps you have seen some of these things done—they are quite common tactics. And yet, now that people everywhere know the grave facts about addictions, have we managed to eradicate alcoholism and drug abuse? Of course not. But many people actually believe that this will work, even though we have tried again and again and it does not.

The reality of our modern world is that knowledge and information are now more readily accessible than ever before. Just look at the Internet—knowledge has never been so cheap and readily available. And yet, have we seen improvements in our moral behavior? Do we make better choices for ourselves? No. On the whole, we do not. The problem is that knowledge alone does not alter our behavior. The only thing that will change our behavior is making the right decisions, and the only way to ensure we do that consistently is to build up the strength of our characters.

I could very easily instruct you in what you need to do to be healthy, just as I could instruct you in all of the practical things you should do to amass wealth. But most people already know what they should be doing; they just fail to actually follow through. We know how to exercise. We know how to go to college and get a job and show up on time every day and do a good job. The hard part is not knowing what to do but actually doing it, day in and day out for the rest of your life.

This is why my goal with this book is not just to tell you what to do to succeed in business—my goal is to arm you with the techniques handed down by ancient Jewish wisdom that will allow you to build yourself up as a person and take ownership of your own character. Only then will you make the right choices, personal and professional, that you already know you should make.

At the end of the day, what we know means nothing; it is who we are, what we do, that matters. This is true in all aspects of life, but it is especially true of business. It is one of the great secrets of business that will lead you to success. Your college professors may have cared about what you knew, but your customers, employers, partners, and share-holders are not going to quiz you at the end of each financial quarter or at your annual performance review. They are simply going to look at what you actually accomplished.

The myth of knowledge solving all problems is repeated like a mantra in our culture. That many people believe something so errone-ous is no reason for you to believe it, too. Do not buy into that which is not true, especially when it will inhibit your capacity to move for-ward and improve yourself and increase your income. Repetition of a statement does not make it true. When assessing what we believe to be true, we must realize that there are multiple ways of looking at things, and we must be sure that we are evaluating facts on a holistic accu-racy, not based on popular opinion or assumption. We must be sure we are not making any oversights. Ancient Jewish wisdom is my guide here, as in all areas of life.

The Bible lays out all of this for us in many places, but one of the most famous is in the Ten Commandments, which are, of course, foundational, and well known by most people in Western societies, whether they are devout or not. The Ten Commandments are pre-sented in chapter 20 of the book of Exodus and later recounted in Deuteronomy, in which Moses reviews all that has befallen Israel dur-ing the past 40 years and discusses the moral implications of each event as he reviews history.

What is important here is that there is an important discrepancy between the Ten Commandments as they appear in Exodus and later in Deuteronomy. Namely, in Exodus 20:8, the Fourth Commandment says, "Remember the Sabbath Day." This is fairly straightforward. But later, when Moses recounts the Ten Commandments in Deuteronomy, chapter 5, he reads the Fourth Commandment as "Guard or observe the Sabbath Day."

Why this discrepancy? Does Moses have a bad memory? Is it possible that Moses thought that God actually said to observe and guard the Sabbath Day? But in Exodus, God clearly said "remember," not "observe and guard."

So which is it?

Moses did not have a faulty memory. And what about all of the people that listened to him recount the Ten Commandments? Why did they not "correct" him? Surely they noticed the discrepancy.

So, again, which is it? How does the Fourth Commandment really read? The answer is that it reads both ways. Both ways are "right."

You may ask, how is this so? Let me suggest an analogy. Imagine we ask someone to draw a teacup. Perhaps this person thinks of a teacup sitting in a saucer and he sketches out his picture and hands it to you. What he gives you is a picture of two concentric circles, one inside the other. The drawing is from a perspective above the teacup. The outermost circle represents the rim of the saucer and the inner circle is the rim of the teacup.

Overhead
view

Now imagine that we ask another person to draw the same thing—a teacup on a saucer. The second person gives you a side view. The drawing is of a vertical rectangle sitting atop a horizontal line, the ends curving up slightly as a saucer does. From this angle you can see the teacup handle.

Side view

So here we have two conflicting sketches of the same teacup. Which one is correct? You may say, they do not match, so one must be wrong. But they do not match only because they are from different vantage points. They are indeed drawings of the same teacup, but you need both of these perspectives in order to assemble an accurate image of a three-dimensional teacup in your mind. Even if you had never seen a teacup, you could begin to form an image of one in your mind's eye . . . but only if you have multiple perspectives to study.

You would say one is wrong only if you thought solely in two dimensions, but teacups exist in a complex, three-dimensional world. In fact, it is difficult to fully convey a three-dimensional shape on two-dimensional paper without using more than one drawing. The full three-dimensional nature of a teacup is revealed only by considering both drawings together. The only way to depict three dimensions on a two-dimensional sheet of paper is with more than one drawing. If you are limited in dimensions, you need more perspectives to see the whole picture. If you are limited in a godly dimension, since we are mere mortals, then you need more than one "drawing" on an earthly level in order to understand God's word.

So clearly both perspectives of the teacup are valid, and both are needed. And so it is with the Fourth Commandment.

It does not make sense to wonder whether God meant "remember" or "observe and guard" in regard to the Sabbath Day. The answer is He meant both.

You might ask yourself now, how could God use two phrases to the same thing? God's word lies beyond our abilities of full comprehension and conceptualization. Trying to concretize a concept that defies being pegged down or quantified or defined eliminates its usefulness as a concept.

Let me give you a more earthly example as an analogy. In mathematics there is a concept represented by the symbol i (like the letter of the alphabet) that equates to the square root of negative one. The square root of something is a value that when multiplied by itself is equal to the value of that something. So, for example, the square root of four is two. The square root of nine is three. The square root of 25 is five. And so on. Now I ask you, what is the square root of negative one—the actual value? The square root of one is one, because when you multiply one by one, you get one. Simple. But what about the square root of negative one? What do you have to multiply by itself that will give you negative one? Take a moment to think about it, but if you want me to save you the pain . . .

The answer is that there is no answer—or rather, there is no tangible answer, no exact answer, no quantifiable answer. In literal terms, there isn't such a thing. There is nothing that you can multiply by itself that'll give you a negative one, because a negative multiplied by a negative, as any elementary math student knows, gives you a positive. Therefore, it doesn't actually exist. This is why we have the concept of "i": to define and speak about a concept that is indefinable and, in a way, does not really exist. Because while the thing itself doesn't exist, the concept of it does.

Now you may wonder why we need a name for something that doesn't actually exist. Without getting too technical, it is because i is a very useful concept in mathematical computations. We use i as a reference point to define other things—because we can define i (the square root of a negative) in relation to something that does exist (the square root of a positive number), we can still use i as a reference point, as a concept. Because i is, in fact, a concept. It's just that as soon as you try to visualize it, as soon as you concretize it in your mind and you say to yourself, "Now what does i actually look like?" you can no longer see it in your mind's eye. For some, this destroys the concept and their willingness to entertain that concept. If they cannot visualize something, trying to do so causes them to shut down the process. They just can't comprehend such a thing, and so they insist it has no use when actually it does if they would only look at it a different way.

The problem with this way of thinking is that it limits you to the bounds of your own imagination. We don't all have equally strong imaginations, and closing off our minds to that which we cannot visualize limits our possibility for thoughts. Sometimes we do this because a thing is too hard or painful to imagine—for example, many cringe at the thought of eternity, which we cannot fully visualize and are thus frightened by. But eternity does exist, as a concept, even if you cannot visualize it. You can think of eternity; you just cannot peg it down and see it all at once in your mind. Doing so causes us to lock up and not try. It is beyond the power of the human mind.

Just because we cannot visualize the square root of negative one does not mean that we cannot use the concept. And indeed, the concept of i is very useful in solving certain kinds of mathematical problems. The concept of eternity is very real and should be considered. So it is with the dual nature of certain things, such as the Fourth Commandment as read by Moses and handed down by God.

If you try to visualize or concretize God's word, you fail to see His word in its entirety—as concepts. God's word transcends the capacity of our minds. Our bodies have limitations, which wise people recognize. You are never, for example, ever going to be able to jump over a house no matter how hard you try because the acceleration required is beyond the ability of humans—even the best athletes can't even come close. It's physically impossible. And our minds have limitations as well. There are some things we simply cannot fully conceive. We can't concretize them. However, if we leave them as theoretical constructs, we can still work with them. Just as with i, we can use them as reference points. We can accept their multifaceted meanings.

"Remember the Sabbath Day" or "Observe the Sabbath Day"? Exodus or Deuteronomy? Which is it? It's actually both. The truth is a synthesis of the two. How did God say both of them? Stop worrying about that. God does not speak in words with lips from clouds on high. God's words transcend the confines of written language. If you try to picture God, you limit your perception of Him. So don't try; it's a futile and worthless endeavor. All you have to focus on is what ancient Jewish wisdom tells us about these two messages, and how they synthesize, and how we should integrate them into our daily lives—you can't and don't need to peg them down.

For 3,000 years now, Jews have observed and remembered and held sacred the Sabbath Day by not working on that day. This is extraordinary: more than 3,000 years ago, God told the Israelites you mustn't work on Saturday and still we hear His words and obey and observe. Of course not all Jews do this, but many do, in all nations, across all generations, after all these millennia.

And they do so at great financial sacrifice, or so it would appear.

It's family knowledge that my own grandfather had a business partner who was not Jewish, and who burst into the synagogue on Saturday telling my grandfather that they had a business opportunity to acquire the patent for a new invention that would sell very well, but they had to move on the deal immediately. My grandfather told him that he would be available that night after the sun had set to work on the deal. His partner was furious, but my grandfather would not budge. My grandfather did go seek out his partner after sunset, but it was too late. "You've blown it!" his partner said. "It's too late. The deal is gone!" It later turned out that the deal went sour and investors lost a lot of money. But no one knew that at the time, and my grandfather truly believed he was turning his back on an opportunity in order to observe the Sabbath.

It is extraordinary to me that people would do something for 3,000 years that, on the surface, is actually quite illogical by human standards. They take one day a week and they quit working. So how did observance of the Sabbath remain so important all this time? The answer is, again, multifaceted. There are two main aspects to understand. First, there is the instruction, plainly seen in Deuteronomy ("observe"). God is telling us what we must do. But also, secondly, He places the instruction in the context of a narrative that allows us a general picture. We have to remember the Sabbath Day, as we are told in Exodus. *Remember* it. He is telling us to consider its context. He is telling us to remember the Sabbath's role in Genesis. God worked for six days and rested the seventh. If we want to be God-like, we must do the same. Remembrance is *how* we observe the command.

Observing God's word here brings us closer to the ultimate creator. It allows us to be creators ourselves. It has been proven that sleep recharges us for the next day. In the same way, resting on the Sabbath recharges us for the following week, so that we can commit ourselves fully to our business enterprises. By observing the Sabbath, we are able to create, on our own mortal level, things such as a successful business, or an invention, or a work of art. For us to be creators, we must emulate Him, the ultimate creator. We must remember way back. We must remember that at the beginning, God didn't work for one day.

So you see, God is not just stepping out and issuing an order (as He does in Deuteronomy), but He is also giving us an internal philosophical structure and narrative so that we understand the history of the Sabbath. In order to "observe," we must first "remember." Furthermore, by observing each week, we are also simultaneously remembering. It is not enough simply to know what we should be doing, we must understand the context and fully internalize it so that we may build up our character in a way that allows us to really integrate His will into our lives.

So do you now see how knowledge alone is not enough?

The knowledge of what to do ("observe") is not enough; we must also remember so that we can know the context for what we are supposed to do. This enables us to place God's will into the context of a narrative, which allows us to integrate His will into our everyday lives. We do this by developing the character necessary to actually do it, but it starts by accepting His word and internalizing it and then acting upon it. We cannot just say to ourselves that we must lose weight; we have to exercise and eat well and make it happen.

In Order to Achieve Success, We Must and Can Build Up Our Self-Discipline, Integrity, and Character Strength.

Let's consider weight loss. Why can't we just decide to lose weight and then simply do so? Because there is very real pain involved in adopting a new lifestyle that holds more sway over us than the imagined—the visualized—gain of future health, vitality, and improved appearance. We all want to be these things, but we cannot feel them. We must imagine them. On the other hand, we can feel the actual pain of turning down dessert. You cannot pit real pain against imagined gain. Real pain wins every time. You are setting yourself up for failure by ignoring the way the human mind works. We have to find other motivators—imagined gain isn't going to deter us when we face immediate pain.

We encounter a similar dilemma when we try to understand the process of making money. There can be very real pain involved in earning money. It requires us to go to work every day. We know that going into work is what delivers us a paycheck and allows us to build out our savings and create the lives for ourselves that we want. But the promise of accomplishing future financial goals is more distant than the fact that I have to wake up when my alarm goes off, get dressed, and spend the day at work. The payoff is distant and gradual and requires our imagination. On the other hand, the television is right in front of us. Turning it off to do something more productive causes real and immediate pain—we can now no longer watch TV! Imagined gain is not the best self-motivator when change is so painful and immediate.

What we have to do then is find a way to make the imagined gains attractive and real enough to overcome the pain of taking action. One way or another, we have to equalize the struggle—our success as business professionals in any professional endeavor depends on it. But how do we do this? How do we overcome our basest human urges and flaws?

The book of Psalms contains a beautiful passage by King David that provides guidance. Psalms 34:13 reads beautifully in Hebrew: *Mi HaIsh Heh Chafeitz Chayim.* The translation is, "The man who desires life and who loves days of goodness where things happen well? Who's that man?"

"Well, it could be you," says King David, "if you turn aside from evil and do good."

Why does he not simply say to do good? Is this not the same thing?

Consider again the example of losing weight. You may think that the most important thing is to "do good"—to exercise. So perhaps you go to the gym and work out a lot. You are "doing good." But wait, because you are doing so well, perhaps you come home and binge eat. What does it matter? You're going to exercise again tomorrow! But as the days go on, you continue to eat too much, which is bad and goes against your diet. But you are doing good by exercising, you tell yourself. Nonetheless, you are seeing no results.

You know, deep down, that what you are doing is an act. You have no right to feel virtuous for working out when any gains are being ruined by overeating. You tout how well you are doing at the gym but gloss over the fact that you are cheating on your diet. I am doing good (exercising regularly), but I am not turning away from bad habits (overeating). The problem is that exercising does no good while still overeating. It does no good to tout your good when you are still doing bad at the same time.

The bad may not negate the good, but the good does not negate the bad either, and God wants us doing only good, not bad, too.

What King David is telling us is that it does us no good to celebrate the good we do if we ignore our transgressions. We must turn from evil in order to reap the benefits of the good we do. This may not be easy, and it certainly denies us the right to celebrate easy victories, but deluding yourself into believing you are virtuous when acting virtuously only some of the time is counterproductive to character growth. You must carve out all of the evil in your life in order to feel virtuous about the good you do.

Make no mistake: this is hard. Doing an act of good is a choice one can make in the moment. You have to make it over and over, but each time it is always a choice made in the moment, albeit a single choice you have to make again and again. (This is why Alcoholics Anonymous tells addicts to take it "one day at a time": because it is easier to make a choice in the moment, which provides immediate positive or negative reinforcement, than to focus on future imaginary gains or pain, which requires using your imagination.) Turning away from all evil thoughts requires you to resist all bad actions forever. This is far more difficult and requires you to really build up your character.

We face this dilemma all of the time in the business world, where we are constantly challenged to do the right thing even when it is not always pleasant. It is hard to find the strength to make another sales call after you've just made seven sales calls without closing on a single sale. This can destroy our confidence and ability to act. We may just wish the phone would disappear. We may look for any reason not to have to make another call. You hope the person you are calling won't pick up. "Let them be out of the office," you tell yourself. If you are really discouraged, maybe you call in to work. Maybe you shirk your responsibilities while on the clock. Selling is a great profession, but it is hard, as all salespeople know. But no one is paying you to do something that is easy! The hard part isn't making any one sales call. You know how to do your job and maybe you're even good at it. The hard part is showing up every day without fail, always smiling, always doing your best. This requires that you make yourself into a strong person who can endure the tribulations of life and the workplace. Such is the life of the successful business professional. You must find a way to always be your best if you want to succeed in business, or any other endeavor for that matter.

This book is meant to give you the knowledge you need to make money just as generations of my people, Jewish people, have done. However, if all I gave you was the knowledge and I failed to provide guidance on how to become a strong enough person to walk the path of good and turn from the path of wrongdoing and evil, then I would have given you nothing at all—because knowledge alone is simply not enough. You need to act upon that knowledge and you need the character and strength to do so.

Realize that *wrongdoing* and *evil* are relative terms. In the world of business, shirking your responsibilities on the clock is an "evil." Not being productive and wasting time are "evils" too, in this context.

So your two goals as a business professional are: (1) to become better at doing hard things that you are not accustomed to doing, and (2) to learn to resist doing things that are easy and often enjoyable. This is the ancient Jewish wisdom borne out in the book of Psalms. This requires you to retrain yourself, because man is not wired this way; we have to make an effort to do the right thing and think the right way. You must be proactive, in business and in all areas of your life.

One thing I advise people to do is thank five people a day without fail. I do this always. It can be hard at first, as it is something you are not used to, but eventually it will become like breathing. When I miss a day now, I feel bad, as if I have missed a workout or a meal. I should be self-loathing and become sick, thinking myself a weak person when I fail to make my goal and keep my promise to myself. This is me actively seeking to do good.

I also actively seek to turn from evil by being more productive. Many people watch television for three hours every day. It may not seem like much, but that is 21 hours each week that you could be being productive! Convert this to productive use! The first step is to recognize where you stand and how you feel about your life and actions. What is your morale like?

What is your morale like? Do you hear that word *morale*? What does it remind you of?

I'll tell you: moral. *Morale* and *moral*, anyone can hear the stark similarity in the way these words sound and know that they are related etymologically. Our morale is and has always been related to our sense of moral conviction and moral worthiness. This is why people so often declare that they are "a good person." I understand the need. We all want to believe that we are good people. We are not animals. We're human beings. Animals have no need to believe they're good. Animals are instinctive creatures. It is very simple to be an animal. Being human means having a desperate desire to know that your actions are good and moral. The occasional sociopath recognized but notwithstanding, the majority of us need to know we are doing good and need to keep a monitor on our morale and how moral we are being. This requires us to do things that make us feel closer to God (good actions) and avoid those things that make us feel distant from Him (evil actions).

I appreciate that you may not be a religious person. That is fine. I want this book and this advice to be accessible to people of every background—I am, after all, a Jewish rabbi who regularly teaches at Christian congregations! Your religious affiliation is not important here. I personally come from a place that draws upon ancient Jewish wisdom, and so I speak and think in terms of morality bringing me closer to God and immoral behavior making me feel more distant from Him. But even if you are someone without a personal relationship with God and are essentially not religious, you should still be able to relate to wanting to be a good, moral person. You probably have aspects of your life and self that make you feel good and virtuous, and at other times, you probably feel as though you have let yourself down. Surely you relate to this?

The important thing is not the language and terms you use or your philosophical positioning; the important thing is recognizing where you stand morally. Why do I say this? Because success in business and life depends upon your ability to withstand temptation. You must resist all temptation that may steer you wrong: the temptation to sin; the temptation to overeat; the temptation to sit another hour watching mindless television; the temptation to relax at the coffee shop instead of squeezing in one more sales call. You must resist all temptations that prevent you from realizing your goals and a better self.

This is a two-way street: The ability to withstand temptation is closely linked to your sense of your own moral self-worth. Resisting temptation makes you feel better about yourself, and feeling better about yourself makes temptation easier to resist. Resisting temptation is easier when you truly think of yourself as a worthy, deserving person who is above bad behavior. It is hard to tell yourself that you cannot hang out at the coffee shop or watch TV if you enjoy those things. But it is much easier to tell yourself that you are not the kind of person who misses out on a sales call or wastes all day watching trash TV. "Who do you think I am?" you say to yourself, indignantly. "No way would I do those things. Not me!" This is you positioning yourself morally, building up your character, to make your choices easier to make and temptations easier to resist.

But beware: The reverse is also true. Succumbing to temptation and experiencing failure beget more temptation and failure. If you over-eat, you may feel less like going to the gym because you feel like you already have blown it. The alcoholic who takes that first drink is more likely to keep drinking until he passes out. If you waste half a day at work playing on the Internet, you are more likely to waste the second half because you already feel guilty anyway. You see yourself as a failure and it becomes a self-fulfilling prophecy. You must break the cycle!

In Victor Hugo's *Les Misérables*, there's a marvelous scene in which a character teetering between a life of crime and a moral life steals some silver from a priest. Later, when the thief is eventually caught, the priest spares the man and tells the policemen that the silver was not stolen but was actually a gift to the man. This act of mercy completely turns around the criminal's life. The priest, who is one of the most positive depictions of a religious figure in all of literature, understands that once the man is branded a thief, he will continue on the path. But by persuading the man that he is not a thief and has stolen nothing, he helps build up the man's morality. The man will have a harder time stealing in the future. The priest understands what I am telling you: Every time you stay firm to the moral course, every time you resist temptation, you will have an easier time resisting next time. But each time you yield to spiritual gravity and act immorally, you will find it easier to continue to do so.

The Bible is very clear on this. In Genesis, chapter 38, Judah takes a wife who is not a very suitable woman. They have three sons, two of whom are bad, and God takes them away. Then Judah is publicly humiliated for consorting with a prostitute. Let's put it this way:

chapter 38 is not Judah's best day. All of this misfortune starts from the beginning of the chapter, when it says that Judah descended from his brothers and turned aside towards an Adullamite man. Judah *descended*. He fell from a moral condition. Right off he is headed in a negative direction. He is not the only person to have ever felt that way. I have, at times in my life, thought to myself, "What are you doing? This is not a good thing. No good will come of this."

In Judges, chapter 14, we are told that Sampson wants to marry a daughter of the Philistines. For a Jew to date a Philistine was simply not allowed and Sampson knew this. Note that the Scripture here says, "Sampson went *down* to Timnah," where he met Delilah. Like Judah, he descended morally. Sampson and Judah did so knowingly and so were complicit in their own downfall. This language of descent, no coincidence, is a consistent pattern in God's message to man. Spiritual gravity hastens our moral descent.

Delilah's primary loyalty is not to her husband, Sampson, but to her Philistine former boyfriends. She asks what the secret of his strength is, planning his undoing, but he lies, telling her that if she weaves seven locks of his hair into a loom, he will lose the strength God has given him. She does this in his sleep and then wakes him, declaring that the Philistines are on him and he must go fight them. Enraged, he smashes the loom, his strength still with him. But later, after much badgering, he tells her the truth: his strength comes from the fact that he has never shaven his head and to do so would be to turn his back on God. This time, when she wakes him to say that the Philistines are again upon him, she has shaved his head in his sleep. So he goes out to fight them, not knowing that God has departed him, and this is the beginning of the end for him.

In both verses where Delilah declares that the Philistines are upon him, the Scripture tells us that "Sampson awoke from his sleep." In English translation, these verses look exactly the same, but in the Hebrew, they are quite different. The first time it is written in Hebrew, there are five letters, two *yudes*, and we know God is with him. In the second appearance, the same phrase is written with only four letters. The missing letter is that second *yude*, which is representative of God's spiritual strength. When both of these *yudes* are in place, Sampson wakes fully in touch with God, whom he has not yet betrayed by yielding to his wife's enticements. But the second time Sampson wakes from his sleep, the word is missing a *yude* and we know that his moral failure has resulted in a collapse of his morale. The missing letter signals that this is no simple awakening, but a shift in his reality. This is borne out again and again in the Bible: Moral failure begets a failure of morale, which begets more moral failure.

So how do we develop the strength that we need in order to maintain our morale and moral center? There are many ways and techniques. One is to allow yourself to celebrate small victories. Do not think victories are insignificant simply because they are small. As you have seen, good acts lead to more good acts and greater rewards. Every small victory lays the seeds for the next slightly bigger victory. And the reverse is also true. Small moral defeats and failures lead to more of the same. You must not focus on the individual points along the path but the path itself. Make sure you are on the moral path.

A technique is to actually use small victories as motivating rewards. Build them into your day as little self-challenges. If you make a sale at work, try to count the days until your next sale. Then, for your next sale, try to close it in less time. Or try to close a slightly larger sale each time. It doesn't matter if the sale is only 1 percent larger. The important thing is not that little victory—it's the string of victories that you will accrue, each one a little bigger than the one before. You grow as you go. That's the big secret.

Another technique is to write your goals down on paper. I don't mean your overarching life goals; those are too big and far off to revel in. Write down small actionable tasks that you can complete in short order. List them on paper. Then, try to achieve them. Having them written out both focuses you on the tasks at hand and also helps you to avoid procrastination. It's helpful to set a specific deadline when possible. Remember, small actionable tasks only. If you have larger projects, you can break them up into smaller pieces. No one carries out a large project in one fell swoop; break it down into steps and put them on a timetable. You will feel like a different person when you do these things. You will be free to make specific and achievable goals, step by step, and you will have motivators and daily reminders to continue to do so.

A final technique that can help is to impose accountability on yourself. Make yourself accountable to someone other than yourself. If you happen to be a person with a relationship with God, you can make Him the entity to which you're accountable. This works for many people. For others, those who are not religious or who need someone physically in the same room to keep them on track, you may find that a trusted person works just as well. Ideally, this will be somebody with something at stake in your performance and who is your true friend. Consider this person a member of "your own *personal* board of directors." Make this person your partner. Remember, you are in business if you are working, even if you are an employee or are unemployed and just working on finding a market for your skills. You've got to see yourself as the business professional you are.

Now, let's take this person to whom you are accountable. Put them on the "board of directors" of your small self-company. Name your business if you like: *Me, Inc.* maybe? Me, Inc. needs a board of directors like any other business, someone to hold the company (you) accountable. Maybe this is your spouse or children, a coworker, a friend, whoever—as long as they are someone whom you trust and respect. Give them the list of tasks that you wrote earlier and ask them to hold you accountable to them. Give yourself a timeline and share it with them so that if you fail to follow through, you will not let down only yourself, but them, too. This will motivate you, because we all want to please and serve others.

Also, offer this service to others. Offer to do it for a coworker if they will do it for you. This is a tremendous service we human beings can do for one another, and you should offer to provide the service to your friends just as you should ask it of them.

I realize that none of this cultivation of your moral character is easy or comes naturally. Being a human being is hard, and being a human on the road to success is harder. But the prize is worth the toil. And making choices about your behavior is what it means to really *be* human. Animals act on instinct. You probably have never met a lazy wolf or an obese elephant, just as you have also never known an animal that overeats or underexercises. Only human beings have these faults and virtues. Only we humans have to hone our discipline and persistence through education and training. None of this is instinctual, and it comes naturally to very few of us. But we do have the capacity for change and improvement, because we humans are special and, as I see it, are touched by the finger of God, whom we cannot let down. But even if you are not religious, you should avoid thinking of yourself in animalistic terms. And you should never yield to "instinct." Doing only what you feel like doing is an animalistic way of being, and resisting temptation is a profoundly human quality. You need not be religious to see this. We see this over and over again in the Bible because it is one of the most important principles that ancient Jewish wisdom teaches us.

Let me tell you a story from Scripture that illustrates these points: In Judges, chapter 7, Gideon is trusted by God to go and fight the Midianites, a mighty and terrifying army. Gideon raises an army of 12,000 men, but God tells him that he does not need so many men. Instead, he needs fewer of the right sort of men—a tight, fast-moving, hard-hitting small group of people. God emphasizes quality over quantity. So Gideon reduces the force to 10,000, but God still thinks it is too large. He dismisses the group as a rag-tag band.

Gideon takes his ten thousand men down to the river after a long day's march and allows them 10 minutes to drink from the stream. The men are terribly thirsty after being drilled all day and they rush to the water. Gideon watches them like a hawk to see how the men drink. He watches to see who lowers their heads to the water and laps it up as an animal would and who lowers their hands into the water and brings the water to their mouth as a civilized man would. You can probably guess Gideon's motives here! He sends home all the men who drank from the stream like animals and then is left with only 300 men with which to battle the Midianites. These 300 chosen men go on to a triumphant victory in battle because they are quality men with God on their side.

These men are blessed and chosen because they acted like men, not like animals, both at the stream and in all aspects of their lives. They are men who make their own choices about how they will behave, and who hold themselves (and their fellow man) accountable for their choices and their behavior. Remember this when you are choosing business partners—you want to surround yourself with men and women such as these, those that resist temptation and animal urges and move through the world like human beings. Choose partners who take responsibility for their actions.

It may seem like a small gesture, bringing water to your face rather than bending for it as an animal would, but it is one small measure of a human. I remember once when I was a little boy. My mother served me chicken soup, which I slurped from the bowl on the table. My mother demanded to know what I was doing. I told her I was drinking my chicken soup. "You're eating like an animal!" she told me. Stubborn, sassy, and stupid, I responded shamefully, "Well, so what if I'm eating like an animal? Maybe I am one." I don't want to tell you exactly what happened, but I will just confide to you that for the next three or four hours, I had four finger marks on my cheek. I never drank soup that way again.

Why would my Jewish mother react so strongly? Because she understood ancient Jewish wisdom and knew that we must resist temptation and behave like humans. We must not act like animals, for animals have no moral compass. What distinguishes us from animals is our spirituality. And where is our spirituality? Our head is its reservoir, that container for our spiritual strength. This is why lowering your head down to the river, or to your chicken soup, is akin to saying, "I am an animal." This is why civilized people use cutlery: so that we may raise the food to a spiritual level rather than lower our spiritual being to a material level.

The lesson of Gideon is that real victory requires us to act as humans, not animals. The military is an excellent analogy for business because, as in business, no one can pull off victory alone. There are no Rambos in real life. We must depend on our comrades and our partners to overcome our enemies. In Scripture, the historic enemies of the Israelites from so long ago are also depictions of the enemies that are found inside each of us that obstruct our triumph and block our success. Ancient Jewish wisdom shows us how the various enemies of the Israelites each represent a different aspect of the spiritual gravity that pulls us down and prevents us from achieving what we know in our heads we need to do. In the case of Gideon, we are shown how to overcome our animal urges and how we must band together and trust in our companions, compatriots, and business partners.

Nobody succeeds all on their own, not on the battlefield and not in the boardroom. What allows us to succeed, in life and in making money, are our connections to one another and the morale we get from following our moral conviction. It is the discipline and character we cultivate that makes it possible to work well together. Have you ever had a coworker who was an immoral person? Then I don't need to tell you that they were terrible to work with! So surround yourself with the right people. And surround yourself with more people. An isolated person accomplishes nothing—such a person will struggle to succeed in mastering himself. The more people you surround yourself with, the more likely you will find the right people. Consider Gideon, who had to first gather 12,000 men to find a mere 300 with whom he could work.

Remember the accountability principle we discussed earlier? Surrounding ourselves with people of moral character makes it easier to hold ourselves accountable and be moral ourselves. And together we all become a rising wave. Teach these principles to your friends, partner, and your children. Deuteronomy 11:9 says, "And you shall teach these to your children." Do not fail to pass these principles and their meanings on to other people in your life, as well. The Hebrew text offers an expanded understanding of what you are asked to do.

Most such passages in Scripture that instruct us to teach things to our children read: "and you shall teach them to your children," or something similar. This means that you shall teach all these principles, all these laws, all these statutes to your children. But what many people fail to realize is that in this particular instance, in Deuteronomy 11:9, the phrase "teach them" is spelled differently. You probably do not read Hebrew, so let me explain again that small spelling changes in a word can change the meaning of a whole passage. In this case, there is a letter missing, which changes a four-letter word to a three-letter word and also changes the meaning to mean "you" so that the correct reading of that verse is not "and you shall teach them to your children." Instead, the correct reading is this: "And you shall teach them to yourself first and then your children."

In other words, there is an obligation placed on each and every one of us to master these principles, each and every one of them. You must first build your own character and moral center so that you may then pass it along and share it with others. But do not forget: Your actions and character must start with you.

Secret #12

Your Authentic Identity Requires Other People

F rom the last biblical business secret, you can see that other people need what we have to offer so that they may build up their own characters. The thoughtful person will of course realize that, by extension, we too need other people in our lives so that we may build up our own characters into an authentic identity. People require these connections. All things in the universe do. Think back to earlier when we discussed the 92 naturally occurring elements of the periodic table of elements used by scientists everywhere. Recall that all useful things in nature are a combination of these basic elements; everything we benefit from is made of these few elements. The air we breathe is made up of nitrogen and oxygen. The water we drink is made of two parts hydrogen to one part oxygen.

As an aside, it is worth pointing out that in the first 34 verses of Genesis, God creates all of these 92 elements. Now, how many Hebrew words do you think are used in Scripture to describe the creation? Would you be shocked if I told you there are precisely 92 Hebrew words? Many of them, of course, are used more than once, but in terms of how many discrete elements are used to recount the story of creation, which involved actually making 92 elements, there are only 92 words. This kind of structural integrity is important to ancient Jewish wisdom and to the Hebrew text of the Scripture, and it is absolutely irresistible. It gives us a glimpse of understanding that which is beyond our understanding in the Bible.

You may wonder why God gave us these elements but not water itself in its complete form. Why is water, something so basic to survival and life, not its own element? Why did God not deliver to us whole and useful things?

It seems that in order to get use out of the world, we have to connect and combine things. God gives us a world in which only connections yield practical results. We benefit from the elements only when they are connected and combined. Likewise, connections with other people are also integral to any benefit we would see ourselves. Connections to other people help us preserve our own sense of virtue and worthiness. Alone, we are nothing.

Consider Adam when he finds himself alone in the Garden of Eden. Never has a man been so alone on the earth and never again will he be, because it is God's desire for people to come together and collaborate. In the book of Genesis, chapter 2, verse 18, God says, "It is not good for man to be alone." This isn't just a statement about Adam's matrimonial prospects. What He is telling us is that if you were the last person on earth, life would be miserable. Living alone is an absolute misery.

After making this declaration that it is not good for man to be alone, God decides to make a helper for Adam. And then He brings all the animals that He has created, all the beasts of the field and all the birds of the sky, and He brings them to Adam and allows Adam to name each one. This is actually the first service man provides other men (before they are even created!), and it is an interesting service: Adam begins naming God's creations.

Note that it is only after the creation and naming of animals that God puts Adam into a deep sleep and creates Eve. Why is there this interruption in the story between the declaration that man not be alone and the creation of Eve? Why must we pause for Adam to name all of the animals? You can just picture Adam tapping his foot impatiently, thinking, this is great, but can we get to the girl already, please?

Remember, there are no accidents in the Bible, so we must turn to ancient Jewish wisdom for insight into this matter. Earlier we spoke about the importance of humans acting as humans and resisting animalistic activities. As you can see, humans are partly defined by what they are not. We are not animals; we are humans. So you can see that before Adam can act as a human, he must name that which he is not. He is defined by what he is not as much as by what he is.

So Adam had to name each animal, and he picked names based off how they appeared to him. For instance, the Hebrew word for a giraffe—from which the English word is taken—is *neck*, because Adam looked at this creature and he said, "My, what a neck!" And on it went. Each and every animal named appropriately. The Hebrew language structure of every animal's name is mindboggling—there is such symmetry to the language and that which it describes.

But don't forget: It wasn't God that named these animals, because these animals were not going to interact with God. They were going to interact with people. You get your identity, your name, that which is and identifies you, from your interaction with others. Our identity does not exist in the absence of others. Total isolation from other human beings erodes our identity.

There is a common trope in contemporary literature about man needing to get away and escape into isolation in order to find himself. We see this popularized by Henry David Thoreau, who lived alone in a cabin by a pond to find himself, and Jack Kerouac, who popularized the road narrative as a way to find one's self. Perhaps you yourself have romanticized the notion of disappearing to a secluded isle.

This is completely misguided. The truth is this: You can only find yourself when you are among others. Isolation doesn't work. People go crazy in isolation. In such a state, what you find is not your identity at all but a distorted perception, because you lose perspective on yourself without others around. Our identity hinges upon connections to other people. We define ourselves by what we are not.

In the case of Adam, we can see this is true. When God asks Adam to name Eve, as he did with the animals, Adam does not say *Eve*. He uses another Hebrew word: *Esha*. This roughly translates to an amalgam of woman and wife. God asks what made him think of this name, and Adam says, through her, he found his own identity as *Isch*. This may seem curious. Prior to this point in Genesis, he is referred to only as Adam. His identity as Isch only emerges in the presence of Eve. It is only through that connection with someone else that Adam's full identity begins to become clear.

The lesson here is that by connecting with other people, by making commitments with other people, by establishing obligations between ourselves and others, we are able to discover and hone our own identity. Alone we cannot know who we are. We cannot know who we will eventually become as we set out in life because it is our connections and relationships with others that mold us. As you set out in life and business, you will make connections to new people who will steer the course of your life and character, so do choose these people carefully. Also, when it comes to meeting new people, cast your net wide. Meet a wide variety of people so you will find those who allow you to grow as you want.

This is one of the greatest secrets of business that the Bible gives us. It is through networking that we find ourselves and grow. Look to others to find yourself. Choose your colleagues and business partners based upon how you want to be and whom you want to grow into.

Know How Business Works; Understand Specialization and Cooperation

There is a widespread belief among the general population that business is unfair. Maybe you have met people who believe this. These misguided souls believe that business is inherently unfair simply because they see some people who do better in business than others. They assume that anyone who has more must be greedy. Business is bad, these naysayers of capitalism suppose, because it rewards greed. If you are reading this book, it is safe to say that you do not hold similar views. But many do. Ask people in your various circles about this and you may be shocked at how many buy into this misguided notion. They believe this because they do not understand what business really is. They believe it because they have not put in the effort to find out how business really works. If they were to put in the effort, they would see business, at least as it exists in free-market economies predominately in the West, for the meritocracy that it is.

Many books have been written that examine why some nations work better than others. To name a few: *The Wealth and Poverty of*

Nations, by scholar David Landes; *Why Nations Fail*, by James A. Robinson; *Civilization: The West and the Rest*, by Niall Ferguson; and *Guns, Germs, and Steel*, by Jared Diamond. I recommend all of these books for insight into this topic: That differences in economic performance are chiefly dependent upon spiritual rather than physical characteristics. We come to understand that this is as true for individuals as it is for nations. The most significant factors in our success are things we have the power to change.

These books show us why some countries perform better than others do. When separate nations are bound by the obligations of economic alliances, as in the European Union, this leads to the less efficient state leaching off the stronger state. Consider, for example, the case of Germany and Greece. These two countries, bound by the European Union, are economically linked, and you have one not pulling its weight. Germany literally pays for Greece to take siestas!

But why is it that some countries simply function better than other countries? Why does Germany's economy function better than Spain's? Why do certain countries in Europe work better than many in Asia? Why does most of North America work better than the vast majority of the nations in Africa? What causes these differences? It is not racial differences, I can tell you that. And I will concede that climate and geography and natural resources have an effect, but the wealth and poverty gap observed between countries is predominately the result of differences in culture. Most scholars and researchers are in agreement: culture is the defining difference. The other factors, while real, are insignificant by comparison.

Culture is influenced by the language with which people of that culture communicate. Culture and language color each other. French is the language of romance, whereas Russian lends itself to brooding epics about the darkest side of human nature; these differences result in a noticeably different aesthetic in the art originating from these countries. The language helps define the mood and political atmosphere as well. As God's language, Hebrew has a very privileged position—it gives us insight into God's culture. By studying Hebrew, we can intuit what God deems important and proper and right.

The differences found within languages give us insight into the priorities of that culture. Different languages allow for different ideas to be communicated, and this has an impact on the lives and mind-sets of the speakers of that language. For example, the English language clearly allows for delineation between "winning a sum of money" and "earning a sum of money." This allows English speakers to discuss the difference between earning and winning—indeed, it allows for a distinction to be made at all. Hebrew doesn't even have a word for "winning money." Why not? Well, ask yourself, what does "winning money" mean? It implies that you did not do anything for the money. God might ask you what you mean by "winning money," because there is no word for it in His language. So you might say, I went to the casino and won money, by which you may mean you gained money that someone else lost. To God, this is not good, and so, in His language, there is only earning money. This teaches us a lesson that is not in the English language and culture. But at least English distinguishes between winning and earning so that its speakers might see the difference.

Now consider Spanish. In Spanish, the phrase for this concept is *ganar dinero. Dinero* means "money" and *ganar* means "winning or earning money." The language draws no distinction between the two. Whether I go to a casino and win money or spend the day roofing houses to earn money, the language allows for no distinction to be drawn. In effect, they are the same to the speaker and listener. French is similar. Their phrase is *gagner argent.* Again, no distinction between winning and earning.

Now, to recap: French and Spanish make no distinction between winning and earning; English uses separate words for both; Hebrew has a word only for earning.

Now, which of these languages positions the speakers to best earn the most money? Obviously, those of the Hebraic culture have an edge. Their language is set up to facilitate earning money. They don't even acknowledge the dreadful and destructive concept of "winning" money for free without earning it.

Earning money is clearly superior to winning money. When I earn money, two parties benefit: the one who earns the money and the one who makes a purchase so that he may receive a service or product. When you hire a roofer to fix your roof, he gains a paycheck, and you gain a roof that no longer leaks. God smiles on the transaction because both the roofer and the customer are better off from doing business together. It is beautiful. Two human beings have come together. They collaborated. They created something. They created a repaired roof. The roofer walked away with his wage; the homeowner has a watertight roof.

Winning money does not create happiness for all involved. When you win money, you are taking it from someone *without earning it.* If you and I play poker and we both put $100 into the pot and I walk away with $200 and you have nothing left, have I earned money or simply taken your money? Was anything created? Was a good or service brought into creation? Are all participants equally happy? The answers are no, no, no, and definitely not. I won, you lost. That is how winning money works, and that is why winning money is such a bad idea. A language or a culture that combines the two words, earning and winning, implies that they are the same thing. They are not. Not even close.

This is just one example of how language affects culture. You may draw your own conclusions about how this effect influences societies. Just note that in England, where they have a word for winning and earning, the people have thrived. The industrial revolution was launched in England, not in France or Spain. Why? Because it was driven by the potential of earning money, not winning money, and cultures that draw a distinction between the two words are better positioned to appreciate the power of earning your money. And so too will you, but only if you accept this truth and integrate it into your everyday life.

Just look at Hebrew culture, which has a word only for earning. This shows you how focused on earning wealth the Jewish people are and also explains why there have been so many wealthy Jews throughout history. The culture is just set up to make money, to focus on it. The Torah, the five books of Moses, contain far more laws about money than laws about kosher food, the dietary laws, about ritual, or about anything else. Why would the Torah have more rules about money than anything else? Because ancient Jewish wisdom recognizes that earning money is essential to life. Each and every one of us must eat and put a roof over our heads and care for our families, which means we must earn a living.

We can either go it alone or we can collaborate with other people, but we must earn a living. We discover pretty quickly that going it alone is a terrible way. Engaging in business with other people is thrilling, exciting, and effective. God wants us to collaborate, and so he makes it more effective to do so. He has put collaboration at the center of the moneymaking process by giving us the principles of business. If we want to succeed in business, we must understand these principles. This is what it means to understand business. You fail to do so at your own detriment.

Indeed, trying to go it alone in business is like running against the current. If not impossible, going it alone is certainly less efficient than specializing and collaborating.

In the eighteenth century Western world, Adam Smith identified the concept of specialization, though he did not invent it, for the concept always existed; it had just not been named. Ancient Jewish wisdom was already aware of the concept; Smith just gave it a new name and popularized it, which, make no mistake, was a great service to his fellow man. Smith observed that specialization provided advantages over independent living. In villages where everyone does everything for themselves, people must sew their own clothing, look after their own cows for milk, look after their own chickens for eggs, grow their own carrots and potatoes. Everybody takes care of all of their own needs entirely. As you can imagine, this is simply exhausting and allows no time for pursuing moneymaking or leisure—it is a harsh subsistence life. And it is lonely. In such a village, the people don't even need to ever get together because they are independent and everyone is self-sufficient. But they are also tired and always working, terribly inefficient, and isolated from their fellow man.

This apparently was not part of God's plan for human economic interaction. Why? Because no one does this anymore unless they have to. It doesn't work. Or rather, it doesn't work well. Imagine two farmers working independently on neighboring farms. They never see each other because each has everything they need on their own farm. Until one day, they bump into each other on the road and visit each other's farm. One farmer notices that the other has better cows that provide the most creamy-looking milk. He asks to try some and notices that it is better than the milk from his cows. But he also notices the other farmer's rough, scraggly clothes. He asks about them and realizes that this farmer has inferior wool and little knowledge of sewing and weaving.

Pretty soon the wheels start turning in their heads. They realize that one is better at raising cows and producing dairy products, and the other better at raising sheep and making wool and clothes. They decide to exchange wool for dairy products. And—boom!—commerce is born! This goes on for a while, but then they realize that the farmer making wool doesn't need his cows anymore and the one making milk and cheese doesn't need his sheep. So they exchange those, too! And now they no longer have to tend to these animals, and they have more time to focus on what they are good at. And—boom!—specialization is born!

This is an oversimplification, of course, and in modern culture we are far more specialized so that only a few percent of the population need to farm *at all*. But in economic terms, this model illustrates how specialization works. All of a sudden, the farmer who is no longer raising sheep still has wool. They also now have the cows and time to produce extra dairy to trade for even more products, allowing them to further specialize and reinvest further time and energy in their burgeoning dairy business. The same for the other farmer—his wool business is taking off!

Furthermore, every time they get together to trade, they talk to each other and exchange ideas. One day, in conversation, they realize a third farmer down the road has the best potatoes around. Together, they come up with the idea of cutting this new farmer in on their trades. Again, they are now all able to further specialize. The more people they trade with, the more they exchange products and ideas. The whole process is viral.

Adam Smith observed this process of specialization and realized that even in the limited experimental arena in which he was able to observe the idea of specialization, geysers of economic productivity were let loose. Of course, ancient Jewish wisdom already knew of this, but now more countries throughout the Western world were recognizing and implementing this knowledge on a grander scale than had ever been done before. But it was always there in ancient Jewish wisdom.

Consider, for example, Jacob. When Jacob died, he gave blessings to his 12 sons and explained what is essentially the principle of specialization that Adam Smith describes. Jacob basically told his children this: "You're all the children of Israel. You're all unified. But each and every one of you is going to fulfill a different function. Some will be in business. Some will provide scholarly research and work in academia. Some will provide shipping and transport."

Each son would provide their own thing, and in this way, all of their individual needs and the needs of their fledging nation would be supplied collectively. But Jacob also said that none of them was going to be independent. Each one of them was going to need the other 11. They were thus tied to one another, combined if you will, and Judaism was founded, Hebrew culture took off, and the economic power of the Jewish people experienced exponential growth—all thanks to specialization, trade, and collaboration. When you make yourself interdependent with other people in this way, as Jacob told his offspring to be, there's no stopping you. Each of you can do something, but together all of you can do everything.

This is what business looks like. These are the principles on which it functions. And so I bring us full circle and I ask you, what is unfair about this? Everyone contributes and everyone reaps rewards. But everyone contributes differently, by their own accord and their own ability, and thus they reap different rewards based on their talents and effort.

The answer, of course, is that there is nothing unfair about it at all. The people who say so simply do not understand business and how business professionals really make their money. They do, however, understand how NFL football players make their money. You very seldom hear politicians preaching the politics of envy against football players. You never hear them saying, "That football player got a 60-million-dollar contract! That's not fair. He's got to pay his fair share!" You don't hear politicians speaking like that about football players. But you do hear this all of the time about business professionals. You hear complaints that the chief executive officer of a company makes a hundred times more than the janitor, but never do you hear that a football player makes a hundred times what the groundskeeper makes, though they do make that much more, if not even more. It's the same with movie stars and pop stars. Have you ever heard a politician say that these movie stars making $20 million for three weeks of working on a movie don't deserve it? No. But when we find out a CEO has made that much, politicians demand to know why. They demand to know how much he paid in taxes—and they are never appeased with the amount, they always want him taxed more.

Everywhere you look, business professionals are demonized for making lots of money while football players and celebrities get a free pass. This is because the general populace understands why a football player gets paid so much. He can throw a ball farther than anyone else, or he runs very fast, or he is good at scoring goals. These are simple activities and we can observe them. We can see the thing that makes him distinctive, which also earns him his money. We can all see that we cannot do what he does, and so we admit that he deserves his lavish compensation. Hollywood actors are the same: they are especially beautiful or charismatic, and we can see that they are a rarity, and so we believe that they are worth the millions of dollars they make. And make no mistake, they are! These people have rare talents and skills, which they have fairly leveraged for handsome pay. There's nothing wrong with that.

But what about the highly compensated business executive? Does he not earn his keep, too? Top CEOs also make a lot of money, often more than actors and football players. The richest people in the world are almost all business professionals, not entertainers. Now consider the CEO's case. The average person looks at a business executive and wonders what about him is so special that he can command a salary of millions of dollars. They think, "What does he do? He sits in the corner office on the top floor, talks to people on the phone, and that's it. I can do that! Anyone can do that!" This isn't usually true, but it is what people think.

This is why business professionals are so easy to demonize: because your average person does not understand what a talented and proven CEO brings to the table. Nobody understands that he brings a reputation. He brings a competence. He brings an understanding and expertise and savvy. He brings connections with other people. People not in the upper echelons of the business world often do not understand how much this is worth. They do not see that it is tremendously valuable.

In 2009, following the stock market crash and during the height of the Great Recession, one of the great brokerage houses of America was in financial trouble and starting to fail. The highly paid executives who'd performed poorly and run the company into the ground were fired and the company needed a replacement. Who did they get? They hired Warren Buffett, one of the greatest business professionals in the history of mankind, to come in and become the head of the brokerage house. They wanted him to save the house. How much was he worth to them? There was almost no limit! He could've asked for anything he wanted because he was going to save a whole company.

So how did Warren Buffett do this? How did he, specifically, save the whole company? He did so through the magic of human connection, through the magic of reputation, through the magic of understanding and knowledge. The global business community realized that Warren Buffett was going to be in charge, a man with a remarkable track record, and so they continued to extend credit to the company. And the company was thus saved by the confidence that creditors and the markets placed in this one man. The world had faith in him. That's right. It's all about faith and reputation and a solid track record of doing good business, but people find that hard to understand.

They just don't get it. Football players they get. Movie stars they get. He can really swing a bat! She has a face like no other! But when a business professional makes an equivalent sum of money, people don't get it. They just see a man in a suit in an office, a man that maybe looks nondescript like everyone else, and people don't bother to understand what he really does or brings to the table. But they could if they tried, if they did a little independent research, if they bothered at all. If you are going to be taken seriously in the business world, you must take the business world seriously. Give your due diligence to understanding business or you will have no place in it.

And you do want a place in the business world. Or you should. Business is a spiritual endeavor, and it brings us closer to one another and closer to God. And we are all in business—all of us who work and provide services to our fellow man. So unless you're independently wealthy or homeless and not looking for work, you are assuredly in business. And this is a good thing. Business brings us closer together. Business is one of God's plans to keep us connected with each other and slowly trudging toward that vision of greater unity that is God himself.

Consider again our farmers from earlier: the wool farmer, the potato farmer, and the dairy farmer. These were isolated individuals forced to take care of themselves independently. But now they are part of a community, a co-op. Specialization has brought them together. And now it keeps them together. They now need each other. If one gets sick, the others will definitely be there praying for his rapid recovery because they are dependent upon him. Before, if one got sick, nobody cared because, economically speaking, it didn't matter. It wouldn't have mattered on a personal level even because without business to bring them together, they did not even know each other. But now they are all bound together into this invisible network of human connectivity that compels them to love each other. It is a fact that people who trade don't usually fight. Trade reduces the incidence of wars.

You can see God's hand guiding us towards business by how He has structured the world and mankind. He created man with almost limitless yearnings. We yearn for the infinite. We have infinite desires. But He also placed man into a world with apparently limited resources. There's only so much real estate, so many fish in the sea, so much oil in the ground, and so on. Most importantly, there is only so much time in the workday. It is only by following God's rules of ongoing and constant cooperation that we can create enough for everyone. Going it alone condemns us a constant struggle for survival. Clearly, God has set up the world in mysterious and counterintuitive ways, but we can intuit His motivations here through ancient Jewish wisdom. Limited time and resources requires us to be generous and giving to one another. It requires us to cooperate.

What ancient Jewish wisdom makes of this is that interpersonal economic interaction through ethical capitalism is good and pleases God. Otherwise, why would He require it of us? There have been other attempts to solve the problem of extracting a living from a world that is often noncooperative. They do not work. Isolation and independence do not work well. Communism coerces us to work together in unnatural ways. God finds these systems evil and has arranged for them to ultimately fail—the game is stacked against them by Him. There has never once in the history of the world been a communist nation that has been successful, and there never will be. It is only the voluntary cooperation between people that free market capitalism encourages that finds favor with God, which is why it is the only economic system that works.

The wise and moral person accepts these truisms and truly understands business and economics as God intended them to look and be. Others struggle to understand how business works, how it works now, and how it has always worked. To swim against the current is futile and will find you in disfavor with God and ultimately unsuccessful at making money, no matter your endeavor.

Each and Every One of Us Is in Business and Should Act Like a Business Professional

A s we have said previously, you must begin to see yourself as in business now. Not later. No one need grant you this legitimacy. You do not need an employer or the stock exchange or the IRS or anyone else to grant you legitimacy. It is a frame of mind you may simply adopt. If you trade services or products for financial gain, you are in business. You are then a business professional. Regardless of what you do to serve humanity, you should strive always to be a business professional, not an amateur. What your particular business is doesn't matter, whether you are an executive or in retail. Whatever you do, just be a professional at it. If your innate talent is that of a rodeo clown, by all means go out and be the most professional rodeo clown that ever existed. But do not be an amateur rodeo clown.

So what is a professional? How do you become one?

First and foremost, a professional is someone who does the work that he must do when he must do it. Do your work and do it on time. Wise King Solomon said in Proverbs 22:29, "If you see a man who is quick to do his work, prompt to do his work, not when he feels like but when it needs to be done, you are looking at a man who's going to stand with kings." Promptness to do your work, to do what you have to do, not what you want to do, is the mark of the true professional.

The professional always busies himself with business only. His true work.

Just because one is not idle does not mean one is actually working. It is actually quite easy to keep busy, but you must be sure you are busying yourself with the task for which you are actually being paid.

There was a man who worked for me as a sales professional, a new employee, who used to produce the most beautiful graphs and charts. His job was to seek out new customers. Several times a week I would ask him, "When are you going to get started on those sales calls?" He had yet to do one. He told me he just had to finish a chart of all the potential customers in the region. The next day he gave me a chart with colors and tables and references. It was beautiful. I didn't even know how he had made it. I asked him, "Are you now ready to make sales calls?" He shook his head no. "I've just got to do a graph that'll show me which are the most potentially profitable customers," he said, nodding his head and clearly excited about his "work." He soon brought me a new graphic detailing where to find the best customers.

The thing about this man is that he was always busy. Whenever I went by his office, he was working. I never saw him around the water cooler. I never saw him hanging out in the break room. He was working and working and working—always. But guess what? We fired him. He wasn't doing what he *must* do. He was doing what he *wanted* to do. He just loved playing with Microsoft Excel and making graphs and charts. But he wasn't producing any value at all because he wasn't doing what needed to be done when it had to be done. He wasn't doing what we had hired him to do. This is not the mark of a professional. Resist the temptation to do only what you want, and do what you must do, and you will find the favor of your employer, your fellow man, and God.

The Latin root of *amateur* is from the Latin word *amor*, which means "to love." That's what an amateur is: someone who does only what he loves doing. A professional does what he must do. Whereas an amateur does what he loves, a professional learns to love what he must do because he takes his professional life seriously. There is a time for play and a time for socializing and a time for hobbies and a time for family—but guess what, the time for all of those things is on your own time. When you are on the work clock, you need to be working. A professional takes his work seriously all of the time, full-time.

I consider part-time work a very big problem and a risky endeavor. It sounds nice to only work part-time and have more time for hobbies, family, and socializing. But working part-time is not the mark of someone who takes work seriously. Sometimes, there are exceptions, as there are to every rule, but examine the part-time work life very carefully before you consider it. If you're planning to make more money, significantly more money, and your plan is to do it part-time, I urge you to examine your intentions. If you have all of that extra time, why wouldn't you put it towards being more productive? Even if you only get part-time hours at your day job, why would you not use your free time to start a business? That is what a professional would do, and if you are not doing this, you really need to examine why.

A professional doesn't look for work that he loves; he makes himself love his work. Reporters on radio and TV are always asking people about their work and how they feel about it—maybe you have seen or heard one of these little segments. They will interview people in all kinds of professions—doctors, policemen, firemen, businessmen, whoever. Inevitably the interviewer asks, "If you had to do it all over again, what would you choose to be?" You can tell that the interviewer expects them to say something grander, like a politician or an artist or actor or something. They expect the interviewees to say they would have picked a profession with more prestige and pay. But, overwhelmingly, most people say they would do the same thing.

Did all of these people luck out and just happen to find their one true calling? No. What are the chances? The fact is they were professional about their careers. And when you're a professional, you invest in your career; you set and accomplish your business goals; and, in the process, you end up loving it. As a professional, you do not find work you love—you find a way to love your work. You may not start off loving it, but by investing in your work, you begin to love it. Just as when you invest in people, you begin to love them, so this is true for your work. Investment in your work leads to commitment, which leads to love for your work.

It's no accident that at the beginning of Genesis, chapter 2, verse 15, God put Adam into the Garden of Eden and said "*Le-Ovdah*," which is Hebrew for "to work it." This may come as a surprise: After all, everything came easily in the Garden of Eden and you didn't have to work. Note that word: Adam didn't *have* to work. In the Garden of Eden, the food came readily and easily. Adam didn't have to do anything to feed himself, not until after he was evicted from the Garden of Eden, but God had him work the garden anyway. God wanted him to do extra things: to make the garden look beautiful, to keep things spruced up and looking nice. It was still going to produce no matter what, but Adam was still put there to work. Why? Because God wanted him to love the Garden of Eden. God knew that only by working the garden would he come to truly love it, which is why He told him to work it even when he did not have to.

Follow Adam's lead and learn to love your work. This is a mark of the true professional—choosing to love what you do to serve others simply because it is what you do to serve others. There's nothing professional about sitting at your job eight or ten hours a day and hating every minute of it. This negativity will reflect poorly in your performance every time. There's no faking it. You must readjust your attitude. Invest in your work. Commit to it. Love will follow, just as it did for Adam. Love will follow and so will money, because God rewards those that serve others, and serving others is what professional business professionals do naturally.

Develop All Four Dimensions of Your Life Simultaneously

From the previous chapter, you may get the wrong idea that I overvalue work and undervalue other aspects of life, such as family, friends, and hobbies. This couldn't be further from the truth. I have a wonderful family whom I love and enjoy spending time with. I cultivate as many friendships as I can, as I have suggested you do earlier in this book. I am an avid boater; boating is one of my greatest passions and joys in life. But this book is called *Business Secrets from the Bible*, not *Boating Secrets from the Bible* or *Hobbyist Secrets from the Bible*. The instructional focus here is on developing your professional life. We are talking about your work life here, not your personal life, and at work, you work. Period.

However, do understand that you cannot, in life, focus on only one aspect of yourself. You must develop all aspects simultaneously.

In Hebrew, there is a word that means ladder: *S-L-M*. And there's another word that is the word that follows ladder—or, put differently, the word that ladder leads phonetically toward. This word is: *SH-L-M*. This word means totality, completion, and peace. The idea is that the ladder, the route upwards, must lead to completion . . . completion of everything. That means all aspects of your life must be complete. You cannot succeed in business unless you have met all of your needs, not just your professional needs.

We all probably know someone who has been deemed a workaholic. I don't like that word because it is often used by lazy, idle people to shame productive people. Why do they do this? Because it is easier to tear down others than to work on improving yourself. Taking your work seriously and giving it your all is noble. But, that said, it is possible to lead an unbalanced life. You may know someone who throws himself into his career to such an extent that he ruins his marriage and neglects his children. If you were to ask him if it is really worth it, you know that deep down inside he understands that it is not. This is true just as it is true that spending all of your time with your family and neglecting your work is not worth it. If you neglect work, you cannot support your family. But it is also true that if you neglect your family, then you may find yourself with nothing worth supporting. You have to strike a balance.

When people become despondent about not reaching a goal, often it is because they have adopted a one-dimensional view of their lives. They have a vision of where they should be, and they fall into a trap of focusing on only one dimension, the development of only one area, and can't see the forest for the trees. You need to consider the big picture and address all of your needs.

Abraham Maslow was a Jewish psychologist who became famous for detailing the hierarchy of human needs in the 1960s. Now, honestly, I don't know if he lifted them from ancient Jewish wisdom or whether he figured it out for himself, but, either way, he got the basic human needs right. However, while Maslow did list the four needs, he did not explain where they come from in ancient Jewish wisdom or why we need them, only that we do. The four needs are easy to forget if you do not understand their origin. So I want to show you how we understand these four needs through ancient Jewish wisdom so that you will be able to understand them within the context of your own life. It is not really important that you know what Maslow called the four needs on his hierarchy chart, but it is important that you understand the four principles of ancient Jewish wisdom on which they are based.

If you understand these principles, you will be able to develop all four areas simultaneously so that they are never out of proportion with each other. Your life will look and feel distorted if it is overdeveloped in one area and underdeveloped in another. Develop them simultaneously and you will cultivate a well-rounded fullness of life that will allow you to remain enthusiastic and excited about your present and future. If you fall behind in one or more areas, you will get despondent or gloomy, but if you develop them all simultaneously, you will feel good no matter what stage of development you are in. The key is to be able to identify what area you are lagging behind in so you can focus on whichever specific area needs more attention, bringing your life back into balance and harmony.

In the beginning, God created heaven and earth. This is how the Bible begins. The Bible is the only sacred text among all the religions of the world that begins with that fundamental statement. Ancient Jewish wisdom notes that, if the story of creation were merely a historic account, the opening of the Bible would have read: "In the beginning, God created everything." Or perhaps: "In the beginning, God created the entire universe." However, because the volume is a comprehensive matrix of the totality of all existence, and is intended chiefly as a guidebook to human existence, both on an individual and a social level, it begins with those words: "God created heaven and earth."

The reason is because there is a maddening duality to our existence. Our lives are complicated by the fact that everything needs to be examined through two eyes: The eye of heaven, namely the spiritual, and the eye of the earth, which means the physical. Spiritual does not necessarily mean holy or sanctified or even virtuous. Spiritual, in ancient Jewish wisdom, means very specifically those things that cannot be measured by means of conventional scientific discovery. For instance, spiritual includes love and loyalty. It includes determination. It includes hope and ambition, and it includes, yes, money.

The physical of course includes everything tangible and visible in the world. The point that is so easy to miss is that much of what brings us the fullness and joy of life is spiritual rather than physical. And even deep insights in ancient Jewish wisdom, in that much of the physical requirements for long, healthy, and comfortable living depend upon mastering the spiritual. My point in writing this book is to unpack the thousands of pages of ancient Jewish wisdom, most of which remained an oral transmission until about two millenia ago. My goal is to make this easily accessible to you in ways that can dramatically enhance the quality of your life.

Allow me to start off with an example to help explain the difference between the spiritual and physical. Imagine a woman eager to discover more about the baby she is pregnant with. Now, I do not know if at the present moment all the tests I am about to describe are already available at your local clinic. However, I am quite confident that those that are not will soon be.

For instance, the woman might ask the doctor, "Is my child going to be male or female?" That is purely a physical distinction and easy to determine. She might ask if her baby is going to have a tendency toward being overweight or being large or slender. She might ask if her baby has a proclivity to any childhood diseases. She might even ask the color of the skin of her unborn child. All of these things are easily determined because they are physical, and the answers lie within the embryo's genetic structure, which is easily examined.

She might continue, since the doctor has been so successful in revealing so much about her future child, and ask, "Please tell me if my child is going to be an honest human being. Is my child going to be a person with integrity? Is my child going to be a loyal friend, whom people will love? Is my child going to be a person of optimism or pessimism? Is my child going to be capable of resourcefulness and determination?" At this point, the doctor shrugs his shoulders helplessly and explains to his patient that she is now inquiring of the spiritual characteristics. No tests exist. These depend on the manner in which the child is raised.

Now, when you get down to the question of that child's future financial success in the world, it should be clear that the physical characteristics about which she inquired are not as important as the spiritual. If that child will one day seek a job, the job will be awarded only on the basis of the child's personality, integrity, skills, communication ability, resourcefulness, optimism, and acquired knowledge and skills. Do you see that all of these things are spiritual in nature? If the child should be raised with an awareness and understanding of only the physical world, that child is greatly handicapped in our hopes for its future success. It is a reality that we humans have physical needs. These are obvious. They include air, water, food, and shelter to protect us from the elements that fatally reduce our bodies' temperatures. However, what is far less widely understood is that we also have spiritual needs. And these are no less vital to our success.

All our success in life is the understanding that we are not merely bodies; we are also souls, and just as the body has its needs, the soul has its needs as well. A well-nourished soul confers enormous advantages in future life, and wise parents teach a child the things that his or her soul needs. Sometimes it falls to us as adults to make up the deficiencies that may have surrounded our upbringing, and thus later in life teach ourselves those things that enable our souls, from the spiritual side of ourselves, to operate effectively.

In the same way that we comprise both body and soul, having both physical and spiritual needs, the world in which we live has the ability to supply both our physical requirements and also our spiritual ones. It supplies our physical needs in the form of water and shelter. It supplies our spiritual needs in the form of intangibles that play such an important role in our lives. We are going to explore all of these needs and all of these requirements in the form of ancient Jewish wisdom's depiction of them in four separate areas.

The first consists of those physical things we need which the earth supplies for us in physical form. These include food, water, and shelter, so necessary for our functioning today.

We're also going to look at the spiritual requirements we as humans have, and which the world nonetheless supplies in physical form. Things that the world supplies physically yet which fulfill our spiritual needs include more material good than mere survival—in fact, enough to provide us with a sense of security and confidence about tomorrow.

Then there are those things that the world supplies spiritually that nonetheless fill a physical need in ourselves. These include connection with other human beings. Indeed, without such connection, our physical survival is threatened.

And then finally there are those things that the world makes available to us in a spiritual form, without which we will not perish, but which add enormously to our chances of success. The things that the earth makes available to us in spiritual form and which fulfill our spiritual needs include a sense of growth, greater understanding in how the world really works, and the connection to the infinite in the form of getting to know the Creator himself.

So what are the different areas of human needs? Humans have both physical and spiritual needs because we are physical and spiritual beings. The physical describes anything that can be measured in a laboratory. My height and weight are physical. The color of my skin is physical. How much hair I have on my head is physical. All of these things are physical measures. The spiritual arena is harder to measure and gauge. Honesty, for example, is spiritual. There's no instrument that can measure that. Or loyalty? No way to measure that. Resilience? Persistence? All spiritual qualities.

As a religious person, I take spirituality as a given, but I understand that not everyone is religious. But you need not be religious to be spiritual. You need not be religious to believe you have a soul. Honesty and persistence—who denies that humans possess these immeasurable qualities? No one. We are both body and soul; we're both physical and spiritual.

As such, we have both physical and spiritual needs. Physical needs are straightforward. In the physical sense, we are similar to animals, such as chimpanzees. We both have to eat and breathe and drink to live. If an animal can recognize and understand a need, it is almost assuredly physical, because animals are not spiritual creatures as humans are. The other way to tell if a need is physical and not spiritual is that when deprived of a physical need, you will always die in short order. We cannot live without water and food, for example.

Spiritual needs are less tangible. Do realize that spiritual is not synonymous with religious. There is an overlap in religious people. Spiritual needs include all needs to feel faith and one with God, but they also include certain desires for human connections. In addition to physical needs, we need the affection and the esteem of other human beings, and we need faith and a sense of spiritual connection. These spiritual needs are unique to humans and not understood by animals because they are intangible. If a chimpanzee sees me thinking warmly about my friendships or hugging my children, it will not be able to understand my feelings or interpret my gestures. This is a wonderful litmus test for the spiritual: an animal's inability to understand it. And of course, deprivation of a spiritual need won't necessarily kill you, though it can be just as detrimental to your spirit—just not your body. Friendship, for example, is a spiritual need. Not having friends really can contribute to less healthy and even shorter lives. In social isolation we care less for our hygiene and defer medical maintenance.

And so I am a human being who has physical needs *and* spiritual needs. And I live in a world that supplies physical needs, with food and water and air, and I live in a world that also supplies spiritual needs, with emotional connections and spiritual connectedness. But the tricky thing to understand here is that physical needs can be supplied spiritually and spiritual needs can be met through what the world supplies physically.

Take a look at this chart for clarification:

	World Delivers Physically	**World Delivers Spiritually**
Physical Needs (required for life)	Food, Shelter, Water, Air, etc.	Esteem from Peers, Friends, Connections, etc.
Spiritual Needs (not required for life, but required for well-being)	Savings, Discretionary Income, Financial Security, etc.	Faith, Spirituality, Understanding, Charity, etc.

There are certain things that are spiritual needs, and there are certain things that are physical needs. The world can supply my physical needs. The world can also supply my spiritual needs. This gives us four quadrants of needs that we need supplied. Let's examine them in detail.

In the upper-left corner, we have physical needs for which the world supplies something physical. If I don't get this thing, I am going to die because it is a physical need. The world supplies this thing in a way that is so clearly physical that even a chimpanzee can recognize the need and that which the world supplies to meet my need. When a chimpanzee sees me eating food, he gets excited. Chimpanzees understand the physical, and since my need and its supply are physical, we share these needs with animals. This corner includes food, shelter, water, and other physical items that meet my physical needs.

In the lower-left corner of the chart are spiritual needs that are met by something physical. This encompasses all things that the world supplies physically, but if I am deprived of them, I will not necessarily die. Are you with me? These are physical things that the world supplies, but my personal need for them is spiritual. This includes things like financial security, investments, savings, and also physical luxuries that are not necessities, such as a nice car or a vacation home. These are physical things that I want and may think I need, but I will not die without them. Do not think these needs are unimportant just because they are not a matter of life and death. I may not die without substantial retirement savings, but financial security is important to my security and sense of well-being.

In the upper-right corner are physical needs that the world supplies spiritually. So what are these? Well, we know that without them, I will die, but the world supplies them spiritually only. My chimpanzee will not understand this need, nor will he have it, because he does not operate on a spiritual level. You are probably wondering what intangible thing could possibly exist that, if I am without it, I will physically die—what could it possibly be? you may ask.

Let me answer with a story. In the early twentieth century, there was a famous English professor of philosophy and ethics in England named Professor Joad. Back in those days, the London Underground (the subway system in London) worked on the honor system. You would just get on the train, and when it was time to get off, you told the conductor how many stops you had traveled. There wasn't a fixed fee throughout the system as there is now; the fare was based on how many miles and how many stations you had traveled. Professor Joad, for reasons that nobody will ever know, got on the subway and lied about where he got on, maybe to save a little money, but the conductor could tell that Joad was lying. The conductor was a professional at his job and good at spotting people who lied about fares. By asking a series of questions, he was able to ferret out Professor Joad's lie. But the conductor, and everyone else, could not understand *why* he had lied and cheated the system. Professor Joad had saved himself eight pennies with the lie. Eight mere pennies! And this was a well-paid university professor and also a BBC radio celebrity. Clearly, he didn't need the money.

Given his high profile, the London Transport had to throw the book at him in order to keep the system honest. The next day, *The Evening Standard* carried this outraged headline: "Famous Professor Joad Caught Cheating London Transport Out of Eight Pennies." Joad was then fired from his university position, and he later lost his radio show. The university couldn't keep a professor of ethics and philosophy who would cheat the transit system for a mere eight pennies. After this, he couldn't get another job because his name was all over the papers, outing him as an immoral thief. He started drinking. His wife left him. His children cut off contact with him. He became a vagrant, and shortly after this incident, he died in the gutter of a London slum.

The reason I recount this sad story is to illustrate that we actually *can* die without the esteem of our friends and associates. The care, concern, and respect we receive from our fellow man are what drive us to take care of ourselves, and while they are spiritual in nature, our need for them can be physical. Without the care and concern of others, we have no reason to take care of our bodies, maintain our hygiene, eat properly, exercise, or to resist abusing our bodies with alcohol and drugs if we feel so inclined. We take care of ourselves for other people. If everybody else removes themselves from our lives, we have nothing to live for and we stop meeting our own physical needs. So you can see we have a very physical need for these spiritual things.

The final quadrant in the lower-right corner is reserved for spiritual needs that are supplied by the world spiritually. These are important needs: Although I do not need them to stay alive, the lack of these will leave me feeling as if something is missing in my life. What is that? That "something" may be a faith connection, a spiritual connection, wisdom, and a deeper understanding of the world and my place in it. The chimpanzee does not see the world giving me knowledge and giving me understanding. The chimpanzee doesn't see the world giving me a faith and a spiritual connection. But as a human, I need these things. If I don't get them, will I die? No. Millions of people live without those things. They don't live completely fulfilling lives, but they do live.

When we fulfill these spiritual needs, we become happier and better people and are better suited to serve our fellow man. We will do so in business and also through charity. That's a spiritual need as well— supplying charity to your fellow man. If you don't give charity, you won't die—plenty of people lead selfish lives, giving absolutely nothing back to the world—but it is a real need. You live a better and a more fulfilling life when you give charity. Giving charity enhances your own ability to make money, because making money is God's way of rewarding us for doing the right thing.

There you have it—your hierarchy of needs according to ancient Jewish wisdom. These four areas of your life must be attended to simultaneously. It is a matrix of physical and spiritual needs and the worldly benefits, which can also be physical or spiritual. They are all important and integral to a successful personal and business life. You may think that you can ignore one, and for a while maybe you can, especially spiritual needs that won't cause your death if they are not fulfilled, but over time, spiritual gravity will drag you down. It will cause you to fail in your personal life and to fail in your professional life as well.

And so, for the purpose of growing your capacity to make money, you need to be simultaneously focusing on making sure that your basic needs are met, such as food and your shelter and the needs of your family. You need also make sure that you earn more money than is needed for your basic needs so that your financial security is in place—insurance policies, savings, investments, retirement accounts. And you need a little luxury now and again that boosts your morale. You also need to focus on relationships so that you may earn the esteem and favor of others. We need family. We need friends. And these deserve our time and attention as well, to bolster our morale and ability to be better business professionals. And finally, obviously, you also need faith and a spiritual connection. You need to have greater understanding. Each and every day, we should be asking, "What did I learn today? What do I understand about the world better than I understood last week?" That is a spiritual need we have, because without it, we will not continue to grow. Ignore any of these needs at your own peril.

And the final point and secret that the Bible gives us here is this: Not only will fulfilling these needs bolster our ability to earn money, but earning a living bolsters our ability to better meet these needs. In this way, our personal and professional lives—when all needs are attended to—feed off of each other with perfect synergy, catapulting us toward success and the fulfillment of our true earning potential.

Secret #16

Earnings and Profits Are God's Way of Rewarding Us for Forming Relationships with Others and Serving Them Faithfully and Effectively

This principle of ancient Jewish wisdom underpins and supports the Bible's intersection with business. You must internalize the fact that personal wealth is the result of doing the right thing. Money is the *consequence* of doing the right things. There. Do not focus on the consequence itself, focus on what causes the effect, which is serving your fellow man. When you serve other human beings, personal wealth follows. It cannot be the other way around. You bring about an effect by activating the correct cause, not by focusing on the effect itself.

This is one reason not to envy others. Often in business, as in life, we will see our superiors and those who have done better for themselves than we have, and we will think, "I want that." When we do this, we find ourselves growing bitter and cynical when we fail to make progress on our goals. This is ironic given that the reason we aren't getting anywhere is precisely because we are focusing on what we want rather than focusing on what we should be doing. Instead of focusing on imagined rewards, focus on serving God's other children, for they are your customers. Let this and only this preoccupy your mind when you are at work. Ask yourself, how do I supply the needs and the desires of as many other people as I possibly can? This is God's will and is therefore the foundation on which the economy is built. Do whatever you have to do to serve your fellow man. If you need to develop a new skill, do so. If you see an unmet need in the market, provide it. If there is an invention that has not been invented but would be useful, build it. Whatever you do, if it provides your fellow man value, they will provide you with wealth.

But you may ask, how do I know what it is that I should provide my fellow man? This is another way of asking, what should I do with my life? Very often people tell me they don't know what career to go into. Young people especially, those entering or leaving college, often say they do not know what they want to do with their lives. So they look to advice from others, and one place they are sure to get bad advice is from the commencement speaker at their graduation ceremony.

Invariably the commencement speaker will advise the graduates to just "follow their passion." The speaker tells the newly minted baccalaureates that they should just follow their hearts and pursue the thing that they most love doing. Do what you love, they say. If they only do what they love, the speaker asserts, they will never have to work a day in their lives because every time they go to work, they will be doing what they love, and that isn't work at all.

Well, they are right about one thing: Doing what you love is not work. Or, at the very least, it isn't what defines work. It's not even a characteristic of work.

Here is a tip for young college graduates: Ignore your commencement speaker.

They are feeding you a terrible and destructive lie. They are misleading you. What they are telling you is this: Think not about what the world needs but about what you really like doing, and do that for the rest of your life. Can you imagine anything more selfish?

Not only is it selfish, it is also impractical and it does them a disservice. Following one's passions professionally, when by *passions*, you mean "what someone just likes doing," you set them up for professional failure. Work is not about doing what you want to do; work is about serving others.

Maybe your passion is orchestra conducting, and so you really want to be an orchestra conductor. You hear your commencement speaker tell you to follow your passion and do what you love. So you decide, "All right, I'll go for it; I'm going to be an orchestra conductor!" There's only one snag in your plan, which you only realize after you've quit your job, and that is that there aren't that many orchestras looking for conductors. And the few professional orchestras that are hiring a conductor want someone with more experience conducting orchestras than you have. You find that there are maybe only two orchestras in the whole country hiring conductors at a livable wage, and they want people who have graduated from the top music schools and conducted for decades. But you? You played the oboe in college and only "air conduct" orchestras in the shower.

Now, given your situation, should you follow your passion and attempt to be an orchestra conductor? In your leisure time, perhaps, but the idea that conducting should be your professional focus, your career goal, is naïve and misguided. Maybe it will work out. But probably not. Almost certainly not. In this situation, you have a better chance of winning the lottery—at least that's random! There's nothing random about the hiring process for orchestra conductors, and you have no chance of just getting lucky.

What do you do then? How do you pick a career?

Look to the Bible for the answer. Ancient Jewish wisdom says, "Delight in serving other people." This is the best career advice you will ever get. You want to choose a career? Take a look and see what people need done. You should look around and find what people need you to do, learn to do it, and then learn to love it. As we have already discussed, you learn to love your work, whatever it is, by committing to it and investing in it. You don't have to follow your passions and find work you love if you just decide that, whatever your career is, you are going to be a professional and commit 100 percent and *choose* to love what you do. That's the thing, you get to choose to love your work. But, sadly or not, you don't always get to choose your work.

And that is the key. You can't always choose your profession, but you can choose how you are going to feel about the profession you have and whether to act professionally or not. It's up to you, but if you want to build wealth, choose wisely.

The unfortunate fact is this: Few of us get to do what we enjoy doing in our leisure time as professionals. I mean, I really love boating. But I wasn't exactly waiting around for someone to pay me to go boating. And this is why just "following your passions" is not good advice for the masses. It works for some, but only a very few.

Now obviously some people are blessed with certain talents, and some people are blessed with certain abilities. Naturally you don't overlook that. If God has blessed you with the ability to conduct an orchestra and your talent has been recognized and substantiated, by all means, go conduct an orchestra. If you can conduct orchestras and have done so in college and landed a job doing it, but there's a local dry-cleaners with a "Help Wanted" sign, I'm not saying give up on being a conductor to be a drycleaner's assistant. If you happen to have a talent like conducting or acting or writing songs and you are able to prove yourself professionally and earn a living at it, that talent should be exploited. One can very much serve one's fellow man as a conductor, if—and this is a huge if—you can actually land a job doing it. But most of us aren't so remarkable, talented, or lucky. The world does not need many conductors or Hollywood actors, but good business professionals are always in short supply.

For those of us who don't have such rare and extraordinary talents, we should not be focusing on what we love because we will not be able to serve people that way. We must focus on what other people need. Build this conviction deep into your heart, no matter your profession. Even if we cannot be conductors or actors, we can still serve God's other children in less glamorous fields. When we fully commit to our careers, humble as they may or may not be, we will find success, wealth, happiness, and a love for what we do. Because all successful people really do the same thing, be they the rare successful conductor or a middle manager working their way up the company ranks: They serve God's children by providing products and services to others. I implore the middle manager not to envy the conductor, but to take pride and joy in his own service to mankind.

You cannot fake this conviction. You must really make yourself feel it. You must actually commit yourself to your work. Why can't you fake it? Because people can tell! Exodus (23:7) states: "Keep yourself distant from any falsehood and do not slay the innocent and righteous. . . ." Ancient Jewish wisdom explains that when you indulge in falsehood of any kind, the innocent and righteous person you are slaying is you, yourself. A lack of conviction will show through in your work.

Imagine that you are an employer interviewing an applicant. The applicant comes in for the interview and you ask them why they would like to work for your company. The applicant says, "I've heard you guys have great benefits!" Right off the bat you are probably not feeling so great about this candidate. Why would you hire them just to give them great benefits? You do give great benefits, but someone's desire for them is not the basis upon which you make a hire. So you ask them to tell you a little about themselves and they say, "Well, you know what I really love is playing jazz music. Oh, by the way, I really need to get off work early every Friday because the jazz club where I play the trumpet is pretty far from here." You're not really feeling great now, and so you ask them if they have any other questions before ushering them out the door. They say, "Well, actually I do. What is the pay? And how many days off do I get a year? I like to take a month off in the summer to tour with my band."

So what do you do? Do you hire them? Not unless you want an unprofessional employee who is not ready to commit themselves to their "day job" and invest themselves in your company. When you are interviewing a candidate for a position, do you really care what they find fulfilling or what they need from you to pursue their interests? Of course not! You care what they can do for you, not what you can do for them. You are paying them, not the other way around! When an employer hires someone and is going to actually start taking company money and handing it over, they need that person to tell them exactly what they are going to add to the company's bottom line.

But all this person is talking about is how they are going to get what they want out of the relationship. An employer understands that a business relationship is a two-way street—it has to be or both parties won't stay in the relationship—but they want to know what you can do for them, not how they can benefit you. They want to know this at the interview, and they want to see it once you are on the job. Obviously, the job has to benefit you, but they know how they can benefit you: they hand you a paycheck. What they want to know in an interview is how you are going to benefit them. They want to see you committed to serving them. Again, you cannot fake this. You must truly invest yourself in being of service.

We see proof of this throughout the Bible. Let's return to the story of Sampson and Delilah in the book of Judges, chapter 16. Remember how Delilah repeatedly asked Sampson to divulge the secret of his strength? Several times he lied to her, and she could tell he was lying. But on the third time, he told her the truth: that it was his hair that gave him his strength, and before she even confirms the truth by shaving off his head, we can see that she already knows that this time he is indeed telling the truth. How did she know this wasn't yet one more lie? How did she know he had been lying earlier?

Consider also when Jacob is shown a bloodstained jacket by his sons, who tell their father that it belongs to their brother Joseph, who is dead. What they don't tell their father is that they sold Joseph into slavery in Egypt. Later, in Genesis, chapter 45, the brothers come to Jacob and tell him that they have seen Joseph in Egypt, where their long-lost brother is now the ruler of the entire country of Egypt! But Jacob rejects this report as a lie even though it is true, and what he has believed up until now is the real lie.

Now I ask you this: Why did Jacob believe his sons' original lie and not the truth they tell him later? And how did Delilah know when Sampson was and wasn't lying?

Is Delilah more spiritually sensitive than Jacob? No. The truth is that there is one big difference between these two stories: When Joseph's brothers sold him as a slave to be taken down to Egypt, they truly and completely believed he was a goner. There was no way a Jewish boy was going to survive as a slave in Egypt, or so they thought. And so they truly believed that if he wasn't dead yet, he was going to be dead pretty soon. So when they said to their father, "Joseph our brother is surely dead," they held a deep internal belief that this was so. They were, in their own minds, not telling a lie here—they truly thought him as good as dead.

In the case of Delilah and Sampson, Sampson was telling a clear lie the first few times, and only the last time did he tell the truth. But Sampson knew his lies to be lies, and Delilah, like most people, possessed enough human sensitivity to recognize the difference between the way Sampson spoke when lying and the way he spoke when telling the truth. This is why the verse says, "Delilah *knew* he was telling the truth." She didn't even have to cut off his hair to prove it; she knew beforehand because she could read his true convictions. That which is a deep conviction in our heart comes across to those around us; they can see it in our eyes and hear it in our voices and observe it in our demeanor. This may sound obvious, but the liar and the deluded do not realize that we only come across as authentic when we are being authentic. When we speak with conviction, people believe what we say. This is a difficult thing to fake.

The lesson here is not just that we shouldn't lie. The lesson is that we must be authentic because lying, over the long term, deceives no one. If we build into ourselves a deep understanding and conviction that serving the needs of other human beings is the reason we profit, that the reason we earn money is because we are focused on serving the needs of other people, other people will see this. We must commit ourselves to these convictions. Then and only then will the money follow. The money comes automatically. The question you have to answer is not, how will I make money? It is, how will I serve my fellow man?

Raise the Limits on Yourself and Others by Imposing Boundaries and Structures

C hildren do not manage their own lives. They are governed externally by their parents. Their perception of what is and isn't allowed is dictated wholly by what their parents allow. As a child, you could not play ball in the street. You had to be in bed by nine o'clock. You had to finish your greens. You had to do chores, attend school, and say please and thank you. You didn't necessarily understand why you had to do these things, only that you did. Children are told what to do and not to do. To many a child, life seems defined by limits, demands, and requirements. They do not necessarily know the reasons for these external limits. As adults, parents understand the reason for imposing the rules. The rules are there to keep children safe and we, as adults, impose them because we know better.

But children are not the only ones that require explicit boundaries and responsibilities—adults do, too. This is because, paradoxically, the more confined and structured you are, the freer you are. By imposing structure upon your own life, you have a better understanding of the function of the rules that govern you. Many adults do not comprehend this because it is counterintuitive. You may ask, how can limitations provide freedom?

God gave Moses the Ten Commandments. Exodus 32:16 reads, "And the tablets were the work of God, and the writing was the writing of God engraved upon the tablets." The Torah uses the Hebrew word for engraved: *ChaRuT*. What you may not know is that this word has two meanings. The first, as we have said, is "engraved," as if marked in stone. When you write something in stone, it is indelible—no eraser can remove it. When you engrave something, it cannot be changed.

The second meaning of *ChaRuT* is freedom, which seems to be exactly the opposite of engrave. As you have seen before, it is always significant when a Hebrew word has two meanings; there will be an intersection between those meanings. This is not true in English. In English, for example, a rose is a flower and is also a verb for standing up. What does this mean? Nothing. It's just a word used twice. Life is too short to ruminate on such nonsense. But Hebrew is different because it is the Lord's language, and in the Lord's language, a word with two meanings binds those two things. So we know then that the concepts of freedom and engrave are somehow related, even though they appear to be opposites.

Freedom is the opportunity to be creative, to be a creator. When we have total freedom, we have infinite possibility to do whatever we want. We have the *potential* to get anything done; but potential does not mean actual. It is only once we restrict our freedom by filling up our workweek with tasks that we actually get anything accomplished. But this also closes off the potential possibilities we had, which in turn further restricts our freedom. As we close off possibilities in this way, our lives become set in stone—engraved. This is where the paradoxical effect comes from. The more we restrict our freedom by setting rules and limitations on ourselves, the freer we are to actually be productive. The idle person who leaves himself free to do what he likes when he likes has the *potential* to accomplish anything, but he actually accomplishes less than the person who rigorously restricts his freedom in order to focus in on what he wants to accomplish. It is he who carves his life and time, his schedule, into granite who is genuinely free.

The people who put no limits on their own freedom, who do as they wish when they wish, are embracing childishness. Children want to stay up all night even though they will be tired the next day and get nothing done. Put another way, children free to stay up all night are not free to get anything done the next day. But children who have their schedules engraved in stone for them, who are restricted from staying up late, are free to enjoy the following day free of exhaustion.

As adults, we force limits on our children, and by setting limits on their freedom to do as they wish, we free them from the consequences of their bad choices. By setting limits on a child's bedtime, a parent gives the child the freedom to be awake and alert the next day. And, in doing so, parents do children another favor: They teach them the value of rules and structure in life. The child can only see that he wants to stay awake. The adult can see how that desire, if fulfilled, robs the child of freedom to be productive the following day.

As adults, we do not have guardian protectors to watch over us. We have to establish rules and boundaries for ourselves much as we do for our children. We'd rather leave our schedules open and uncommitted, our days free to do as we feel, but this would be doing ourselves a disservice. By limiting our freedom, by requiring ourselves to be organized and forcing ourselves to use time wisely, we are giving ourselves the freedom to be creative and productive.

This is why time management is so important. Commit to time management. Engrave your schedule in granite so that you might be free to thrive in business. Lock yourself into productive commitments as much as possible. Every day on your calendar should be full of productive work. Block off every day, except, of course, the Sabbath, as you want to give yourself one day off a week. Many people take off two days a week, Saturday and Sunday, but this is, in my opinion, excessive. God did not create the Earth and then on the weekend rest—he rested on the last day only.

Buy yourself a calendar if you don't have one and start making commitments. You may give yourself one day to rest and remain free to do as you wish. Mark that day on the calendar—every Saturday if you are Jewish, or Sunday if you are Christian, or whatever. But on the remaining six days, you must lock yourself into commitments as much as possible—you must be productive. This is how you will succeed in business—fail to do so, and your competitors will outpace you. I also encourage you to keep a journal in which you can keep a record of whether or not you completed your goals. It is not enough to set goals; you must meet them. You have to hold yourself accountable.

There are two common reasons people do not reach their goals. One is that their scheduling is overly optimistic and they need to set more reasonable goals. The other, which is far more common, is that people fail to focus on what actually needs doing. At the end of each day, I want you to take an honest inventory and ask yourself if you worked as hard as you could or if you goofed off or procrastinated. Be brutally honest with yourself. Did you not get everything done that you set out do because it was too much, or did you simply fail to fully commit yourself to working all day long? Take an inventory of what you did that day. If you failed to get through all of your sales calls, and yet found time to watch a funny animal video on YouTube, send e-mails to friends, and play a game of chess on your phone, then the problem is not that you didn't have the time to finish your work—it's that you simply failed to do your work.

True freedom is not the opportunity to do as we please, but rather, it is the opportunity to lock ourselves down into the things that need doing. True freedom is the ability to be creative, by which I mean, to create. Remember, making money through creating commerce and business is one of the most thrilling and creative things we can possibly do. We don't win money, we earn it—we make it. Business creates money and it creates good in the world. That is creative, the ultimate act of creation that man is capable of. When two or more human beings serve one another by trading, they are literally creating money, bringing it into the world, and there is nothing better than this. But to be able to earn money, we must set limits on ourselves and our freedom. Earning money requires focus and a plan.

Imagine I place a rifle cartridge into a vise and clamp it firmly in place on my workbench. Now imagine I take a nail and hold it over the percussion cap on the back of the cartridge and hammer the nail into the cartridge. What happens? There's going to be a big bang, no question about it, and a flash of light. Where is the lead bullet from the cartridge going to go? How far will it travel? The answer may surprise you: about two feet or so. The bullet is going to plop forward and drop onto the floor at your feet. But how is this possible? When I fire that same round from my rifle, pulling the trigger causes that same bullet to travel hundreds of yards at the rate of 600 feet per second. So how is it that it now just plops to the floor? What is different?

When the round is inside my rifle, the explosion is confined on all sides, and all of the chemical energy stored up in the powder causes the bullet to burst out of the brass casing and fly down the barrel. All of the energy is focused down and out the barrel. All of this energy is applied to the rear end of the bullet and the bullet goes flying out. But when the cartridge is held in a vise and not in the chamber of my rifle, its being fired causes the casing to burst open, dispersing the energy in every direction. Nothing productive happens. The bullet goes nowhere. The difference is that the barrel of a gun confines, restricts, and focuses the energy all in one direction.

In the same manner, true power is achieved by confining our own selves. When we focus our energies in one direction rather than many, we can accomplish great things. Freedom is obtained from direction, not from the potential to move in any which way. Without a goal and narrowed focus, without placing limits on our potential, our energies are wasted, dissipated, and ineffective. In our work, we must make our goals explicit. If we have a destination then we will, like the bullet that is restricted to one option, know where to go.

You have probably heard people—indecisive, noncommittal, unproductive people—say that they prefer to keep their options open. A man who avoids marrying in order to keep his options open in case something better comes along will never marry. Ever. He is waiting for an opportunity that he would not seize even if it came—because there is always a better *hypothetical* option down the line. What good is keeping your options open if you aren't ever going to settle down?

Other men may keep their options open as a way of intentionally playing the field forever. This is a childish urge. These men, too, will never settle down, never marry, and never have a family. They will drift from one woman to the next for no reason, with no purpose, and no end in sight.

This same man will probably have a hard time investing his money because the ability to be productive, whether through getting married and creating a family or investing money and creating a business, is only possible when we limit our options and freedom by choosing a direction and focus. You want to confine yourself by making purposeful choices and following them through to the end. Freedom, potential, options—these are traps. They rob us of the chance to be productive and creative. Narrow your freedom, limit your options, choose your path, and you will be free to pursue your goals to their ultimate end.

Sometimes we overcomplicate matters. Avoid this pitfall. We immobilize ourselves when we view our lives, circumstances, and choices all at once. It is a panorama too vast to consider or handle. The view is overwhelming. If you begin to feel this way, take a step back for contemplation and to seek outside counsel. Both quiet deliberation without distraction and thoughtful discussion with a trusted and more experienced advisor can provide a simpler and more accurate perspective on the challenges you face.

For instance, consider the incredibly complicated problem of inflation and its potential to cripple the economy. I sometimes pose the following question to economists: Given that the British Empire had far-flung outposts spread across the known world at a time when there were no computers for tabulation or sophisticated communications, how did they avoid the ills of inflation for over a hundred years? How did they print the correct amount of money that would neither induce inflation or deflation for hundreds of years? Doing this required them to keep tabs on countless vendors across several counties and relay that information back to the Mint in a timely fashion. Doing so in that day and age was, of course, impossible. And yet they did it. But how?

These professionals will inevitably overthink the question. They seek a solution that fits their preconceived notions of how the economy works. But nothing fits. The true answer eludes these highly learned professionals. However, when one considers inflation in its most basic terms, the devaluing of a currency, and one remembers the almost mythical power of a marketplace, the solution becomes more visible, almost obvious.

Furthermore, in seeking the simple and direct solution one avoids the paralyzing fear we have of large-scale problems. Similarly, limiting our choices is the simplest and most direct way to focus our efforts in the direction our heads and carefully considered plans demand. The answer is that the British Mint did not keep tabs on all of the economic transactions at home and abroad. They used a different method to balance the printing of money. To understand the method though, you must understand a little bit about how inflation works.

Inflation happens when the prices of goods and services rise. This happens when the government prints too much money. We are told this is a bad thing. But I ask you, what is too much? Who decides how much money is too much?

There was a period in history when the British Empire had virtually no inflation for nearly a hundred years. The price of a bushel of wheat, a pair of shoes, a haircut and shave, and everything else remained the same for a hundred years. For a hundred years, the prices for all goods and services remained the same respective to gold. Back in those days, pounds sterling were convertible legally and at any moment into gold. This may sound miraculous. No inflation! That's great, right?

This was no easy task to accomplish. The government has to print just the right amount of money to cover all new commerce. The mint had to print enough money to cover the total value of what every human being in the empire was doing for every other human being. This is because every single time a citizen sells a good or provides a service, money is created by the transaction, and therefore money worth the equivalent value of that transaction must be printed.

Remember, in those days, the British Empire included all of Great Britain, South Africa, and parts of Canada, Australia, and India—this is a lot of people and transactions to account for. The Bank of England has to know exactly how many pounds sterling to print, which requires knowing about what everyone is doing and creating. Keeping up with this correctly is a massive and notoriously difficult undertaking; even today, with the assistance of computers, governments struggle to keep track of and predict commerce accurately.

So how did the British Empire manage it? They simply kept track of how many people came into the Bank of England to exchange their pound notes for gold. The bank understood this to mean that there were too many pound notes in circulation, which made them feel uneasy for fear of inflation. When people began asking for gold in exchange for pounds, they stopped printing any more money. Eventually, people would start coming into the bank with gold to purchase pounds. They needed the pounds to conduct business, which told the bank that the market in London, which was at the center of the whole empire, was feeling that more good deeds were being done, more economic transactions were being made, and more value was being created than there was printed money. When this happened, they would again print money until people started wanting their gold back. In this way, inflation was defeated by the collective wisdom and ingenuity of human beings.

And during the entire time that the Bank of England scrupulously printed no more money than citizen's creativity warranted, the Empire's economy thrived. Through this honest discipline, the Bank surrendered the power to print money whenever political purpose suggested. The great Bank of England imposed limits upon itself and through those limits and restrictions, it achieved greatness for itself and empowered every British business professional to reach for greatness.

The Importance of Service Is That You Cannot Lead If You Cannot Follow.

W hen we are young, we enter the workforce by going to work for an employer who is hiring in our field. In order to move up in the company, or even to hold onto a job, you must have the ability to take orders, which means recognizing that you are subservient to someone. In other words, you must accept authority. You must not only accept it; you must respect it as well. Service need not be unpleasant. Embrace service and learn as much as you can from others. Successful business professionals seek out mentors.

A major flaw with the United States educational system is that it does not prepare students for the job market or the workplace. The public school system utterly fails to teach the single most important skill necessary to avoiding poverty: obtaining and retaining a job. We do not teach our children how to take orders. Instead, we nurture their independence and self-esteem. We make sure they feel good about themselves. We remind them that they are special and unique. But we forget to impart the one quality that employers most want to see in job applicants: a will-do spirit. Supervisors and bosses detest attitude and they want to see demonstrated perseverance and commitment.

Showing that you have held down a job, any job, will do more for your resume than a semester of midnight basketball and almost all other extracurricular activities. Do you know what extracurricular activities tell an employer? That you can spend time doing what you feel like doing. That's really not all that impressive. But if you can show an employer that you held down a retail job throughout high school and college while also completing internships, you have proven that you know how to take and carry out orders.

Our colleges and universities aren't doing much better than our public school system. Half of the time, universities aren't even teaching students usable skills as part of their "liberal arts" core education. Even those students that are learning practical and useful skills aren't receiving everything they need in their education. Useful skills are important, but they are not the only things employers are looking for in new hires. Most employers will teach you skills. On average, at least 95 percent of what you need to know you learn on the job. This is true for doctors, lawyers, nurses, investment bankers, and everyone else. What employers are really looking for in a job candidate is the right raw material—good character. Most employers are willing to train if you can show you have the right attitude. If you have the right attitude, they can mold you into what they need. No one wants to try to mold someone with a bad attitude; you can't do it.

But our schools aren't teaching the ability to accept authority. They aren't even teaching practical skills, either. Instead, they teach the concept of independence. Would you believe that today it is standard practice to issue students teacher evaluations on which to assess how well their teachers have done? We have the *students* evaluating the *teachers* these days—this is completely backwards! The culture of students addressing teachers as sir and ma'am that was so entrenched decades ago is gone. We used to prepare students to be subservient, to serve their superiors, and they were thus ready to go to work for someone. Who wants to employ somebody with attitude? Not me. Not anyone.

Another thing our schools teach students is that they must have tolerance for all views. They teach children that all opinions are equally valid. But this is simply not true. When you work for someone, be they an employer or customer, your view is not as valid or important as theirs. Period. If your view is as valid as your bosses, why should you listen to them?

Ancient Jewish wisdom shows us that the only route to wealth is in serving other human beings. People are not going to voluntarily part with their money and give it to you unless you have done something for them. Therefore, earning money is always an act of service. This is true of employees and it is true of business owners too, because everyone in business has customers to serve. A retailer must understand that the customer is his boss. So too must the store clerk.

You have probably had the experience before of dealing with a salesperson with a bad attitude. This kind of person isn't necessarily a bad person, but they fail to realize the debt they owe to the customers they serve, or should be serving. Instead of serving the customer, they view their customers as nuisances—just irritating people preventing them from goofing off behind the sales counter or in the break room. Though this can be infuriating, we probably should pity such a person. They will never move up in business behaving this way. And neither will you if you adopt such a negative and entitled worldview.

Nordstrom's, one of the world's most successful department stores, starts all executive-track employees out on the sales floor in the shoe department. They do this because they want their executives to understand customer service. They do it because they understand that going down on your knees in front of a customer is wonderful training. It teaches even their highest-level executives that the customer is the true boss. Every Nordstrom's vice president has experience serving customers firsthand; they know that the little old lady looking for the navy-blue high-heeled shoes, and everyone else that patronizes their store, is the final boss. Not them. Not even the CEO. Not even the majority shareholders. That is why Nordstrom's executives and the Nordstrom brand are so successful. If you want to progress and succeed in business and in making money, you too need to accept subservience.

Service to others never ends. No matter how high up you are in your company, you must still embrace subservience. True leadership means letting the people around you see your ability to be subservient. Even CEOs and other executives have someone to serve—customers, stockholders, God. It never ends and it never should. Serving is a blessing. In Judaism, a belief in service to a higher authority is passed down almost from birth. Jewish children are taught to always thank the Lord for returning their souls to them in the morning when they wake up. They say a blessing before going to sleep, too, and when they get dressed. They are taught to say a blessing before and after they eat. This service is built into their lives from day one. Jews understand right away that they are not the ultimate boss—God is.

In Judaism, arrogance is seen as the ultimate wrongdoing. Displaying arrogance insinuates that you are the most important person in the whole world. You are not. God is more important than you are. And serving others is more important than you are. Everyone else you meet is somebody whom you have the opportunity to serve. You should view this as an opportunity, an opportunity to serve, not as a shackle.

The Fifth Commandment tells us to honor our father and mother. We must do so for their sake, but also for our own children's sake—and our own as well. You are your children's role models and they will learn to treat you (and others) the way you treat your own parents. If your children see you acting in impatient, rude, resentful, and angry ways toward your parents, how do you think they will behave toward you when you grow older? They will treat you just as poorly as you treated your parents, and why shouldn't they? They'll be faithful to your own teachings. If you can treat your parents with genuine service, then your children will learn to treat you the same way. They will learn to serve others, as well, and they will prosper for it.

As children, we have our parents to thank as our mentors. But adults need mentors, too. Successful business professionals always seek out mentors, people from which they can learn. And, later, when you climb to positions of leadership, you too should be a mentor to others. True leadership means showing others your ability to be subservient to higher powers. Just as you set a good example for your children, you should also set a good example for your partners, colleagues, and employees.

Vision Is Necessary; Sharing That Vision Is Not Always Necessary.

The Hebrew word for face is pronounced "*Panim*." The "im" sound at the end of the word signifies that the word is plural. For example, the Hebrew word for water is pronounced "*mayim*." The word *water* is a mass noun, meaning it is always plural, never singular. You would never tell someone to "bring me a water" any more than you would say "bring me a bottles." You would say, "Bring me a bottle of water." What this tells us is that the word *face* is always plural, which means we cannot have only one face because there is no such thing as a face in the Lord's language. There are only faces. In Hebrew, you would never say, "Look at my face." You would always say, "Look at my faces." The reason for this is that everyone is multifaced. This may remind you of the English phrase "two-faced," which obviously has negative connotations. That is not what we mean by multifaced in ancient Jewish wisdom. We all put on multiple faces and there is nothing wrong with doing so—in fact, it is proper.

When my children look at me, they do not see exactly the same face as the manager of my bank does when I am applying for a loan. I do not have the same face when I am speaking to one of my employees as I do when I'm praying to God. You do not show the same face to your superiors as you do to those you lead, and neither of those two faces will be the one that your spouse sees. This is quite proper and acceptable. You do have more than one face and you should not feel dishonest about this fact, as it is the only way to move through the world. Our face is the portal into our soul and the window into our heart. Because we do not share the same things, the same parts of our inner lives, with all people in the same way, we must therefore ensure that our face does not expose all sides of us for all to see. We should not wear our heart on our sleeve, which is another way of saying, if you will, that we should not wear our heart on our face.

Long ago, there was a wonderful student with whom I studied the Torah for many years, a young man named David who lost his job suddenly. He was a married man and he and his wife had just had their second child when this happened. He had been laid off very suddenly because his company ran into difficulties that the owner had been trying to conceal. One morning he came in for work and was told by his boss that the company was closing down, effective immediately. He came to me shaking with anxiety and asking what he should do next. He only had three months of savings. He didn't know how to tell his wife.

I told him he had two choices and that I would give him the best advice, if he could handle it and follow through. He said he thought he could. I told him the best thing to do would be to not tell his wife that he had lost his job. She would be rightly nervous and worried, which is not healthy for a young mother. Her worrying would do nothing to help him find a new job. Only he could fix this situation and so it should be his burden to carry alone. I told him that what he needed to do was get up every day as if he was going to work, put on his suit and tie, and kiss his wife good-bye, and then head down to the library and conduct his job search from there. He was to look at every company within a commutable distance, not just those hiring, but any company that he might be an asset to. And then we would network with people at the synagogue to see who worked where, and we would find him a job. I promised to help teach him ancient Jewish wisdom on how to properly interview for a job. He had three months to get it done before he would need to tell his wife and worry her, but he would have to be able to hold it together for the sake of his family.

When I asked him if he could do this, he asked, what other choice did he really have? I told him plan B was this: Tell his wife now. He would worry her, but if he couldn't hold it together and she was going to have to carry the burden anyway, it was best if she did so now.

He told me he could handle it, and handle it he did. He asked his former boss not to tell his family what had happened and, should they call him, to take messages for him as if the company was not defunct. He hit the library and then the streets looking for a job, and within one month of searching and interviewing, he found a new job . . . with 20 percent higher pay! Only then did he go home and tell his wife they were going out to dinner to celebrate. They hired a babysitter and went out alone. Over dinner, he took her hand and said, "I hope you won't be angry, but I have been keeping a secret from you." And at this point he told her everything, because there was no longer any reason to worry. She was happy for his new job. She was also proud and grateful that he had done so much for his family, had carried the weight alone. His wife appreciated what an incredibly tough time he'd had for the past four weeks. She could see in his face how much he had silently endured for his family, and their marriage was stronger than ever before.

So you see, not everyone need see the same face, for you have not one face only. In the case of David, I saw the face of a shaken, frightened man. His wife saw the face of the husband she loved who had made sacrifices for his family and remained on top of everything. She saw a man who had carried the family's financial burdens alone so she could tend to their children without worrying. He was able to show one face to me, one face to his wife, and yet a third face to the company where he was interviewed—that of a competent business professional worthy of a job. You don't have to share everything with everybody. Not everyone must know about all parts of you—just the parts they need to know. There is no shame in compartmentalizing your life. Certain things you have to keep to yourself and bear alone. This is part of true leadership. David was a husband who understood what leadership was all about.

I knew another couple, Matt and Sandy, who were not married and had only been dating a few months. Sandy came to see me one afternoon very troubled about her new relationship with her boyfriend, Matt. Though they had only been dating for a few months, she had thought they were very compatible. They shared common goals, beliefs, and values. She thought a shared future might be possible. That is, she had thought so until the previous Sunday when she and Matt had attended a barbeque hosted by his old college buddies. She had been having fun and had thought everyone seemed nice, but one thing had disturbed her: Matt had avoided giving any indication of their special relationship to his friends. He had introduced her as if she were a friend or some random neighbor. He never once had called her his girlfriend or anything like it.

She came to me for advice. She wanted to know if she was making a mountain out of a molehill or if this was a real cause for concern.

I opened the Bible and read to her from Genesis, chapter 24, verses 2 through 8, a passage that details instructions Abraham gave to his servant, Eliezer. Abraham was sending Eliezer to a distant land to bring back a wife for his son. Later in the story, the Bible spends valuable ink detailing Eliezer's arrival at the home of Rebecca. Rather than summarize what Eliezer tells Rebecca's family—which we have already heard straight from Abraham's mouth—the Bible repeats the story in detail. In any normal book, a repeated story like this would just be summarized. The author would write something along the lines of, "Eliezer related to Rebecca's family everything that his master Abraham had told him." An author would do this so as not to bore the reader with pages of dialogue repeating what the reader just read a few verses earlier.

Why would the Bible do this? I will tell you one thing—it is not because the Bible is sloppily written! Everything in Scripture is there for a reason. Ancient Jewish wisdom tells us that anytime a story in the Bible is repeated in this way, we must search for any differences in the story as they will be important. If a story is repeated twice in detail, you can bet that it will not be verbatim. There will be differences, and they will be of significance.

In this case, there is a major variation between what Abraham originally said and how Eliezer recounts his master's words. According to

Genesis 24:3, Abraham said, "Don't take a wife for my son from the daughters of the Canaanites, *among whom* I dwell." But when Eliezer repeats this to Rebecca's family, he says, "Don't take a wife for my son from the daughters of the Canaanites, *in whose land* I dwell." Abraham said "among whom I dwell" because the land had already been promised to him by God. His statement reveals his belief that the land is his and the Canaanites are in his land. Eliezer, a servant, misses this point and misquotes his master as having attributed ownership of the land to the Canaanites.

The difference is that Abraham was a leader. He fully believed with a clear, unshakeable vision that the land was promised to him, and therefore he already visualized that it was his land and spoke of it as such. Eliezer was a follower who could not see beyond the readily evident reality of the here and now. He thought of the land as the Canaanites', who had made a claim on it and still resided there even though God had promised the land to Abraham and their time there was short. The story is repeated twice to highlight this fact. On the surface, the two statements are similar enough, but if you dig deeper, you can see that the minor differences in phrasing reflect a massive disparity between the two men. One was a visionary and a leader. The other was a follower.

My advice to Sandy was that while she shouldn't terminate her relationship with Matt just yet based on what had happened at the barbeque, she was wise to pay such close attention to small details. This is something you must train yourself to do as well.

God gave us one mouth but two ears so that we might listen twice as carefully as we speak. We have two ears also because God knows we need to listen more often than we need to speak. People reveal their inner thoughts by the words they use, and you must be attuned to the words of others because their words betray their real thoughts and feelings. What was clear was this: Matt had either a different view of their relationship than Sandy held or he had difficulty communicating how he felt about their relationship. Some men are like that, unable to use the word *girlfriend*, perhaps because they think it trivializes the relationship, or because they do not know if it is proper or expected of them. Maybe he didn't know what to say, or perhaps they really were on different pages. Whatever the case, clearly some mismatch or discord was being communicated, and Sandy had picked up on it.

When things go wrong in our romantic relationships, family lives, or, indeed, in our business interactions, we often say that we should have seen it coming. We are perhaps being jocular, but in fact, yes, we probably should have seen it coming. Do not miss the premonitions and red flags. You must be listening for when people inadvertently reveal themselves in their words. People do this all of the time. You do it. I do it. Everyone does. We all give hints to what we are really thinking and feeling by the words we use and the way we say them. The astute listener will pick up on these reveals and be able to use them to better serve his fellow man. It is actually possible for a good listener to better know how to best serve a speaker than the speaker himself knows.

The trick is learning to listen well. Never confuse what you want to hear with what the other person is really saying. Read between the lines. Do not minimize the importance of what people say and how they say it. Learn to read people and you will be well served in business interactions and in other areas of your life as well.

At the same time, a strong leader understands that he himself gives vocal cues and must be careful not to reveal all of his faces. The great military writer John Keagan called this ability the Mask of Command. Commanding officers don't allow their followers and soldiers in on information that they need not know and that may harm them. Very often, they know frightening information, and there is no good reason to demoralize people. The job of a leader is often to carry the burden of worry and concern alone to spare his followers worry over that which they, as followers, cannot change or influence even if they had all of the discomforting facts.

The Most Important Organ of Leadership Is Your Mouth

This principle may seem counterintuitive or hyperbolic, but I assure you it is not. You might have thought the brain was the most important organ for leadership. The brain is obviously very important to everything we do, but the mouth is the organ with which we communicate with others.

As in all professions, some doctors make more than others. Some doctors make a fortune, while others barely make a living. It may surprise you that some doctors struggle financially, as the medical field is generally thought to be a very lucrative profession. And, over all, it is . . . but not for everyone. What's the difference between those doctors who earn well and those who are barely eking out a living? Is it that the poor doctor went to a bad medical school and the rich doctor a good one? I can assure you this has no bearing on the matter. I will bet you the farm that you cannot name the medical school your favorite doctor went to. It is also unlikely that you know what percentile or rank he was in his graduating class. You probably don't know much about your doctor's professional history at all other than that he went to medical school!

So how did you pick that doctor? If you're like most of us, you found your doctor by word of mouth, either from friends or from reading reviews. Either way, you chose him because his other patients spoke well of him. That's the only reason you started seeing him. And why did these people like and recommend him? Probably for the same reason you do: because of the way he communicates with patients. He probably has excellent bedside manners and knows how to comfort patients, and not only using medicine, but with his words and general countenance. Doctor's hands are very important tools in their work, but the gift of speaking and communicating well will make all of the difference when it comes to running a good practice that makes money and best serves patients.

For doctors and all business professionals, good communication skills are what make the difference between earning a lot of money and a little money. Speech is God's great gift to us. It's a unique gift that God gave to humans. Obviously, he didn't give it to animals. Animals can communicate to some small degree, but not with words. Human beings are able to communicate ideas with words, which allows for nuance, detail, abstraction, and specificity. We are not born as good communicators, though. We have to learn how to communicate effectively.

This is one of the most important secrets I could reveal to you: the importance of learning to communicate effectively. It doesn't matter how you make your living. However you serve other people, you will do so better by speaking more effectively. It doesn't matter if you're a bus driver or a salesperson. Whether you are a waiter, plumber, book-keeper, landscaper, veterinarian, or landscaper—whatever you do for a living, you will perform better and make more money if you learn to use your mouth more effectively than you do now.

Some people claim that they are simply not that articulate. They throw up their hands and say they are just not good with words or public speaking and they never will be. Maybe they hesitate, search for words, have trouble projecting, or can't maintain eye contact when speaking. Maybe they mumble. Does any of this sound like you? Whatever your shortcoming may be, you can correct it. You can improve.

One of the very important insights of ancient Jewish wisdom is that our souls are enormously impacted by that which our ears hear our own mouths speak. So if you want to improve your speaking, here is what you have to do: Listen more and listen better. The best way to do this is to listen to yourself speak. Get to know how you speak and how you should speak.

Here is some homework: Find three occasions a week, at a minimum, more if you have the time and inclination, to read aloud to yourself for half an hour. You can't read just anything; you need to select a good book. You could read *the* good book, the Bible, but it doesn't have to be that, but if you have no particular relationship with God, reading the Bible, while it won't hurt, may not inspire you as it should. There are many other good, intellectual, moral, well-written books out there to select. Just don't read garbage; don't just grab a tabloid magazine off the checkout stand at the supermarket and think that this will do. Pick a good piece of literature or an important book of intellectual discourse—anything intelligent and well written. You can find recommendations on the Internet or from a librarian. What you want is a book with advanced vocabulary, great style, and good prose.

Reading aloud is an excellent way to train yourself to speak better. When your ears hear your mouth shaping those words, your tongue wrapping itself around the correct pronunciation and delivery, and your whole mouth articulating fluently, you won't hesitate for words. You won't have to pause to seek words because, when reading, the words are right there in front of you. Even most people who stutter are fine when they are reading aloud from a text. No matter what your problem is, you will improve, and it is going to sound and feel terrific to hear your lips and tongue shaping those words. The goal is to enunciate clearly and deliver the text naturally and powerfully. All it takes is a half hour three times a week, and in no time, you will begin to see—and hear—improvements. People will compliment you on your improved speaking, and you will be able to smile and chalk one up for ancient Jewish wisdom.

The second thing you need to do is acclimate yourself to speaking in front of others. Jump at any opportunity to speak in public. Public speaking can be frightening, but you can overcome this stage fright with practice. The better you get at speaking in general, the easier it will be to speak in front of others. You may want to try spending some of your three weekly sessions of reading aloud by reading to someone else. The process is more enjoyable this way; moreover, it will allow you to practice speaking in front of others while you practice skills. This will be less scary if you start with someone who already loves and respects you. Your spouse may love to be read to—mine does! Or maybe you have a child you can read to, though you need to pick the material carefully. There are many great books written so that a child can enjoy the superficial plot while an adult can take delight in the deeper meanings.

As you get more experience and practice reading aloud and speaking publicly, you will begin to develop as a speaker. Initially, you may be speaking at a small family gathering, perhaps proposing a toast at an event, but the better you get and the more opportunities to speak publically that you seize upon, the more often that better opportunities will come your way. People will recognize your developing talent and start coming to you when they need a speaker. Don't miss an opportunity to speak in public: Speaking publicly is valuable training, and often it is free—eventually you may even find yourself getting paid for your efforts!

If you don't have family events you can easily attend and speak at, there are other options. There are organizations, like Toastmasters, that offer opportunities to regularly speak publicly. Also, you can accost your friends about opportunities or even form a club where you get together every few weeks to practice giving speeches in front of each other. Do not be afraid to ask—every participant will benefit, not just you.

Let me offer you two tips on public speaking. Practice these techniques while training yourself to speak in front of other people. The first tip is this: Do not bring notes. You may think this sounds crazy and terrifying, and maybe it is, but it is the only way to deliver a good speech. You do not want to practice *reading* a speech (that's what your three weekly sessions are for). You want to practice *giving* a speech. Reading your speech from notes will bore your audience because you will not make as much eye contact, and you will fail to fully reveal the window to your soul. If you read straight from notes, people will wonder why they came at all—you could have just given them your notes to read during their morning commute! A speech is not just the words but also your personal delivery of them. It is a performance, an interaction. When you look into their eyes and speak from your heart, they will connect with you. This is the essence of being a good public speaker. Speakers draw off their audiences for inspiration.

The second tip is a small practical matter, but one that can pay big dividends. When people start out speaking in public, they often do not know what to do with their hands. Sometimes, they let their hands dangle, which is awkward and unnatural looking. Other people lock their elbows down and then allow only their forearms to wave around. This can look as though you are doing a half-windmill motion—not good, either. Some people clutch the podium, which can make you look scared and timid, which, in turn, makes you feel scared and timid, which turns into a vicious cycle. Other people shove their hands into their pockets while they speak, which can make you come off as aloof, unconcerned, or unprepared.

What you want to do is this: move naturally. Gesture naturally. Let your arms reflect the words that are coming out of your mouth. But don't overdo it; you want to appear natural and comfortable. My advice is to watch videos of great orators and notice how they move—natural and unencumbered, but expressive. Their hands seem to mimic the feeling of what their mouths are saying. Study videos of famous speakers giving famous speeches and you will see what I mean. Keep in mind, though, that giving a presentation on your company's performance in the previous financial quarter to your coworkers in the boardroom is different from delivering the State of the Union address. Make sure your countenance and delivery is appropriate to the venue and audience.

So practice reading aloud and jump at opportunities to speak in front of others, and you will see improvements in no time. If you are in business or sales or any profession that requires interaction, which is basically all of the lucrative career fields, what I am telling you now is priceless. You may find that it is worth $10,000 to you in your very first year—maybe tens of thousands of dollars, maybe more. Follow this advice, put in the work, and it will pay dividends like you cannot believe because, again, your mouth, your ability to speak, is one of your greatest tools when it comes to making more money.

Change Is Scary

We humans would prefer things, for the most part, to remain unchanged forever. There is comfort in the known. We would just as soon not keep aging. We would prefer our neighborhoods to stay the same. Some of us would even prefer our children to stay children so that we could be with them forever. In our quest for wealth, we would rather money just come to us without the need for change. Putting in effort to change our speaking skills, for example, takes effort, as you saw in the last section. We would rather our jobs last forever, but just pay us more. And wouldn't it be great if our clothes never wore out and we already had everything we would ever need?

But all of this is fantasy. Things do and will change. That we feel stress when they do does not change the fact that change is inevitable. The more permanent the impending change, the more stress we feel. You cannot stop change, but you can learn to cope with the stress, and the approaches you will find in ancient Jewish wisdom can help.

In April 1998, *Fortune* magazine ran a cover story, "Out of the Holocaust," which recounted the stories of five men who survived the Holocaust death camps and then came to America to start new lives. They were young men in a strange land with nothing but the shirts on their backs, but each one of them eventually built up enough personal wealth and became rich philanthropists. From Europe's death camps to Stalin's Gulags, from Cambodia's killing fields to Rwanda's corpse-filled lakes, the twentieth century provided us with a lamentable catalog of cruelty and crimes against humanity. If there is any silver lining to all of this brutality, stomach-churning horrors, and needless suffering, surely it is that we now have what amounts to a survival study guide.

As a Jew brought up knowing the names and stories of relatives who perished in the Nazi Holocaust, I am naturally most familiar with that tragedy. The Holocaust is also perhaps the most exhaustively documented and best-commemorated instance of modern genocide. But I will confess that I personally do not typically read the many accounts of death and torture that transpired during the Holocaust. I don't attend movies that depict these horrors and I shy away from Holocaust museums, with their ghoulish death chambers and morbid exhibits. I see little value in surrounding myself with nightmarish images and storing away in my brain indelible visions of appalling destruction. My reason for this is not born of a desire to remain ignorant of these tragic events. I already know what happened, though I fully recognize that while I know *of* what happened, there is no way anyone who has led a life of relative comfort and security such as mine can ever really understand the full scope of what took place—not without living it for yourself.

Absorbing such hideousness does not even make its repetition less likely. We told ourselves "never again" after the Holocaust, but the full catalog of twentieth-century genocide has cured me of the naïve notion that we can prevent such atrocities from ever occurring again. In the same spirit, I shelter myself from the images of terror, death, and destruction that saturate the news media and the products of an often-vulgar entertainment industry. Those hideous images darken each moment of spontaneous gratitude I may feel in my life. To me, Judaism is a life-affirming practice, just as I know Christianity is. With so many atrocities carried out falsely in the name of religion, I do not want even a subconscious association of my faith, a good and moral thing, to be tarnished by images of death camps and gas chambers. Horrible things happened and they will happen again before the last page of human history is written, but I choose not to dwell on that which I cannot change when doing so would sully my day-to-day observances and my life-enhancing religious practices. No, I would rather protect myself from the overwhelming, albeit subconscious, awareness of death and destruction. Instead, I practice optimistic joy, and I do not want to poison that optimism. Without it, I would be in no mental shape to serve God's other children.

But I do favor one genre of destruction-related material. There is great value in those accounts of heroism and survival that are told by the lucky few who made it out of the valley of the shadow of death. Unlike accounts of ghoulish torture, there is much useful insight to be gleaned from these accounts of survival.

In her book *Ravensbrück*, Micheline Maurel gives a harrowing account of the notorious concentration camp of the same name. She writes,

> Be happy, you who live in fine apartments, in ugly houses or in hovels. Be happy, you have loved ones, and you also who sit alone and dream and can weep. Be happy, you who torture yourself over metaphysical problems, and you, the sick who are being cared for, and you who care for them, and be happy, oh how happy, you who die a death as normal as life, in a hospital bed, or in your home.

Maurel is telling us that no matter how bad we think our lives are, we should remember those who have had it worse. I do not need to be shown the nightmares that this brave woman endured and that inspired her to write those searing words. The words speak for themselves. They remind me of the beauty of my life and the value of all life.

I was initially drawn to such "survivor literature" because I wanted to understand how some managed to survive such horrible times while others perished within a few days of arriving at the concentration camps. One very powerful truth of survival surfaced repeatedly in my studies, a truth we must all surely apply to our own dealings with the constant and distressing changes we face in our busy, professional lives. What I observed was that we humans can become accustomed to almost anything, no matter how awful or dreadful, just so long as it develops gradually. What stresses us past the point of breaking is sudden change.

According to folklore, if you drop a frog into a pot of boiling water, the frog will immediately leap from the pot, shake himself off, and be okay. But if you put the same frog into a pot of cold water before turning on the burner, the frog will sit there until he boils to death. The water just gets hotter and hotter, but gradually, until it is too late. I will freely and proudly admit that I have never tested this myself, but the story does contain a certain metaphorical truth about humans.

When put under stress, we are like the frog that acclimates to the increasing temperature, even when that temperature is hot enough to eventually kill us. But if the change comes on slowly, we can handle it (assuming that we eventually use our human brains to reason, in a way that no frog can, that we should get out of the pot while we still can). But when change is too rapid, our minds and bodies are put under great stress and we are unable to cope. The frog cannot sit in the boiling water when tossed in—it is too hot for him to handle and he must leap to safety immediately.

Imagine a pre–World War II family living comfortably, as many did, in a town like Vienna or Warsaw when it was invaded by Nazi forces. At first, the many middle-class Jewish families in the town might experience little direct discomfort when the Nazis first arrive in town. But eventually, their mansion is forced to accommodate several other families. Then Jewish areas are quarantined and turned into ghettos, but life continues. Little deprivations turn into bigger ones. Food becomes scarce. Casual indignities in the street turn into blood-chilling humiliations and outright threats. It might be several weeks or months before physical violence begins to occur. Sometimes a year or two passed between the invasions, when middle-class Jewish people lived in comfort, and when life turned into a struggle for survival. Only then were many sent off to death camps. The very gradual decline of life, that gradual slow deterioration that they experienced over the past years, gave many the opportunity to endure what they eventually faced at places like Auschwitz. Those who saw gradual deterioration, gradual change, had the best chance of survival.

Contrast the above experiences with that of the family who has their home invaded unexpectedly one night by military police. They are taken from their home of polished hardwood floors and gleaming white china straight to the degradation and life-threatening filth of a death camp. Such a family is almost shocked to death. Such a family is less likely to be able to adjust to the horrors that await them.

What this tells us is that in order to manage change—any change, be it the change wrought by war or changes in the marketplace—we must avoid sudden, dramatic changes in our lives. Such change most shocks us. With sufficient time to acclimate, we can adjust to almost any condition.

In Genesis, chapter 29, verse 27, Jacob must work for seven years before he is allowed to marry Rachel, his betrothed. When his wedding day finally comes, he realizes that the woman behind the veil, the woman he just married, is not Rachel but is in fact her older sister, Leah. The girls' father has substituted Leah for Rachel. Jacob realizes he's been duped and demands to be allowed to marry Rachel, too. Their father says he will allow this, but only if Jacob works another seven years and completes the seven days of celebration.

A Jewish wedding then was seven days long, which was wonderful, if exhausting. It also had the advantage of softening the shock of marriage. Getting married is a big change. It's wonderful, yes, but also shocking because everything is suddenly different. As we have established, our bodies, minds, and souls do not handle sudden change well. This is why we have a seven-day period to adjust to marriage—it allows us to come down from the big emotional high of marriage. Rather than one big celebration, we have a celebration every night, each one smaller and more intimate than the previous, until on the eighth day we are eased back into normal life and may return to work. This allowed Jacob to adjust to not only the shock of marriage but also to the huge shock of seeing that his bride was not who he thought she was!

Jewish people also observe a seven-day mourning period for the dead for the same reason. We still do this today. Losing somebody we love is very painful and stressful. It's especially shocking because there is no change more permanent than that of death. It is hard to lose someone, bury them, and go to work the next day as if everything is normal. So instead, Jewish people observe a seven-day period of staying home and mourning. We get a little better each day until the eighth day, when we are a little bit more accustomed to what has happened, and we return to work.

Back in 1967, a psychologist by the name of Thomas Holmes led a massive study in which researchers attempted to measure and assign numerical values to the levels of stress induced by different life events. The death of a close loved one resulted in a stress level of 100. A divorce was scored at 70, also high. Retirement, it may surprise you, caused a stress level of 45. You might have thought that work would be stressful, not giving up work, but ancient Jewish wisdom tells us that work, which is in the service of our fellow man, brings joy and a sense of purpose. Coming out of retirement reduces your stress level back to normal! Job change results in a stressful rating of 35, relocating from one city to another is 20, and getting issued a speeding ticket results in a stress level of only 10, except in the case of a certain unnamed rabbi who get stopped so often that he just gets used to it.

There is, as you can see, no shortage of opportunity for stress in our lives. There's no avoiding it. The trick is to learn to cope with that stress. But how? I wish I could give you a simple answer, but life is complicated and there is no set of simple aphorisms or mottos that can safely guide us through every circumstance. For every clever motto or slogan advising you on what to do, there is another one saying you should do exactly the opposite. For instance: look before you leap. Have you heard that expression? That may seem like good advice, until the next day when you read the Sunday horoscope and it informs you that "He who hesitates is lost." This is telling you the exact opposite! So which are you supposed to believe? Both seem as though they might be true in the right set of circumstances. Also, they might be terrible advice in the wrong set of circumstances!

Or consider the case of the person whose boyfriend is being deployed overseas for the next nine months. You are worried that the two of you will drift apart because you haven't been dating that long. Your friends tell you not to worry because "absence makes the heart grow stronger." You nod your head and conclude that, yes, your friends are right, you have nothing to worry about. You feel just dandy until someone else lets slip that old saying: "Out of sight, out of mind."

Again, which do you believe? The answer: neither. Such hackneyed advice is useless. Life is too complicated for pithy, glib mottos. You can't make life decisions on the basis of little slogans. If you could, we wouldn't need ancient Jewish wisdom to guide us.

Now, the cynical among you might say, "But wait, Rabbi Lapin, isn't this book nothing but 40 little slogans?" To which I would answer, no, not in the least. The biblical secrets in this book have stood the test of time and are derived from the teachings of the Bible and ancient Jewish wisdom. But moreover, they are, by name, biblical secrets. They are always true. Take, for example, the current biblical business secret under discussion: "Change is scary." When is that ever not true? Even relatively good fortune, like getting a new job, introduces the uncertainty of the unknown.

All of these biblical secrets are always true, regardless of the particular circumstances you find yourself in. They are not hollow slogans. They are not telling you what to *do*, but rather they describe how the world is and how you *should* be in turn. But they do not give you direct advice on what course of action you should take in any given situation or circumstance. Situations and circumstances change. Luckily, ancient Jewish wisdom does not. By following the principles laid out in this book, you may be able, not merely to avoid stress and change, but to mitigate them, cope with them, and continue on with your life.

As Painful as Change Can Be, It Often Contains the Seeds of Growth

You may think, given everything I have told you thus far about how scary and stressful change can be, that you should avoid change. Avoiding change leads to stagnation. If you don't embrace change, you cannot grow and you won't ever be successful. There are many circumstances of sudden change that people seeking to increase their wealth should rush to embrace. Most people assume they will be more economically prosperous in the future than they are now. This is often true—people do tend to earn more money as they get older. But such growth is not automatic. It is going to involve effort and it is going to involve, pretty much by definition, some degree of change.

You cannot stand in place. Resisting change does not prevent change; such passivity simply prevents you from taking the reins. Change is inevitable. No matter what you do, you are going to get older. One day you are going to die. And between now and then, many things are going to happen to you and around you. Change is coming. It is constant. It will involve stress, and stress involves pain. You must learn to deal with change so that you may embrace it in order to seize upon the opportunity that it provides. Realize that change means the possibility of improvement.

During his presidency, Richard Nixon appointed Walter Annenberg to the position of U.S. Ambassador to the Court of St. James in London. Prior to this, Annenberg was best known as the creator and publisher of *TV Guide*, though he also had a hand in other highly successful commercial enterprises and was very wealthy. When Queen Elizabeth II of England visited Reagan in California, she also accepted the hospitality of Walter Annenberg at his palatial Palm Springs estate. Annenberg took Queen Elizabeth out on a golf cart tour of his extensive property. Of this, he later told the press that he just wanted to show her majesty "how the average American lives."

Hold it, you might be saying. Walter Annenberg is no average American! He's filthy rich! Well, yes, but it was not always so. His grandfather, a Jewish gentleman, had emigrated from Prussia along with his 11 children. They lived all together in a small apartment in Chicago. The most enterprising of the children was Walter's father, Moses, who helped to feed the family by catching fish in Lake Michigan. Moses went on to start his own family and amass wealth in a variety of publishing businesses. By the mid-1930s, he owned the *Philadelphia Inquirer*, among other papers.

Everything was going well until Moses was sentenced to three years in federal prison for evading taxes. At this time, Walter, his only son, was only 32 and had inherited $5 million of unpaid tax debt from his father. In a flash, his life was in shambles. Walter was at a loss. His mom, a practicing Jew, may have helped Walter absorb the central Jewish ideas on how to deal with this change. What we know for sure is that Walter came to know both frightening change and change that contains the seeds of opportunity. Often these two kinds of change are the result of the same event. Embracing change is another way of saying opportunity.

When change makes the future look scary and bleak, ancient Jewish wisdom tells us to look to the past for guidance. Walter Annenberg once found a quotation in a prayer book that had belonged to his father. It read: "Cause my works on earth to reflect honor on my father's memory." Walter had the words engraved on a bronze plaque for his office, and to this day, those institutions that benefited from Walter's generosity (he became a famous philanthropist) carry his father's name. The sad past spurred Walter into a creative drive of entrepreneurial fury that he might never have discovered within himself had he not had to grapple with the changes brought about by his father's incarceration.

This is a very common story. How many times have you known someone, maybe yourself, who was laid off or fired unfairly only to bounce back twice as strong? People often not only find a new job after losing their old one, they often find a better, higher-paying job that they never would have even looked for if they had not had the misfortune of losing their old job.

This lesson is taught again and again in the Bible. Change begets opportunity.

Consider 2 Samuel, chapter 20, in which an unimpressive individual named Sheba launches a rebellion against King David. The king sends his best general, Joab, to kill Sheba, who has been holed up in a city close to the Jordan River. Joab's forces storm the city walls and are about to pour into the city when a mysterious old lady appears and demands to speak with Joab. She reprimands him for attacking the entire city without first giving them the opportunity to hand over Sheba peacefully. General Joab agrees with the woman's words and quickly apologizes. They strike a deal to hand over Sheba. The elderly woman returns to the city, and soon thereafter, Sheba's head is delivered to Joab and the city is saved.

What made a powerful general apologize to an old lady and change his battle plans? Ancient Jewish wisdom explains that this vulnerable woman was a daughter of Asher, who was a son of Jacob. This elderly woman was a granddaughter of Jacob. And she had quoted to Joab this law from the Torah: "When you approach a city to make war against it you shall call out for a peaceful surrender" (Deuteronomy 20:10). As a general in King David's army, Joab had to obey the word of God, the highest of all authorities, even when it came from the mouth of an elderly woman. Joab knew his purpose. He did not confuse his plan with his purpose. He was a wise leader who was able to recognize that his plan did not match the situation, and he willingly changed course, seizing upon the opportunity to take back Sheba's head without having to sack the entire city.

Let's look at another case. In the Book of Jonah, we see the prophet Jonah at sea when a terrible storm arises. The sailors and passengers on the boat are all terrified, save for Jonah, who retreats to his cabin to sleep as if he has not a worry in the world. The sailors suspect he has something to do with this unexpected, unseasonal storm. They demand to know where he is from. He could have given some simple lie, but he did not. "I'm a Jew and I fear the Lord God who created sea and land," he replies simply. His answer seems very strange and yet it satisfies them. That was all he had to say. The sailors understood that Jonah had a purpose, and if he was avoiding it, that could explain the cause of the storm.

Being a general and being a prophet were Joab's and Jonah's ways of serving God. We all serve God by fulfilling our destinies and serving our purpose in His plan. Both Jonah and Joab recognized that their purpose was to serve God in this way, but they were flexible in how they did so. They allowed for and embraced change. They did not allow change to affect their purposes, but they did allow themselves to adjust their plans based on changing circumstance so that they could still carry out their purpose. Both men had clear visions of what their mission was and this made it easier for them to cope with the sudden changes that came their way. They were able to cope with the fear and the stress that change brings by maintaining a sense of purpose. What's more, they were both given the opportunity to change their plans for the better. Joab was given the opportunity to take Sheba's head without having to destroy a whole city. He knew his purpose was to kill Sheba, not to destroy the city, and when he saw that these two things did not have to go hand in hand, he changed course, though not his purpose, in order to spare the city.

The lesson is that change, while scary and stressful, can carry the seeds of growth and good fortune. This is as true in business as it is on the battlefield. We must remain true to our purpose but accept that change will happen, and adjust our plans, behavior, and business tactics so that we may not lose sight of our underlying purpose. Embrace change and you may find fortune where you thought there was only misery.

Secret #23

Because Change Is a Constant Reality, Life Is More Accurately Depicted by a Video Than a Photograph

I magine I show you two photographs. In one picture, there is a couple who look extremely happy together. The man and woman are holding hands and smiling at each other on a sunny day. The second photograph is of another couple. This second couple also looks happy. The man has his arm around the woman's shoulders. She has her arm around his waist. Same sunny day. Same big smiles. We have two pictures. A different man and different woman in each one, but they both look happy. You might think these photographs are more or less the same. They certainly appear that way.

What you can't tell from looking at the pictures is that the first photograph is of a married couple who are dedicated to each other and their family. They are looking forward to living out their lives in love, harmony, and tranquility. Regarding the second couple, what if I told you they were also married, but not to each other? Here we have two married people stealing an afternoon of illegitimate bliss in the local motel while their unsuspecting spouses are home tending to the adulterers' kids and houses. Two absolutely different situations here, but you would never know that from looking at the photographs.

Now imagine that, rather than looking at a still photograph of these couples, we were watching a long video of the same two couples. You would see one couple go home to their kids, thank and pay the babysitter, and lie down in bed to read side by side. If the video were long enough, we could watch them grow old and live happily ever after. But we would watch the other couple, the adulterers, emerge warily from the hotel. We would see them go home and feel bad kissing their betrayed spouses with the same lips they kissed their lovers. You would see them struggle to lie to their children. You would see them crying in the shower by themselves, and in time you would witness their eventual divorces. You would see them remarry each other only to cheat on each other and divorce again. These couples are still in the same situation, only now we can see how their lives drastically diverge from that deceptively similar-looking moment. The key thing to realize here is that the photograph is wrong about both the particular moment and the long haul.

A photograph cannot capture reality as well as a video because a photograph is merely a snapshot of one moment in time with no context. A video captures the truth for all to see because a viewer can see the consequence of the actions that follow the moment the snapshot is taken. The video captures a moment in context. A video captures the passage of time. Life is far more like the latter, a video, because we live in a world where time passes. We live in a world where change is continual and ceaseless.

When examining and assessing your finances, business, or the course of your career, do not use a snapshot of what you are looking at. Examine your personal and business matters as if you are watching a video. In other words, don't focus just on the here and now. Consider where you are headed, look for trends, and track your direction. You want to know where you are and where you are headed. And do not think for a moment that you can stand still in life. Life involves change, and change means that a snapshot cannot provide you the truth about anything. The truth is only visible when you consider the passage of time.

A few years ago I was doing consulting work for a struggling factory. This kind of consulting requires that you know a business from the bottom up. So I spoke with a number of the factory workers to get a feel for the workplace before I began my formal retraining sessions. One of the people I interviewed, Miguel Rodriguez, had just emigrated from Mexico with his wife, two children, and mother in-law. He was very happy to have found work at the factory even though the job paid minimum wage. It's hard for me to imagine raising such a large family on minimum wage, but, with a little ingenuity, Miguel was able to just get by. He worked overtime when he could, which paid time and a half, and his mother-in-law watched the children during the day so that his wife could take a job, too. She made only minimum wage, also, but on a dual income and with free childcare, they were just able to make all of their bills. Now you might have thought that Miguel would be stressed and bitter about his situation. He was not. On the contrary, he was happy, hopeful, and grateful for the opportunity to have found a job—any job—in the United States. "We do real well," he said, genuinely. "We are as happy as could be to be here."

Miguel was a pleasure to speak with, a real inspiration, and so I looked forward to talking to him again when I returned to the factory a year later for an annual review. I arrived early just so I could steal a few minutes to speak with him before going about my duties. I went to the human resources office to look up my old friend. This was a big factory with hundreds of workers, but the HR lady knew him by name. His good attitude made him very popular around the factory. Now, I had known with his good attitude and outlook, Miguel was going places. But I didn't know how far! Miguel was now in charge of maintaining all the forklift trucks.

But how did he get the promotion? Miguel had been a menial assembly line worker in an unskilled position before. The story was this: One day, the company that the factory owner contracted with to maintain the forklifts raised their prices. It was more than they could afford and they didn't know what to do. Miguel offered to try to fix them. He told the boss that everyone in Mexico was an amateur mechanic because you had to learn how to make cars run forever. He said if he couldn't do it, they could always hire someone else, but that Miguel could try to keep them running for now. So the boss gave Miguel a chance and he was able to pull it off. Miguel now makes four or five times minimum wage because his boss values his work more highly. Miguel never plans to leave his job, not at that salary, which is of course why the boss is paying him so much. He wants to keep Miguel around. With his new wage, his wife no longer has to work, a fact that had Miguel beaming with pride.

Now let me ask you this: If I had looked at Miguel Rodriguez's life as a snapshot when I first met him, what would I see? Both he and his wife were working overtime and the mother-in-law had to look after the children, whom the parents barely ever saw themselves. All of that and they were still just scraping by. That would be a pretty hard life to lead. I probably would have taken pity on him. But life isn't a snapshot. Life is like a video. Miguel was able to remain unfailingly cheerful and positive because he knew that he wasn't stuck making minimum wage forever. The "video" of his life up to that point showed him moving from poverty in Mexico to a minimum-wage job in the United States. He knew that more change was possible if he continued to seize upon the opportunities presented to him. And he was right. A mere 12 months later, he was making five times what he was before. He was done with overtime. His wife was staying home with the kids. His mother-in-law was free to relax in her old age.

This is what life looks like when you see it as a video, not a snapshot. Don't despair about your current situation. Change it! If you put in the work and seize upon opportunity you can see great change. So don't despair. Remain cheerful. Stay positive and, like Miguel, seize upon opportunity when it presents itself. Your life doesn't have to stay the same. In fact, it won't! It never does. As we have seen, change is inevitable, so there is no benefit to letting your fear immobilize you.

We have also seen that change is scary, even when it is a change for the better. A major promotion can be almost as scary as losing your job. No doubt Miguel had anxiety over the future. What if he got to the United States and couldn't find a job? What if he couldn't keep the forklifts running—would he get fired and then not have the security of his old job? You bet he worried about these things, but he didn't let it paralyze him. Change is inevitable because God placed us in a world of time. Every ticking second, every minute, every day heralds the arrival of the new. Our ability to live safely and comfortably depends upon cultivating an easy adaptability to new circumstances. Change is scary because we are most comfortable when we live under stable and predictable conditions, but everything is ephemeral. Changes in health, in financial, and social circumstances, in the well-being of your family—all of these things are as scary as they are inevitable.

Change is best managed by acquiring courage. To guide us through change, the Tanakh, the collected Hebrew Scriptures, tells us that change teaches us to be strong and of good courage, *chazak v'ematz* in Hebrew. Every time this appears in Scripture, a major change in someone's life circumstances is about to happen. When God promotes Joshua to be Moses' successor, He says, "Be strong and of good courage"(Deuteronomy 31:7, Moses charging Joshua; Joshua 10:25, Joshua charging Israel; 1 Chronicles 22:13, David to his son). You see this phrase also when King David hands over the kingship to his son, Solomon, and whenever Israel confronts its enemies in war.

You can break this phrase down into its composite parts. *Chzak* refers to the strength it takes to overcome obstacles. The word *chzak* first appears in Genesis (41:57) in reference to the famine that drove people to Egypt to buy food from Joseph. Scripture notes that "the famine was strong in all the land." The famine was strong enough to overwhelm the land and the people needed strength to survive—they needed *chzak*.

In Hebrew, *V'ematz* means "and be courageous." This instructs us to have the courage and willpower to use our strength, to use our *chzak*. In Proverbs (31:17), we read a description of a righteous woman that includes this phrase: "with strength she girdeth her loins and invigorates her arms." *Ematz* is often translated here and elsewhere as "invigorates." This suggests that having arms isn't enough; one need also have the fortitude and courage to use them. For example, Winston Churchill claimed that World War II need never have taken place. When Hitler invaded the Rhineland in the spring of 1936, violating the terms of the agreement that ended World War I, Britain and the Allies could have confronted Hitler there and then and precipitated his fall from power. Instead, they hesitated. They possessed the military capacity. They had the *chzak*. What they lacked was the courage and the willpower, the *ematz*, to do anything. Instead, they chose the path of appeasement and much suffering followed. The Scripture teaches that we must first have *chzak*, strength, and then we need courage to do whatever needs doing. Gaining strength is a matter of strategy. Gaining courage is more complicated.

Here are three pathways to developing courage. First, analyze each challenge that you face separately so that you are not overwhelmed by fear. Problems often come in groups and tackling them all at once can leave us feeling overwhelmed. If you are trying to start a business and you have to get zoning approval for a store, find suppliers for inventory, and a loan from the bank, do not attempt these all at once. Separate them into steps. You can do them simultaneously if need be, but separate them out into the separate problems that they are in your mind. Use your journal. Use pen and paper. Separate them out and analyze each one by itself.

The second way to cultivate courage is to realize that cowardice is contagious. Cowardice is our natural default condition. Cowardice is the result of spiritual gravity sucking us down. It is a well-known fact that once the first soldier on a battlefield turns and flees, the whole unit might soon break. Terror and fear are contagious. They spread. When we see our comrades running in fear, we too begin to feel fear, whether it is warranted or not. Perhaps you know this bit of tactical battlefield minutiae. But did you also know that the opposite is also true? Cowardice is contagious, but courage is equally contagious. On a practical level, this means you should find people with courage and surround yourself with them. They will bolster your own courage and spiritual fortitude.

And finally, the third way to cultivate courage is to proactively seek strength in ancient Jewish wisdom. When you feel yourself faltering before fear, let the magic of the Lord's language wash over you. Repeat the phrase *chzak v'ematz* in your head. Let it be your mantra—a meditation. Be strong and of good courage. Be strong and of good courage. Be strong and of good courage. Repeat this to yourself over and over again. Be strong and of good courage.

Scary, inevitable change is constant. But courage becomes constant with exercise and regular use. Courage will always be the best way to handle fear and cope with change.

The More that Things Change, the More We Must Depend Upon Those Things That Never Change

T his is perhaps the principle I repeat more than any other on my radio show. While there are things that change extensively, constantly, and perpetually, there are also things that remain constant, like these biblical secrets, for instance. They comprise ancient Jewish wisdom and are God's biblical blueprint. They are unfaltering. And we may lean on them in the face of change.

And change we will face. Change is ubiquitous. It seems to be accelerating in the modern world. These days we see change that is more rapid and profound than we have ever seen before in recent history. When is the last time you saw a working pay-phone booth? Or a phone with a dial? When we say phone, we tend now to think of cell phones, not home phones. This may surprise some readers, but a majority of young people no longer have a landline at all, and use only their cell phones. Those are nice changes—the progress of technology, which has been going on forever. You can date a photograph down to the decade just by looking at it and examining the buildings, cars, and clothes people wear and the gadgets that they carry.

Some change is constant and forever, a slow forward march of time that seems and is ceaseless. The things that change fall into three categories and I encourage you to think of them as existing on a triangle.

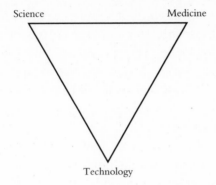

Technology, science, and medicine change; careers change; even people change. Human advancement and personal progress are amazing and exciting things, and progress in these areas brings great opportunity. It also brings great disruption, which is why it is also scary. All change, good and bad, creates uncertainty. Fortunately, we may take comfort in the knowledge that there are some things that do not change ever and we may draw energy, power, wisdom, insight, and courage from these steadfast truths. We can use those things that never change to help us withstand the many things that do change.

During the dot-com bubble of the early 2000s, investors and professionals were excited about the new business opportunities unleashed by the burgeoning Internet. New websites and dot-com startups emerged daily. The markets may have been bullish, but they failed to realize that the driving force behind these websites was not dollars, but eyeballs. Investors were getting excited by the number of eyeballs on the websites, not the cash they were bringing in. The more eyes you had on your site, the more unique visits, the better you were supposedly doing. All of this was new: websites, web traffic, the Internet itself! All of these were big changes to the way business was done.

But something that hadn't changed was the fact that everybody needs to make money. Making money is fundamental to business. Everybody has to eat. Everybody has to buy clothing. Everyone has to take care of their responsibilities, even people who own websites, it turns out! Paying bills takes money, not "page hits." You can't keep the lights on with page hits. You can't buy milk and bread with page hits. You can't buy *anything* with page hits. This was a major problem for the industry and the stock market as a whole, because people had invested vast sums of money in all kinds of websites that, while they were good at getting eyeballs, had not found a way to monetize their presence. People were coming online and leaving without paying for anything. A lot of people lost a lot of money when the market realized this. The stock market bubble burst and many websites and their owners went out of business. The equity stockholders held in these companies vanished practically overnight.

The dot-com bubble is an example of the failure to cope with change that results from not remembering that which never changes. One thing that never changes—and business owners should always remember this—is that a business cannot last without making a profit. A business can float by on loans and investment capital while getting established, but it has to eventually turn a profit. The creation of wealth is the underlying foundation for all societies. The creation of wealth is always a positive, desirable thing for a society and for individuals. Wealth creation is necessary to society and neither can exist without the other. Ancient Jewish wisdom recognizes this tenet, which is enshrined in the Lord's language. The Hebrew word for wealth is spelled O—SH—R, which is pronounced *osher*.

One thing you must understand about the Lord's language is that certain important words that mean one thing will mean the opposite when read backwards. For instance, the Hebrew word for rubbish is R—P—SH. Now, reading that backwards, we have SH—P—R, which means "super." So the word meaning rubbish spelled backwards gives us the word meaning super or valuable. This is because something that is rubbish is the opposite of that which is super. A word having the opposite meaning when read backwards is a common occurrence in ancient Hebrew and is meant to draw attention to the polarizing connection of opposites.

So what is the opposite of *osher*? You might think poor, but you would be wrong. The opposite of a wealthy person is a poor person, but *osher* refers to wealth as a concept. *Osher* is the principle of wealth. So what is the opposite of the principle of wealth? Spelled backwards, *osher* reads R—SH—O, which gives us the word *RaSHaO*, which means evil. The opposite of wealth is evil. In this way, ancient Hebrew tells us that it is God's will to create a healthy, vibrant, successful society, which requires wealth, because wealth is good. Remember from earlier that we learned that wealth is God's reward for doing good. If wealth is not being created, then evil is being done, which means people are making mistakes in their behavior. When people make good choices, when they serve one another, wealth is created, so we know that the absence of wealth, on a societal level, means an absence of good.

This understanding has a profound impact on how we should do business. You probably already knew that wealth is a good thing. Everyone wants wealth! What you may not have realized is that a lack of wealth is not just a lack of good, but is actually evil. In other words, God's natural ideal default condition would be people in society creating wealth. Poverty and destitution are the results of society making mistakes and disobeying God's plan. Societies that are not prospering are engaging in behavior and practices they should not be doing, otherwise God would reward them with wealth. Again I want to stress that I am not by any means suggesting that an impecunious individual is evil. In no way should those individuals enduring financial stress see themselves as lacking in virtue. The formulation I am discussing applies chiefly to a society or an economy. If an economy is struggling and wealth is not being created, the reason is not, as the old-time Soviets would suggest, the weather. It is nearly always the consequence of corruption and following a destructive economic model.

There is a common myth bandied about in famous literature and popular culture that poverty is somehow virtuous. This is fallacious. Never associate poverty with virtue. Never assume that those living in poverty must all be holy, good people. The truth is actually the reverse. If a society appears not to be blessed economically, we must take a hard look at the society and question whether they are truly behaving as they should. Note that I am definitely not saying that individuals who find themselves in poverty are evil. Sometimes individuals are doing all they can, but they live in a hopeless, degenerate society or area or neighborhood that precludes wealth. The poor are not evil; poverty is evil, for it is the lack of wealth. Similarly, just as the poor are mistakenly viewed as virtuous, the wealthy and successful are portrayed as evil.

It wasn't until about 1934, due to a book by a man called Matthew Josephson that men like Andrew Carnegie, who donated a library to each of hundreds of smaller towns across America, began to be referred to as "robber barons." Until then those titans of commerce and industry were seen as worthy of admiration and emulation. Of course, to this very day, the envious do-nothings who malevolently defame those nineteenth-century wealth creators as robber barons never actually identify just whom they are supposed to have robbed or how they robbed them.

And so you can see that ancient Jewish wisdom shows us that wealth is and always will be the foundation of society. It is something that will never change, even as the instruments of business evolve to accommodate and make use of technology. But this is only one of many things that will never change. There are others. You may then wonder how it is you are to tell the difference between those things that undergo change and those that do not. Let me simplify the matter for you. In order to function in this world you only have to know three things. Think of these three things as existing on a second triangle.

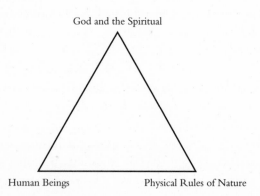

Things that do not change include everything about human beings, everything about God and the spiritual, and everything about the environment, this place called Earth. That is not to say that individual humans or the environment do not change—clearly they do—but that the principles governing human behavior and the way the world works are unchanging. And so those two things, along with God and the spiritual, form the three points of a triangle of things that never change.

You want to understand them totally because they are tools to help you cope with the onslaught of change in the world. They are your pillars and you must seek to understand them, through the principles of ancient Jewish wisdom, as best you can. Our knowledge of these things does not change over time, though your personal knowledge of them is something you must develop. This is, in fact, the way in which personal growth (change) happens—by understanding the unchangeable principles that govern your life.

Unlike our collective knowledge of science, technology, and medicine (which we learn more about as time goes on), our collective knowledge of God, humans, and the Earth remains constants. It is up to each person to learn as much about these areas as possible so that they may lead better lives, but there is no more to learn now than there was at any other point in history. It is all already out there and enshrined in ancient Jewish wisdom. For example, consider your knowledge and contrast it against that of your grandparents. You almost certainly know more about science and technology than your grandparents, but it is completely possible that you actually know less than your grandparents about raising children. It is possible that families of years ago had a better understanding of how marriages should function because they may have put in more effort to learn than you did. But there is no way they knew more about technology that had not even been invented yet. If we have insufficient knowledge of parenting, we may comfort ourselves by saying, "Well, times are different! Things are more complicated today!" But this is exactly the point. As we learn more about science, technology, and medicine, we find it increasingly incumbent upon ourselves to develop our knowledge of that which does not change so that we may not be confused or led astray. You have no excuse for not learning to raise your kids properly—the knowledge is there, all of it, to be had now just as it was at any point in history. But it is up to you to seek it out and master that knowledge.

So as you see, that which does not change and that which does change are invariably linked. Look what we get when we place them on top of each other.

Here we see the two triangles converge and we may observe the two different areas of knowledge: the changeable and the permanent. Now you may recognize this shape as the Jewish star, the Star of David, which

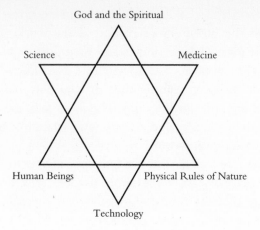

is a symbol that dates back all the way to the miraculous and mystical information that Moses brought down from Mount Sinai over three thousand years ago. The triangle is a symbol of great power and strength. There is a reason that bridges are usually built with triangular struts and that roof trusses are built in the shape of triangles. The triangle plays an important role in engineering, especially civil engineering, because, with only three sides, the triangle is rigid and will not collapse under weight.

You can see how the above triangles hold together these things that provide the totality of all our existence: God in the spiritual world, humanity, and the physical environment. We have that strong triangle that will not shift because it is built upon certain foundational principles given to us back at Mount Sinai. This triangle reinforces the second triangle of things that do change—medicine, technology, and science. When one triangle is superimposed over the other, the result is this massively powerful structure called the Star of David, or the Jewish star, in which everything that changes interlocks with everything that doesn't change. This reinforcement illustrates how the more that things change, the more we must depend on those things that never change. They are interlocked.

Now let's look at the spheres of knowledge on each point of the triangle. As illustrated, there are two types of knowledge in the world—that which changes and that which does not. But why does one group change when the other remains static?

The areas of knowledge that change over time do so because human beings can accumulate more knowledge of these areas as time goes on. Technology falls into this realm. So do medicine and science. We know more about medicine today than our grandparents ever did. We know more about electronics. We know more about computers. We know more about nuclear power and alternative energy. We know all kinds of things our grandparents did not know, and so it is very easy for us to start thinking we are smarter than our grandparents simply because we know so much more about these new and expanding areas of knowledge. But the only reason we know more about these things is because there is now more to know. We can learn from those scientists and thinkers who came before us and build upon their achievements. That is because these fields expand and change. There is always more to learn about technology as new types of computers and gadgets are invented.

Then, of course, there are the areas of knowledge that do not change—knowledge of God, humans, and the Earth. Everything to know about these things God created long ago. They are unchanging. So while our personal knowledge of these areas may expand as we pursue studies into the spiritual, there is not necessarily more to know, just more for you or me to know. But the principles that underpin these areas are the same now and forever.

Let's return to the example of childrearing. It is never good to spoil your children. It does not matter whether you live in Beverly Hills and you spoil your children with gadgets derived from twenty-first-century technology, or if you lived in Montana in the 1800s and you spoiled your children with ponies and rock candy. Then and now, spoiling a child is a bad idea. Give a child things they do not earn, and you will spoil them. Period. You can spoil a child in any generation, in any century, anywhere on Earth. There is no technological information that changes our understanding of how to raise a child because raising a child is an issue of morals. It is a spiritual matter and is thus governed by the principles of ancient Jewish wisdom, which do not change. Whether it is the twenty-first century or the ninth century, those principles are still going to apply.

Understanding that all spiritual matters are governed by the principles of ancient Jewish wisdom, you should see that the existence of cell phones, automobiles, and personal computers does not affect the principles by which children and parents should interact. Nor do the trappings of the modern world change the way siblings should relate to one another. The process by which two people enter courtship, marry, and build a life together is similarly unchanged. Technology has no fundamental impact in any of this or other such spiritual matters. The biblical secrets of ancient Jewish wisdom will always apply in these areas the same as they have before and do now.

That is not to say, however, that modern technology does not appear to complicate these matters. That children have access to all kinds of immoral material on the Internet is something that parents must consider in our current day and age. There are now websites on which married people can meet other married people for extramarital relations. There are positive changes as well. Cell phones allow us to stay in better contact with our children and business partners. In the business world, we see radical change brought about by technology. We now have smartphones, Skype conferences, online investment trading, online job application systems, e-commerce, and many other changes to the way that business is conducted. But all of this technology does not fundamentally impact the way we *should* or *should not* behave in life or business; these technological advances merely impact the *how* and *can* of that behavior. The means by which I do right or wrong—whether with a wooden club, a modern rifle, a homemade computer virus, or my bare hands—is ultimately immaterial. What matters is whether I have done right or wrong, not how I have done right or wrong.

Thankfully, we have a toolset for coping effectively with the drama and the change that technology brings and that toolset never breaks or rusts or gets outdated. It is the principles of ancient Jewish wisdom and, because they rest on the top of the unchanging triangle with God, they will never fail you. We may use those pillars of unchanging wisdom to help us cope with the areas of our life and modern world that are in constant flux. This is why we must rely on that which does not change in order to cope with that which does. We will always be able to face that which comes tomorrow by looking at the past for guidance. We look to ancient Jewish wisdom to make sense of the modern world.

Tomorrows are important—they are the future. If we view tomorrow as something bright and positive and exciting we can go to sleep tonight, in the present, with a completely different attitude than if we approach tomorrow with fear and trepidation.

Press Forward Even When the Road Ahead Is Not Clear

By now you should understand that tomorrow will bring change but that, with ancient Jewish wisdom as your guide, you will be able to face whatever comes. In Deuteronomy, chapter 28, there is a verse that reads: "And it shall come to pass that, if you harken to the voice of the Lord, your God, to observe and perform all His commandments that I command you this day then the Lord, your God, will bring all these blessings upon you, but only if you harken to the voice of the Lord, your God." The Scripture then lists all of the rewards we can reap—prosperity, happiness, success, fulfillment, a life without want, a life without worry. But we are also given a warning of all of the bad things we will face if we do not follow the commandments, if we do not look to ancient Jewish wisdom, the unchanging principles of the world, to guide us. God tells us that we will face these things if we fail to serve Him in joy and jubilation in exchange for all the good that He has done us. This sense of excitement, happiness, positivity, and optimism are absolutely essential to facing the change that tomorrow brings in both business and life.

Let this knowledge buoy your spirit so that you may accept this truth: even though you may rely on those things that do not change to guide your way, they will not necessarily light your way. By that, I mean that you should be able to use these biblical secrets to find your way through the dark, but this does not eliminate uncertainty; it simply allows you to better face uncertainty.

In Exodus, chapter 14, Moses must lead the Jews out of Egypt and to safety by parting the Red Sea. This story teaches us a valuable lesson about how we must face the future. I want to draw your attention to two verses in particular. Exodus (14:15) reads: "And the Lord said to Moses, 'Tell the people of Israel to march forward.'" Exodus (14:16) reads: "Lift up your rod and stretch out your hand over the sea and divide it." The thing to note here is that Moses is instructed to raise his rod to divide the sea only after telling his people to march forth into the water. The Israelites were actually in the water, some of them up to their necks, and were told to keep marching before the water split. And yet no one complained or feared drowning because the message from God was very clear: walk first into the water and the ocean will split afterwards. Had the Israelites waited around for the waters to part, they would have been waiting a long time—perhaps forever. They had to bring about their own miracle, a truth we can deduce from the peculiar order of these two verses, which is no accident as there are no accidents in Scripture.

To succeed at life and business, you too must face the future as the Israelites did at the Red Sea. Get moving now. Do not wait for the bridge. Cross now and the way through will present itself.

Such a leap of faith requires us to view the future as if it had already come to pass. You must have faith that, somehow or another, you will cross that ocean, that river, that obstacle, that challenge. As you navigate your professional life, you will be faced with all kinds of trials and tribulations for which there will appear no feasible solution. Do you sit there trying to figure out what to do? No, you get moving. Problems—all problems—are solved not just by sitting and thinking, but by moving and doing. No one ever solved a problem by thinking about it forever. You eventually have to get in motion, and you had better do so right away, because your top competitors will. You can think while you walk! Get out there and test your hypotheses. Use trial and error to find the way. You find a path by exploring. Remember, a path must be cut through the forest, not found. You know that somehow you will overcome the challenge even if you do not know how or when. It may be later today, or tomorrow, or next week, or next year when you solve the problem. You will take however long it requires you to do so, that is a fact. Dallying will get you there no faster. The solution presents itself en route. This might seem like a counterintuitive way to approach problems, but it is not if you recognize the complexities of time.

There are four basic dimensions to the physical world that God created for us. We as human beings are able to measure these four physical properties. They are: length; weight; temperature; and time. For our purposes, length encompasses all physical measurements. We may measure length alone. Or we may measure length by width to get the area of a two-dimensional space. Or we can add height and calculate the volume of a three-dimensional space. Weight and temperature are straightforward measurements of how heavy and how hot or cold something is, respectively. The fourth measure, time, also seems straightforward (though, as we will see shortly, it is not). Time is measured in seconds, minutes, hours, days, years, centuries, and so on.

These measurements may also be combined to give us other important measurements of the physical world. For instance, you can combine length with time to determine how fast something is moving. When you drive on the highway and see that the speed limit is 70 miles per hour, you are using a measurement of both length and time combined. Density is a combination of volume (length cubed) and weight. Lead sinks when put in water because it is denser—it has more weight per volume—than water. Wood floats because it has less weight per volume than water. Such measurements are very important to engineering planes, ships, cars, and other pieces of machinery.

These four measurements, used alone and in combination, can tell us everything we need to know about the physical world. We can use various instruments to take these measurements, but most people are pretty good at sensing these measurements intuitively to a certain degree of accuracy. Most people can eyeball a table and doorframe and know instantly whether or not a particular table will go through easily, need to be tilted to make the passage, or unable to fit through at all. Weight is not always as easy to eyeball, but by reference and memory, we learn to intuit what something will weigh. You can probably guess about how much a book or a brick weighs. You may not know how many ounces and pounds it is, but you can imagine how it will feel in your hands just by looking. Temperature is also relatively easy to judge. You may not be able to tell that it is exactly 78 degrees outside by feel, but you can tell that it is somewhere in the upper 70s because you know what that feels like.

However, one measurement is less intuitive than the others—time. Time is far more difficult to intuitively judge because it is so subjective. The same span of time can feel different based on conditions and circumstance. When a child is waiting for an approaching summer vacation, their perception is that every day seems to drag. On the other hand, when they are actually on vacation and having fun, time seems to speed up. Time doesn't actually speed up; it just appears to.

Similarly, years seem to pass differently as we age. A year seems like a very long time to a 10-year-old child. And why shouldn't it? A year represents a whole tenth of the child's experienced life! But by the time that same child turns 50, a year seems like not so much time anymore because a year, while it is the same objective length of time, only represents 2 percent of the child's experienced life. A year represents a smaller fraction of our lives as we get older, and so our subjective experience of a year is that it feels shorter the older we are. The year does not change, but our perception of it does.

The main reason that time is harder to intuit than the other measurements is because time is simply far more complex. When Einstein began to study the speed of light, he described strange distortions of time and space. Light travels at 186,000 miles per second, a tremendous speed that, while seemingly quantifiable, leads to distortions of time and space. Without getting too technical, something moving that fast creates substantial distortions in time. Nothing other than light can travel the speed of light, so that speed is approachable, but impossible to reach. Much like "i," the speed of light is more of a theoretical construct than an achievable speed, at least in terms of space travel. Einstein also tells us that it is impossible for two people to experience the same simultaneous moment of time and that the exact speed and location of an electron cannot be measured simultaneously, which is the foundation of quantum mechanics. These concepts are very difficult for humans to understand or visualize, just like the concept of infinity, because time is complex in a way that temperature, length, and weight are not.

Have you ever paused a videotape or a DVD? What you see is a still picture of the landscape or scene. Nothing moves, but you can still view the DVD as a still image frozen in time. Now try pausing your radio while listening to music or speech. What do you hear? Nothing. This seems obvious, because it is a phenomenon you are so accustomed to, but what accounts for this difference? Why can we pause an image but not a sound? We are so used to this phenomenon that it seems normal and so we don't afford it a thought, but when you stop to think about it, why does an image not vanish when we pause a video in the same way that sound disappears when we pause a recording? The image is there. You can look at it. It's not moving, it's not contiguous, and there is no movement through time, but the image is still there. So why can't I see or hear frozen speech or paused music when I hit pause? It is the strangeness of time that makes music and speech meaningless without the passage of time. This is why rhythm and beat are so important in music. If you remove the element of time, all other aspects of music become meaningless. There can be no notes or tune without beat, without time. Time and music are inextricable.

Words and conversation also cannot be divorced from time. You cannot pause a sentence in mid-speech without causing it to disappear. A ten-word sentence might take a few seconds to relate, and if I tried to stretch it over a year, it would become meaningless. It would just be low rumbling sounds, imperceptible to the human ear. Likewise, highly compressed speech is inaudible; it is too brief and high-pitched for the human ear to hear. Time is absolutely inextricable from the delivery of speech and music. What this tells us is that, when we fail to properly appreciate and relate to time, we cannot fully understand language or communication. In effect, we cannot fully appreciate the entirety of existence and the human experience without also experiencing time.

As humans, we enter the world and begin passing through the stages of life. We are born into a world as infants and over time we grow up. We become toddlers, then teenagers, and finally adults. The passage of time is so intertwined with our day-to-day existence that we hardly notice it at times. Often, we become blasé about our own existence. We get bored. We fail to appreciate time and its passage. This is one reason the Bible relates the experience of Adam in the Garden of Eden. Adam is brought into the world right at the beginning of Scripture. But, unlike us, he plops down into existence as a full-grown man. Adam experiences creation in all of its glory all at once.

Try to put yourself in Adam's shoes. Imagine if you yourself had been just dropped into the world at the age of 25, suddenly brought into existence with the snap of His finger. With no earlier memories, you look around at creation for the first time. Everything is wild and unbelievable. You have a hard time understanding what anything even is or means. This is what happened to Adam. Everything, even the most mundane things, were blissful, wondrous, and amazing. God gives Adam a strawberry and the sensation is utterly indescribable—such a small thing to us, but to Adam the strawberry is *literally* like nothing he has ever experienced before.

Of course, that is not how we ourselves enter creation. We enter the world as infants and experience creation as a slow unfolding. When we first experience a strawberry, we have similar experiences against which to compare it, such as eating baby food or tasting breast milk. By the time we hit 25, we have been desensitized to experience by two and a half decades of taking things as they come. This causes us to miss out on a whole lot of beauty and wonder right beneath our noses. We simply don't appreciate it for how amazing it is. By age 25, a strawberry is simply a strawberry—old hat. Right? To us, maybe, but not so for Adam! He had never known such a delight.

Adam also has never experienced fear before. When Adam notices the shadows getting longer and the sun beginning to drop in the sky, he asks God what was going on. Soon it grows dark and he is terrified—the beautiful world he just encountered has vanished. And this is when Adam is brought to understand that he is not in a static world. This is a world constantly in movement and flux. And so he comes to a *sudden* appreciation of time. He undergoes a sudden inoculation of change, which he now must learn to cope with. Adam must learn to understand and handle time and its effect upon the world.

And you too, dear reader, must learn to do this as well. By doing so, you are going to learn from Adam. Moreover, I want you to become like Adam. I want you not only to be able to cope with time, but to also be able to fully appreciate it. When you fully appreciate time, everything can be just like the first time you saw or experienced it. By appreciating time for what it is, by understanding how our view of it is distorted by our own circumstance, history, and perception, we can overcome our own innate limitations. We can overcome the distortions of time our human perspective imposes upon us.

This understanding is absolutely imperative to good business sense. We must be able to look upon things with fresh eyes, as if experiencing them for the first time, like Adam did, in order to see them as they truly are. So much of proper business interaction and accurate economic analysis is born from an ability to appreciate and understand change for what it is. And because change is a process, understanding change requires an unintuitive understanding of time and its passage.

In an age past, iron was crucial to the world's economy. Iron smelting was big business and there were ironworks everywhere in the developing world in both America and Europe. And then, all of a sudden, steel was invented. It was a revolutionary innovation. Iron combined with carbon and nickel and various other elements allowed man to create steel, which was far superior to and more useful than iron. Steel revolutionized the manufacture of countless goods and tools. For example, cannons had always been made of iron, but because iron is brittle, the more times a cannon was fired, the more likely it was to fracture and explode, killing the operators rather than enemy combatants. But steel was far less brittle and suddenly militaries had at their disposals cannons that could be safely fired indefinitely.

Overnight, thousands of iron factories went out of business. New technology had come to the world, through the metals industry, and most of the iron producers were finished. Steel was the future. Or at least it was for a little while. The first generation of steel plants soon went out of business as a new and better way of making steel was discovered. This is how it has always been: one cutting-edge technology and its purveyors usurping that which came before, over and over again. In 1900, over a quarter-million Americans were employed taking care of horses, shoeing horses, building harnesses, making buggy whips, and scooping manure off the streets of America's cities. But then 1908 rolled around and with it, the Ford Model T, the first consumer car developed by Henry Ford. By 1914, the Model T was rolling off production lines at a staggering pace, and almost overnight the entire horse and buggy industry vanished.

Hundreds of thousands of people were suddenly out of work. What a tragedy, yes? No! Some people saw the change coming. Some people didn't wait until the last minute to figure out to whom they could still sell a wagon wheel or horse harness. These people abandoned the horse and buggy industry and started up businesses in supplying car parts and petroleum products. Some learned to work on the new machines and opened the first mechanic shops. Some opened gas stations and travel centers. Others learned to pave and repair roads. But what all of these successful people had in common was what they *didn't* do: they didn't go to school to study horseshoeing—that was the past. The automobile was the future of business.

Of course, this process did not stop with the Model T, nor has it stopped yet, nor will it ever stop. Time will continue to march on, and the successful business professional understands this truth and is always looking ahead. The successful business professional is trying out new paths *before* they become ubiquitous. This is how you corner the market, by getting in on the ground floor. The agile business professional is always looking to provide new services and the next product before the public even knows they need them. If you wait—to turn to ancient Jewish wisdom and speak metaphorically—until the sea has parted, you are too late. Your competitors will have already swooped in. You must be able to go forth even when the road ahead is not clear, nor even visible. We do this by grasping time, understanding its mysterious ways, and taking control of our perception of it. We need not exist at the mercy of time. We can make it our ally.

In Hebrew, the Lord's language, the word for time is *ZeMaN*, which is linked to the word for *invitation*. This serves to remind us that the passage of time is an invitation to make the most of it, to manage it effectively, and to integrate our understanding of how the world works with a true and accurate perception of the reality of time.

Do Not Let Your Fear Conquer You—Press On

L et me be clear that I am not telling you that pressing on when the path is unknown is easy. I am simply telling you that it is necessary to being successful in business and life, even when it is scary. So how do we eliminate our fear?

The answer is that we do not.

Like Moses and the Israelites, you must step into the ocean before it is split, but do you think they were not scared to walk into the water up to their necks? Of course they were scared! But they did it anyway.

No one said that following these biblical secrets will make any of this easier or less scary. But no one promised you an easy life, either. There is no reason to believe that life need not be scary. Every person who has ever lived has experienced fear. That does not mean we cannot overcome our fear. The dirty little secret of true heroes is that they do not overcome fear by eliminating it. They overcome their fear by learning to cope with it. Courage does not come from eliminating fear; it comes from the ability to act and plow ahead in the face of fear.

Consider the job of a fireman. Do you think a fireman ever overcomes the fear of stepping into a burning house? Not if he has any survival sense! Stepping into a burning house is and should be scary! A courageous firefighter understands the danger but is able to do what must be done in the face of his own fear. So do not feel small or weak because you experience fear—that is the sign that you appreciate grave situations. Courage is all about understanding the direness of a situation and forging ahead anyway.

Let me tell you a story about the shipping industry. I love boating and I spend a lot of time on and near the water. My wife and I are accustomed to seeing huge ships piled high with freight containers. We were very fearful of these containers because, if one fell off a ship, it would float just at or below sea level and present a hazard, especially at night when you couldn't see them in the water. And these container ships were everywhere! But it wasn't always this way. Freight used to be loaded onto ships by longshoremen, a process that took forever. Not only that, docks experienced a lot of inventory shrinkage due to pilferage of the cargo. It was a real problem that caused greater loss of stock than piracy, until 1956, when a man named Malcolm McLean came up with a better way. He invented the standardized freight container, which can be loaded at a warehouse or factory, locked, put on a truck, and taken to a harbor. There, the container is lifted with a crane and put on the boat without ever needing to be opened. Nobody actually has to touch whatever is inside the locked container.

In no time at all, the overwhelming majority of the world's cargo was being shipped in McLean's containers.

How do you think the longshoremen felt about that? Not great! Loading a ship now took only a fraction of the time that it had before. A single crane operator could now do the work of hundreds of men. Literally 90 percent of dockworkers were suddenly in the same situation as all of those people who used to make buggy whips. They were no longer needed. It was a new world and it was a new era. The men were scared. And, as you can imagine, quite angry at this Malcolm McLean, who had invented the freight container, founded the Sea Land Company, kickstarted everything we now know to be the shipping industry, and put all of these dockworkers out of business. It was a huge change. It was scary. But this incredible change also ushered in much opportunity.

Such changes are inevitable. We must learn to understand and cope with this because we cannot prevent change. Remember what God showed Adam—that this is not a static world. But how do we face this fear? Simple: You just face it! Despite old folktales, no one ever died of fear. The fact is you are always going to experience unease and fear in the face of change. We feel more comfortable with a stable, static situation, but understand that such a situation is never permanent. Some are better at facing change than others, but all have it in us to learn to face change and fear and stand our ground. Each and every one of us has the capacity for this self-improvement.

One of the enormous differences between people and animals is that a cow or a cat or a camel or a kangaroo will be exactly that in five years' time. Nothing's going to change for them. But a human being is different. We can change. We must change. The excitement of life comes about through change, and success in making money comes about through an ability to change and deal with change. Now, if we fear change, and if we know change is inevitable, then we obviously must learn to overcome fear. As I have told you, the answer is simply to stand up to fear and press on. But where do we gain the strength and courage? You guessed it—from ancient Jewish wisdom.

Chapter 37 in Genesis deals with the life of Joseph. You'll remember that Joseph's brothers sold him into slavery to the Midianites out of jealousy because their father favored him the most of all of his sons. In the final verse of the chapter, the Midianites took him to Egypt and sold him to Potiphar, an official in the Court of Pharaoh. It is not until the next chapter in Joseph's life that we find out that Joseph quickly rises through the ranks in Egypt. Only this is *not* the next chapter of the Bible. It is not until chapter 39 that we pick back up with Joseph in Egypt. In the meantime, chapter 38 in Genesis follows an entirely different story about Judah, Joseph's older brother, and has nothing to do with Joseph at all. The chapter is a massive interruption to the story of Joseph, which is just getting interesting when we leave off in Genesis, chapter 37. But instead of following Joseph, Genesis, chapter 38 is about Judah's life, his marriage, and his public embarrassment for ending up with a woman whom he should never have married. From this embarrassment is born Scripture's second set of twins.

Why would the Bible change focus like this? While chapter 38 may seem like a huge departure from chapter 37 narratively, the similarities between chapter 37 and chapter 38 of Genesis are unavoidable. What did Jacob's sons use to deceive their father? They used the blood of a certain animal—a goat. They dipped Joseph's coat in the blood of a goat and then they took it to Isaac and said Jacob must have been killed. And what happens with this woman who is actually Judah's daughter-in-law, though he does not know it at the time? She deceives him. And what animal makes an appearance here? Once again, it is a goat. The appearance of a goat in the Bible is a rare occurrence, but here we have it in two chapters that stand back to back. This is meant to draw a parallel between the two chapters.

Furthermore, we observe Jacob lose two sons. Joseph has only gone to Egypt, but Jacob believes him to be dead. Later on, Joseph imprisons Simon to obscure his own identity. So Jacob, having lost two sons, tries very hard to save the life of his third son, Benjamin, because this mad ruler of Egypt (whom he doesn't know is really Joseph) has insisted that Benjamin be brought to Egypt. Jacob is beside himself with fear. Now, for comparison, consider Judah. Judah has also lost two sons. God killed Er. God killed Onan. And now Judah is trying to save the life of his third son. The similarities are again striking.

What are we to take from this?

Jacob did something wrong by favoring Joseph, which initiated the whole fiasco. Judah did something wrong as well. And yet both men manage to put it right. In Jacob's case, his mistake lead to Joseph taking a position of leadership over all of Egypt, which allows him to later save the lives of his family. Because of all of this, the children of Israel are formed. The rest is history! It is very easy for us to look at Jacob and Judah's behavior and call them mistakes. But were they? Yes, they were missteps, but all was not lost.

Too often, people fear making mistakes. They think if they make a single mistake, all will be lost, their lives will be ruined, that it will be the end of everything. Thankfully, life just doesn't work that way. We all sin from time to time, but rarely do we sin intentionally. And we don't try to make mistakes, either; they just happen. We are all fallible. The thing to accept is that, in life and in business, you are going to make missteps. You will do the wrong thing from time to time and it will cause bad things to happen. But we cannot fear these mistakes and we cannot fear their repercussions. If we do, we will lock up in fear of the future. We will fail to act, we will fail to carve ourselves a path through life and out of our own mistakes.

In Ecclesiastes (7:20), King Solomon says: "There is no utterly righteous man on Earth who achieves any good without sinning." Solomon is not saying that there are no righteous men. There are plenty. He is saying that there are no righteous men who achieve anything without sinning. You must interact with the world to achieve things and doing so means inevitable sinning and inevitable missteps because we are all fallible. The only way to avoid doing anything wrong ever is to do nothing. Do not build a family. Don't start a business. Lock yourself away in a cave and don't do anything. Then, I suppose, there is the likelihood that you will be able to die totally without sin, other than the sin of locking yourself in a cave, of course. (And doing nothing is a sin, make no mistake. I would argue it is the worst kind because it means you are not serving God's other children.)

If you're out there in the world living life passionately, committed to your life, passionately committed to your family and your community, passionately committed to your career and your business, you are going to make mistakes. It's going to happen. And you know what? So what! You will make a mistake, suffer a setback, and then move on from there, wiser for the experience. There is no need to fear the path forward. Eliminate the fear that you have of making mistakes and simply travel forward and be the best working professional, the best husband or wife, the best father or mother, that you can be and it will all work out in the end.

Make fear your friend. Now that you know it is an inevitable part of a busy life filled with passion and creativity, read these two verses in Proverbs. "Be not be petrified of (even) sudden fear . . ." (Proverbs 3:25), and "Happy is the man who fears always . . ." (Proverbs 28:14). With these Proverbs, wise King Solomon is communicating this very principle. We cannot allow ourselves to be paralyzed by terror, yet remember that ordinary fear is quite normal. Don't allow fear to terrify you and what is more important, know that you can find happiness in fear. It is evidence that you are not a vegetable. Were you not striving toward goals and if you had no dreams, you'd have little fear. The presence of fear can bring a small private smile to your face. You know what is going on and you know how to allow it to lift you to new heights.

Become Strongly, Even Radically, Open to New Directions, Soft Sounds, and Faint Footsteps

I often work late into the night after my family is fast asleep and it's only me awake in the house. Often, I sit at the kitchen table where all is quiet. I have a beautiful office to study and work in, but late at night I prefer the kitchen table because the presence of my family can be felt there. That kitchen table is the core of my family's existence. I feel surrounded and supported by the cocoon of their love, but I don't actually have to endure the noise they make bustling all around me as they would during the day. So sitting at the kitchen table at night, I get the best of both worlds.

An experience I have over and over is that I will be sitting there at the kitchen table, deep in my work, when suddenly I notice the refrigerator cycle on. The compressor kicks on and it clicks away and hums in the background. It isn't terribly loud, but it can be terribly distracting when it is so quiet in the house. However, I have never noticed the refrigerator running during the daytime. I know it runs during the day, but I never hear it. You have probably had this experience as well. Everyone has. Why is it that we hear the refrigerator working only at night? Because the house is loud during the day and all the other noise around you, the hustle and bustle of your family, blocks out the soft hum of the refrigerator and other appliances. They are drowned out completely. It's not just that these noises are hard to hear over the commotion of the day—you actually hear nothing. You don't notice them at all. The noise from the refrigerator doesn't even register during the day. But when everything around you is quiet, individual noises are easier to hear. You hear every little change. You can, in other words, detect the faint footsteps of approaching events. The more noise and bustle about, the less attuned we are to small changes in our environment. This can be a healthy thing to experience from time to time because it reminds us of how we perceive the world.

For this reason, I encourage you to block out a certain amount of time for yourself on a regular basis. Make an appointment with yourself. This need not take up an inordinate amount of time. Once a week is fine for most people. And it doesn't have to be very long; 10 to 15 minutes is plenty of time. Fifteen minutes alone with no distractions actually feels like quite a long time. So not much time is required, but you do need to be absolutely, entirely alone. No one should be around at all—you shouldn't be able to see anyone or even have to worry that they might interrupt you. Put away your computer. Turn off the ringer on your phone. You may find that finding a time and place where you can really truly be alone is more difficult than you think. You are probably going to have to plan for this. Make sure that once a week, you calendar into your schedule 10 to 15 minutes when you actually have access to a place where nobody is around, there are no disturbances, and no one is going to interrupt you by banging on the door.

Once you find a time and a place to be alone where it's quiet, I want you to just sit and make yourself open. Do nothing. Turn down the light so it's not bright, as you don't want to be bombarded by too much visual stimuli. Then just spend that time with yourself. It is a wonderful rare experience for a busy person. None of us do this without being taught to do so. High school does not teach you to do this, nor college, nor most parents. So you have to teach yourself to just sit and be open. Try to stop your mind from thinking about the last movie you saw or the last book you read. If you have been arguing with somebody, block that from your mind. Put everything out of mind. You want to put yourself into a 100 percent receptive mode. That is very, very helpful and it is really the key, the essence of the entire ancient Hebrew principle of the Sabbath.

This is, in fact, what the Sabbath is for. Observance of the Fourth Commandment does not mean we cannot do anything on the Sabbath. Observing the Sabbath does not preclude rearranging the furniture on Saturday (or Sunday, if you are Christian) at my wife's behest. It's not that you cannot do any work. You simply cannot do what is known in Hebrew as *Melachah*, which refers specifically and only to specific creative work where you apply your energy and ingenuity to the world around you to affect change—it also applies to business. If my wife wants me to move all of the furniture around, for example, that doesn't count. No real change is affected. Moving my furniture around isn't business.

What the Sabbath does is give me 25 hours every week to pull back. I'm not putting out anything to the world. I am just being receptive. But the Sabbath is not, for most people, acute focused receptiveness. So I advise you to also take 10 to 15 minutes once every few days or once a week, and go into a room by yourself, dim the lights, make sure you're not going to be interrupted, and just allow thoughts to come in. Just hear the faint footsteps of approaching events. These few minutes I set aside for myself are extra special. There's no phone, no Internet, no fax machine, nothing at all. I am in a receptive mode but there is, ideally, nothing around for me to receive. I am by myself and turned off.

During the 1970s, two good friends, Ben Cohen and Jerry Greenfield, opened a business together. They wrote out a comprehensive business plan, put everything into place, and then Ben and Jerry started their first bagel delivery company. Now let me ask you, have you ever bought any bagels from Ben & Jerry's? Probably not. The idea was not very profitable. They knew they needed to do something different. So they looked around. Because they were in Vermont, there were a lot of cows around, and perhaps that is why they decided to create a brand of ice cream. Whatever the reason, their ice cream company went on to be one of the most successful ice cream companies ever. But the thing to take note of is that they didn't start out with that idea. They started out with the idea to deliver bagels, but when that didn't work, they allowed themselves to be receptive to change.

There is such a thing as intrinsic instinct, and Ben and Jerry listened to it. We don't always want to trust our instinct, especially our animal instincts, but we do want to trust our human intuition and we do want to be receptive to the idea of changing course.

Ben & Jerry's Ice Cream isn't the only such story, either. One Mr. Toyoda in Japan spent the early years of the twentieth century trying to build a fabric weaving company because he saw that the standards of living were rising in Japan. People were going to want fine clothing, he thought. He tried to invent a new and better way to weave fabric, but none of his ideas worked. Then, one day in 1937, he repurposed the machinery that had been devoted to building weaving looms and started building cars instead. The mighty Toyota Company was born from the ashes of a failed weaving business. And perhaps you have heard of Wrigley's gum? William Wrigley started off his company trying to sell baking soda and soap, but he never turned a profit, and so he turned to making and selling chewing gum instead.

These men share one thing in common—they were open to change and they listened to their intuition. Sometimes we hear a whisper in the air that guides us positively. This whisper we hear, it is not passive—it is a response to our own enthusiasm, passion, and commitment. We put in the effort and we get back a divine message. Call it inspiration if you want. Call it an entrepreneurial muse. But it feels and sounds like a whisper in your soul. If you hear it, listen to it. You must be willing to change course when it tells you to.

This whisper is not restricted to business enterprises at all. Often spouses hear a similar whisper when they realize their relationship is faltering from lack of attention. They may realize they need to change directions, which, for a marriage, can be a very good thing when done properly. Sometimes a couple realizes they've fallen into a rut. The marriage may have lost its spontaneity. Perhaps the spouses have not nurtured their enthusiasm for each other. They can see it in each other's eyes, which no longer light up when they see one another after a long day. That's never a good sign, and when this happens, a wise couple will sit down and say, "We need to reengineer our marriage. We have to change directions completely." I mean a change of direction within the marriage, a reengineering of the way you and your spouse interact. This can be a very exciting process. It can be scary, yes—change always is. It may be painful, too. But pain is a part of life. You must be open to experiencing both pain and fear to make big changes. Don't allow yourself to succumb to the very natural human instincts of complacency and inertia. If there are changes that need to be made, make them, no matter how scary or dramatic.

There is an old John Huston movie from 1951, *The African Queen*, starring Humphrey Bogart and Katharine Hepburn. Bogart's character is a drunkard who runs *The African Queen*, a steamboat. One day he wakes up drunk on the boat to find that a missionary, played by Hepburn, has tossed all his alcohol overboard. He scolds her for this and demands to be left alone. "It's my nature to be drunk," he tells her. The missionary looks at him and says, "Nature, Mr. Nutley, is precisely what we were created to rise above." This is absolutely true and one of my favorite moments in all of cinema. It is our nature to be fearful. That is the default condition. Human beings default to fear, which leads us to inertia and complacency. Courage takes an enormous amount of spiritual effort. We've got to be able to face and overcome the fear we have of change. That is how we impact our tomorrow— by overcoming fear today. How do we accomplish this? Ancient Jewish wisdom provides a very important principle that helps guide us.

In Genesis, chapter 28, Jacob leaves home to go out and make his fortune and embark upon a new destiny. Genesis (28:10) reads: "and Jacob went out from Beersheba, which is in the south of Israel, and went towards Haran." The thing about this verse is that we all already know that Jacob is in Beersheba. Why didn't it just say, "And Jacob went on a journey to Haran?" Why does it say, "And Jacob left Beersheba and went to Haran?" There are several references, such as Genesis (26:23), that leave no doubt that Jacob is in Beersheba. Why does the Bible not save a few words here? Saving words is always a good idea. There is a principle in ancient Jewish wisdom that states that there is not a single unnecessary letter in the Torah. In this book every letter counts. Needless to say, every word and every sentence do, too. This tells us that the words "and Jacob left Beersheba" must not actually be redundant at all. So what do they tell us then? What new information do they provide? These words indicate to us that, before you can embark on your new destiny, your old destiny must be left behind. You will never get to Haran if you are not willing to leave Beersheba.

Fear can make this leaving behind, this breaking away, very difficult. Fear causes us to clutch the familiar close to us. Fear causes us to hold on to that which we have, rather than to go out and find what is waiting for us. But you must let go of the old to reach out as far as you can for the new. Imagine yourself crossing a suspension bridge over a little canyon. You don't want to leave solid ground so you put one foot tentatively onto the bridge, which causes it to start rocking and shaking. And you say, "Well, I can't do this!" But once you put both feet on the bridge, it becomes steadier. Things get easier and the path becomes clear. But this requires you to first step away from solid ground.

This is how our minds, hearts, and souls work, too, not just our bodies. You must leave one psychological place before you can reach another. Our hearts want us to stay where we are. They want us to stick to that which we know, that with which we feel confident and comfortable. But you will never get ahead in business if you don't expand your outlook. Overcoming this feeling, this fear, is a tremendous obstacle to succeeding in business and life. We see this in Genesis (28:10), in which Jacob is on the threshold of the most incredible things that are waiting for him—marriage, wealth, family, a future—but at first he is still in Beersheba, where nothing is going to happen. He's got to get to Haran first. This is not a purely physical departure. Nor is it purely symbolic. Jacob has to get this straight in his mind. He has to get Beersheba out of his head before he can really get to Haran. He has to leave it totally behind. To parody a phrase that I'm sure you have heard before: It's easier to get the man out of Beersheba than it is to get Beersheba out of the man. But you have to be able to leave this place before you're going to make it to that place. It's against our instincts, goes against our nature. What do you say to that?

I say: But nature, Mr. Nutley, is precisely what we were put here to rise above.

At the risk of seeming vulgar (though I point this out not to be vulgar, but to be candid), I will remind you that it is in our nature to relieve ourselves whenever we feel like it. Relieving yourself is perfectly natural. But as human beings in civilized society, we are expected to wait until we reach an appropriate room that has been designated for that function. By doing so, we overcome nature. The whole idea of civilizing a baby is to train a baby to overcome its nature. The nature of an infant human is to scream for people to do what is wanted until he or she is blue in the face. That's what babies do. Which is why civilizing a baby, showing a baby how to become a spiritual being, involves teaching the baby to start overcoming its nature. This training is essential for every baby, every man, woman, and child. Our natural instincts are very often going to pull us in the wrong direction; we must resist them.

We must be able to move ahead in life with no preconceived notions—this is what it means to truly be open to the myriad possibilities of life.

The Book of Numbers opens with the words: "and the Lord spoke to Moses in the desert of Sinai." Here, the Lord tells Moses to count the Israelites and deduce how each of them must position themselves around the tabernacle. This is before God decrees that they spend 40 years in the desert; the Israelites are anticipating arrival in the Promised Land in three days' time. Despite their belief that they will be in the Promised Land soon, much time and several chapters of the Book of Numbers are devoted to counting and positioning everybody, all of this taking place in the middle of the desert. This seems nonsensical—why would they waste so much time?

What you must realize is that the children of Israel are being vectored toward their destiny. A vector is a principle of geometry that combines both direction and movement. A vector gives us the direction of a force. For example, the wind blowing 10 mph from the northwest can be measured as a vector. This can also apply to people and their destinies. The Israelites are being told where and how fast to move towards the Promised Land. They are told what position to assume. We can literally see them physically vectored into their destiny.

But remember, they are in the middle of an arid, inhospitable desert; no place to spend time, if you ask me. Find a beach, I say! And yet God chooses to give the Israelites all of this important vectoring information in the desert. This wouldn't have been my first choice and probably not yours. I will guess that the Israelites were none too thrilled about it at first, either. But the reason God chooses the desert to impart this information is because, in ancient Jewish wisdom, a desert isn't just a dry, hot place with lots of cactus, sand, and not much else. The desert is a symbol for total emptiness. Nothing grows or lives in a desert. When deserts appear in Scripture, we are supposed to understand

that their metaphorical significance is that of total emptiness. In order
to go forth into a new destiny, one must leave everything behind. We
cannot envision a destiny filled with potential, opportunity, and unlimited possibility as long as we are still clutching to some other vision
from the past. By speaking to the Israelites in the desert, a place where
there is literally nothing else and no distractions, they are free of their
past lives and thus free of any conceptions of the future, which, perhaps
paradoxically, opens them up to be able to accept their new future.

When contemplating your own future, you need not hop in the
car and drive a thousand miles to Arizona. We are speaking of
the desert metaphorically. You may find that a cleared-off table in a
quiet room at midnight is all of the emptiness you need to contemplate
your life, conceive of new business plans, or envision a new entrepreneurial enterprise. And when you have a business plan in place and you
are ready to start a new enterprise, or a new job, or even just a new
routine at work, be prepared to leave your old ways behind for good.
Get them out of your head so you can focus on your future.

Use the Power of Words, Sentences, and Sound

The exodus of the Israelites from the slavery of Egypt and deliverance into the Promised Land, which we have just discussed, is the Bible's most dramatic transformation from darkness to light, from oppression to happiness, from hopelessness to promise. God takes the Israelites from Egypt into the desert, that place of metaphorical and literal emptiness. The desert is not just an empty place though—that is only half of the story. Ancient Jewish wisdom has more to tell us about the desert as it appears in Scripture.

But first, let me relate to you the etymological meaning of the holiday we call Passover, on which we celebrate the exodus from Egypt. The word Passover is a translation of the Hebrew word *Pesach*, but as is always the case with the Lord's language, much is lost in translation. *Pesach* doesn't only translate to Passover; *Peasch* also means "talking mouth." *Pe* means "mouth." *Sach* means "talking." Put them together and you get "talking mouth."

You may be asking what that has to do with deliverance. In the opening of Exodus, chapter 14, the Israelites cross over the borders of Egypt and stop over at a place called *Peh HaChirot*, which translates literally into "the mouth of freedom." As you know if you are Jewish, we observe Passover by holding a Seder, which is governed by a book known as a Haggadah. The word *haggadah* is also Hebrew for "a talking," "a telling," and/or "a recounting." One of the first rituals carried out at a Seder involves somebody asking four questions, which is usually done by children, though ancient Hebrew knowledge demands that an adult ask the questions if no children are at the table. You do not skip the questions. They are crucial.

Ancient Jewish wisdom shows us time and again that asking questions is important. All relationships begin with a question. Have you ever courted anyone without first asking them a question in order to engage conversation? Don't all business dealings start with some variation of the same question: "What can I do for you?" Questions beget conversation and communication, the foundations of human interaction and business. Questions are too irresistible to be ignored. Consider how the serpent begins his seduction of Eve not by telling her to eat the forbidden fruit, but by asking her why she thought it was that they were forbidden to eat of the fruit of the garden? Eve looks quizzically at the fruit, inquisitively drawn to them, and by this point the battle is already over. A question is an irresistible force. The essential part of Haggadah begins with four questions precisely to stimulate conversation.

And now I want to reveal the second meaning of desert. The Hebrew word for desert is *midbar*, which doesn't just mean an empty place, but also means "speaking." Do you see the convergence? The mouth of freedom. Talking mouth. Speaking. Everything about Passover and the exodus, that ultimate transformation from slavery to redemption, revolves around talking. It revolves around using our mouths. The mouth is a vital tool that takes us from slavery to freedom. It is a vital tool to move from darkness into light. As noted previously in this book, the mouth is the most important organ for leadership— and now you see why. Speaking carries us out of the desert inside of us, the desert of our own solitude.

Much modern research has been devoted to improving the academic performance of our nation's student bodies. The SAT is the most commonly used test for objectively evaluating the academic performance of high school students. Because SAT scores play a central role in college admissions, there has been an enormous amount of research into performance on the SAT. Researchers have tried to isolate the most important factors in predicting high SAT scores. Can you guess what the number one most important factor is? The quality of a student's teachers? No. A good school district? No. The one factor most positively correlated with high SAT scores was whether or not the student had had family meals at home that involved conversation in which the child was allowed to participate. This was even more strongly correlated to high test scores than a high IQ! Understand that family meals were not enough. A family meal taken with the TV blaring in the background or family members on their cell phones had little effect. But a family meal where there is actual interaction between child and parent and child and any siblings made a substantial impact in a child's future academic success and, consequently, overall performance in life.

Knowing this, it would be sheer folly for a concerned parent to come to a family meal without a list of conversation starters. I encourage you to start doing this as a parent. It is best if these conversation starters come in the form of questions, because, after all, nobody can resist a question. They give a child the chance and the invitation to speak up. Parents should come to the dinner table having made mental or physical notes to themselves of four or five great questions to present to the family. These questions should be specifically designed to bring your children out of their shell, out of themselves, out of the metaphorical desert inside themselves. In a sense, that's what a desert is: a lack of stimulation. A desert is where nothing else is going on inside you. Nothing but sheer emptiness. A desert is where you are alone because there is no one to help tease you out of yourself.

Have you ever noticed how hard it is to endure silence in a conversation? It makes us feel awkward and uncomfortable. It is unsettling. And here is where internalization of this principle becomes directly and practically applicable to your business life. Know that you should avoid such silences in your professional (and personal) conversations. These awkward silences are a sign that you are not communicating effectively. You are not reaching out. You are not encouraging the person with whom you are speaking to open up. Sales professionals are often taught that there is a certain point at which they should stop talking and just be quiet. This puts immense pressure on the other person to start talking. That's the silence of the desert. It draws out the person you are speaking to, and if that person is a customer, that is to your advantage. It encourages the customer to engage with you.

Speech is the ability that enables us to bring about deliverance, to bring about hope and optimism, to bring about communication and commerce. There isn't a single financial transaction or exchange that wasn't initiated by one person speaking to another. And while cell phones and the Internet have given us the amazing ability to speak from afar for the sake of expediency, I will contend that there is no replacement for face-to-face conversation.

That is why the airline industry exists to this day and why it thrives on serving the "business class" passenger. Sure, holidays are the busiest times of year for the airline industry, but their meat and potatoes is the year-round business of ferrying business professionals across the globe to hold in-person meetings. People have to move from place to place to do business in this globalized marketplace. Sure, they could rely solely on video chat and cell phones, but they don't. They are marvelous tools that have a place in the modern world, but when it comes to the final analysis and exchange in an important business transaction, two or more people need to sit face to face. A valuable deal that brings profit and prosperity to both sides almost always takes place with two or more people sitting across from each other at a table with nothing in between. Speech is what it's all about and we have to understand the power of that. No matter how technology progresses, there will never be anything that totally usurps the place of direct communication by talking.

Words, sentences, and questions—the building blocks of conversation—are the most powerful tools we have at our disposal to do God's work. Words and sentences are the building blocks of plans and ideas. Language allows us to give order to our lives and world by placing things into a narrative. We can use words to take control of time by inscribing our schedules in words. Whether you are writing a long-term business plan or simply filling up your day planner, you can employ written language to give order to your days and your greater life. Think of this process as plotting your own life against the passage of time. In doing so you avoid procrastination and allow yourself to focus in on what needs doing. Like God did for the Israelites, you too can vector your own destiny by focusing your energy in a single, planned direction. The best way to stay on track is to put your goals and obligations into writing.

Your goal is to commit yourself to a planned course of action and sign off on it. You want a string of actions that build a narrative. One action should lead into specific following actions. These actions need not be grandiose projects. We aren't putting a man on the moon here. We are simply planning out our workdays. The biggest most grandiose goals, which you should have, require many steps. And each step is made of many small actionable tasks. Whatever your long-term business plans are, you will have to take small steps to get there. That is the nature of large projects; they are made up of small parts. No one founds a successful business in a day. You cannot cross "Found successful business" off of your to-do list. But you may research a few potential markets for your new enterprise over the course of a few days. Maybe you pick one and write a business plan the next day. Then the following week you look at one possible business location per day until you find the right storefront. Assemble a list of vendors another day, open the store on opening day, and market to twelve customers a day for the first month you are in business, and so on and so forth.

Oral communication is just as important as written language. No matter what specific business project you are working on, you will have to use the principle of the talking mouth, the principle of Passover. Every business transaction along the way will require communication. The whole system of monetary prosperity given to us by God is only there to get us all communicating with each other. The economy is there to get us talking to one another and also talking to ourselves.

Don Isaac Abarbanel, one of the great transmitters of ancient Jewish wisdom, was the minister of finance for the Court of Ferdinand and Isabella, the king and queen of Spain in the fifteenth century. In 1492, the Jews of Spain were expelled from Spain with short notice. They were barred from taking any possessions with them. This included even someone of the high rank that Abarbanel held, who hit the road with nothing but what he could wear or carry on his back. When Passover came, he found himself alone and friendless in the city of Genoa, Italy, where he had escaped to as a refugee. Being alone, he held a Seder of one. Did he skip the questions? No! As we said, child or no child present, you do not skip the questions! If you are the only one at your Seder, then of course you ask them of yourself. But Abarbanel was an ambitious man, and he did not only ask four questions of himself, he asked hundreds. He later wrote these down and they are now collected in one of my favorite books. The great Abarbanel Haggadah comprises a hundred thought-provoking questions about the exodus of the Israelites from Egypt, a hundred questions I had never thought of on my own. He then proceeds to answer all one hundred. He did this with no one else around to observe him. It is a fantastic act and work that shows the power of the question to initiate conversation. Even in the desert of his loneliness, he was able to reach out by writing down his questions in a conversation with posterity. And before that, he carried on the conversation with himself.

Don't underestimate the power of this. When your own ears hear your own mouth say things, those words penetrate deep into your soul. Speaking aloud is very different from just thinking something. This is why I told you earlier that the best way to practice public speaking is to do so out loud. Walking around and thinking is mere contemplation. Putting your thoughts into words, even if they are just for you, gives order to those thoughts. Oral language requires chronology and order and simply putting your thoughts into words will help you organize your thoughts. It is a way of "orally inscribing" your thoughts.

The importance of language to ordering your thoughts is why I encourage you to not just use words, but actual sentences, when writing out notes to yourself. And when you are thinking out loud, use full sentences. When planning out a speech, whether on paper or by talking it through, use full sentences. Even when filling out your day planner or writing to-do lists, use full sentences. And don't just use bullet points; form paragraphs. If you need to write a note that you need milk later, don't just write down: "milk." Write down: "Pick up milk." Don't ever write: "meeting 9:00." Write out: "You have a meeting at nine o'clock in the morning." Our minds are accustomed to connecting words into sentences and paragraphs and doing so imposes order upon our plans and thoughts. This does not take much effort and you will find that, not only are your notes more useful, but your thoughts will be better composed in your head because you took the time to write them out in your mind. When you start looking at your journal, planner, or calendar, everything will fall into much better place.

You will see the meaning in your actions written out explicitly. What does "milk" mean? Who knows? You wrote it two days ago! But "Pick up milk"? That you understand immediately, no time wasted. The process of trying to recall your intent and reassemble the sentence in your mind slows you down and weakens your energy. Furthermore, it is simply redundant—it requires you to do the mental work twice. This may seem like a small thing, but it adds up over time with each and every action you do. So put down the entire sentence the first time.

If you do all of this regularly, you will find that your schedule and your calendar begin to make more intuitive sense and that you begin to become more productive and, especially, more focused. You will be more motivated when the way is clear and plotted. Looking at a sequence of sentences, rather than lists, motivates us to get into action because sentences and paragraphs have actions, instructions, and direction. "Go pick up milk." Do you hear it? It's a command to yourself. Sentences seep into our souls and minds; individual words simply do not. Words, while powerful building blocks for sentences, lack narrative, and thus focus, when used individually. As God creates man, He breathes into his nostrils the breath of life (Genesis 2:7). In ancient Jewish wisdom, that breath of life is the ability to speak. Cherish your ability to speak and constantly work on improving it. Understandably people religiously attend exercise sessions at their gyms. It is less understandable but just as indispensable that we engage in exercise for our speaking ability.

Feeling Right About Money
Makes You Act Right

S ay you have to make a trip to New York City. You know that certain parts of New York City, as is the case with all large metropolitan areas, can be dangerous when walking around alone at night. The bad news? You're going to be walking around alone at night and you are going to be doing it in the bad parts. There is no preventing this—your business requires it of you. If you are not willing to travel to the seedy parts at night you might as well cancel your flight altogether. But you are a committed business professional, so you are going. You are also a responsible person who believes in being prepared, so you decide to visit your local bookstore and pick up a book on self-defense. It has detailed illustrations and chapters on every martial arts style. It tells you what to do when your assailant has a knife, what to do when they are carrying a gun, or if they attack in numbers, or from the rear. It's a long book, a real compendium, 20-something chapters, but you go ahead and buy it because you don't want to be caught defenseless during your nighttime perambulations through New York City. You tuck the book into your briefcase and head out of the store confident in your choice.

Sadly, the story takes a turn for the worse sooner than you had expected. You are walking out to your car in the parking lot when suddenly the cold steel of a gun is pressed into your back and a voice behind you says, "Your money or your life."

What do you do in a situation like this? Ask your assailant to please wait one moment while you read up on the relevant chapters of your book about being attacked from behind and being assailed by a gunman? Not likely. Chapter 17 of your new book may totally cover this situation, but that does you no good now. It's too late. Had you known right away to swivel around, grab at the gun, and sweep him off his feet in the first place, that would be something different. But you didn't know how to do that. Your book may have been a great guide, but you should have started studying it before you needed it. The book is no help now.

What's more, the book would have been no help during your trip to New York City the following week, either. Such quick action must be instinctive, an impulse with no conscious thought involved. Thought would slow you down and trip you up. Such quick reactionary movement is only possible when there is a unity of body and soul. And the only way to achieve such unity is through repetition. A week is not long enough to internalize something as complicated as martial arts. To act quickly, assuredly, and appropriately when you are attacked, you internalize your knowledge of self-defense. Through repetition, you move the knowledge of martial arts out of your head and into your body and soul, but this takes practice.

What you want is for your heart and soul to tell your body to act without your mind getting in the way. Those 18 inches from the top of the head to the heart is what we are talking about here—you have to close that distance. In a situation like this, in any trying situation, you must be able to travel those 18 inches instantaneously and automatically. This is when you know that you have really internalized a discipline or a principle: when you can act properly and instantaneously without involving your mind. Your soul takes over and tells your body to move. You do not decide what to do in situations like this. You feel what to do. And through study, training, and repetition, you can teach yourself the *right* thing to do.

This is a very important principle in business. The lesson is that you cannot think your way out of some problems—you must feel your way through to the solution. As a business professional, we must know how to feel right about money, not just how to think right about it. It is not enough to know intellectually how to handle and view money if our hearts don't feel that knowledge naturally. We cannot fake this.

Have you ever known someone who was visibly uncomfortable giving you the bill for their services? This is very common among younger people but you can find transgressors of any age and experience level. They have been so indoctrinated to feel bad and wrong about money that they will look down at their feet and mumble what you owe. They don't feel right about money, which is why they come across as unduly apologetic. They feel like accepting money for a job well done is equivalent to taking something away from you. Under this misguided notion, of course they feel bad and ashamed! But they shouldn't, and neither should you.

If you feel this way about money, you need to overcome these feelings. They are misguided and they are holding you back in your professional life. They are making you appear like someone who does not understand the business world. Neither of those things is good for your bottom line. What you need to do is the same thing you need to do to teach yourself self-defense. Learn the right way to feel about money and practice those principles until they are integral to the way you feel. If you feel right about money, you don't need to think right about it, though you will think right about it anyway. Feeling right about a thing, in this case money, leads us to act right about it. This is as true for business as it is for all things. This is where business sense comes from. Good business sense is a practiced intuition.

Let me give you an analogy. I have a beautiful car—a BMW with a 12-cylinder engine. I am of the firm conviction that every man should own a 12-cylinder vehicle at least once in life. One thing about my car is that it is congenitally unhappy when in operation under 70 mph. It just is. Now, it's also my strongly held belief that a happy car makes for a happy driver, and so I regularly take my BMW out on long winding roads in western Washington where the landscape is so breathtaking that it is hard to keep your eyes on the road. I take corners at 75 or 80 mph. The feeling is fantastic. The car just grips the road. Now, I'll say that I do not advise you to do this, but I will also go ahead and say that I enjoy it.

Now let's suppose that one day I am driving along and all of the sudden I see a police car on the side of the road. I'm going to tell you right now that this is all hypothetical! The officer has pulled over some other unfortunate motorist to issue them a ticket. What do I do at that point? Do I slow down? Of course not. My head has done the math. I don't know exactly how many police cars they have in the area to catch speeders, but I know it is a finite number. It's a rural area, so maybe there are three, or maybe five, I don't really know. But I do know that there is now one less squad car in the area, lying in wait with a radar gun. My odds of getting a ticket have just gone down. So I put the pedal to the metal. I'm on my way. I have thought this over very carefully and logically.

Around the next bend I pass an accident on the side of the road. Police cars and ambulances are everywhere. It's really very disturbing. How do I drive now? Slowly and carefully. But wait, aren't *all* of the police cars in the area now here and busy? Yes, but I don't care about that. I am very impacted by the disturbing scene. I *feel* like I should drive slower because I have seen the repercussions of reckless driving. And so you can see that how I feel about my bad behavior is much more powerful a motivator than what I think about it. I may know I should change my behavior, but I don't do so until I feel that I have to. It makes all the difference in the world. And the thing to realize is that this decision was basically automatic. My soul told my foot to lighten up on the gas—my mind had nothing to do with it. This is why we have to develop the correct feelings about money in our hearts. Otherwise we aren't going to act correctly around money and in circumstances where we are able to actually produce wealth. You cannot rely on thinking to do this for you. When a job offer or a business opportunity presents itself, you don't always have the luxury of limitless time for analysis. You must develop your intuition. You want to be able to feel the right course of action. You cannot think yourself into a place where you are comfortable with money, by which I mean you cannot trick yourself in the moment to believe money is good when deep down inside you are uncomfortable with money. You have to accept this as true and internalize it now so that, in crucial moments, you will not have to convince yourself that making money is a good thing.

For a few decades now, scientists have been mapping out the human genome, which is quite fascinating. Scientists want to understand DNA better so that we can better understand ourselves. They have told us that we humans share about 95 percent of our DNA with chimpanzees, which is meant to be taken as proof that humans are descended from chimpanzees. Regardless of where you stand on that particular issue, I want you to know that we also share 97 percent of our DNA with whales. As a matter of fact, any male human, like me, actually has a more common genetic relationship with whales than with human women. So this stuff is complicated and I implore you not to jump to simple conclusions based on half facts.

So clearly genetics are not the only thing that dictates who we are. One other important factor that scientists have identified is what is known as epi-genetics. Every single gene has a little on/off switch and some of them have a slider switch like a volume control or a dimmer switch that controls how strongly a gene will manifest itself. Your epigenetics influences which of your genes are turned on and off. It is like nature's circuit breakers! So while you may technically share much DNA with another of God's creatures, you do not share the same percentage of *functional* and *active* genes. What differentiates human DNA from animal DNA is not just genes, but also our epi-genes. This is a very new and exciting area of scientific discovery right now because it's not altogether clear exactly what makes these epigenetics work. Scientists don't know what causes genes to turn on and off.

During my research into all of this, I encountered the story of a researcher who isolated himself from other humans by retreating to a remote base camp in Antarctica for three months every year. One amazing thing he noticed was that, two or three days before he was preparing to return home, his beard growth would suddenly accelerate. He and his colleagues studied this bizarre phenomenon and concluded that it was due to a change in testosterone. Physical intimacy with a woman releases a flood of testosterone, a hormone that affects beard growth and other secondary sex characteristics in males. Testosterone really gets a beard growing!

But here's the surprising thing: Not only does the aforementioned activity produce testosterone, but mere anticipation of sexual relations appears to be enough to raise testosterone and promote beard growth.

What was happening was that the researcher, knowing he would soon return to his wife, was producing more testosterone as if he were with her already. This anticipation induced a switching on and off of certain genes, triggering the release of testosterone and accelerated beard growth. In other words, his body was reacting to something that was going on inside of him, inside his soul. This is truly remarkable! What it tells us is that how we feel affects our physiological state. Furthermore, since hormones also dictate feelings and behavior, what we think and feel further affects our states. This can create feedback loops. Have you ever noticed how when you force yourself to smile, you eventually start feeling happy and then you start smiling for real? This is the same effect. How we feel about a thing affects how our minds and bodies react to that thing! This is why it is imperative that we control our feelings. Taking control of our feelings means taking control of our thoughts and bodies, too.

Now, you have probably heard the phrase "crass commercialization" before. I very much dislike this phrase. It is one of many examples of people unfairly ascribing a negative connotation to anything to do with business. Negativity about wealth is quite common in modern society and so, not surprisingly, we tend to feel and therefore think of money as a negative thing. Money is not a negative thing, though. Wealth, as we have discussed, is how God rewards us for doing good and serving his other children. But we live in a society where many political and social forces try to condition us to think of wealth as bad, as an evil, though you and I now know, thanks to ancient Jewish wisdom, that evil is actually the opposite of wealth. But not everyone knows that, and when people allow themselves to internalize these negative associations with wealth, they cause themselves to perform poorly in business, for very obvious reasons. The point of business is to make wealth by serving your fellow man—you can't very well do that if you're walking around thinking wealth is a bad thing and loathing and lamenting every dollar in your pocket!

The bottom line is this: Feeling right about money is what separates the best business professionals from the rest of the population.

All Olympic athletes are at the peak of human performance. No athlete even gets a shot at competing in the Olympics unless they're already at the very top of their sport. The differences in their abilities, physiques, and talent are negligible because their bodies are all so close to the absolute peak of physical conditioning. Top runners win races by milliseconds because all contestants are approaching the same peak of physical perfection. They are all at the right age for competition. They train perfectly. They do everything exactly right and by the book. Each competing athlete has a reasonable shot at taking home the gold. So what then dictates who will come in first, second, and third? Any athletic trainer or veteran Olympian will tell you the answer: The winner takes home the gold because of his spirit, not his body. The winner is simply the one who is able to demand more of his perfect body than anyone else. They all have the right body at this level of competition. But the winner has the body and the right spirit, the spirit that allows him to extract just a little bit more from his body.

This is the same as in business. You can train and study until the cows come home. You can get an MBA. You can get an MBA from a top-ranked program. You can learn to do fancy business models and do an internship with a Fortune 500. These will hone your business skills and knowledge and they will increase your chances of success. But to really get into the upper echelons of your industry, you must also work on your spirit. You must develop the correct business spirit. Part of that means viewing money in the right way, not as a product of greed, but as a product of creation and subservience. You must 100 percent understand money.

So what is money? Physically, money is an economic marker of wealth that facilitates business transaction. But what is it in a spiritual sense?

One Hebrew word for money is also the same word for blood: *dahm*. As we have discussed previously, a word with two meanings in the Lord's language is never accidental. The two meanings are always merged in a way that provides us with a unified concept that tells us something about their connection. In the case of the Hebrew word *dahm*, what is the connection between blood and money?

Let's investigate. What similarities can we find? Note that we have banks for both—blood banks and financial banks. Not surprisingly, both carry nutrients. Blood carries nutrients throughout the body. Money carries nutrients throughout the economy. Both are crucial to the functioning of their respective systems. Another similarity is that blood and money are both mass nouns. Nobody asks, "Can I have a money?" Nobody says, "I need a blood." There is no singular form because both blood and money are limitless. You can give away an infinite amount of blood as long as you space out your donations. Likewise, giving away money and spending money on a business always results in greater dividends. You can always earn more money by putting in more work.

And finally, blood and money are both fungible, meaning they are both mutually interchangeable. If I borrow your car for the day and bring back a different one, you are probably going to be upset (or really happy if it is a more expensive one!). This is because cars are not fungible. Now on the other hand, if I borrow a 20-dollar bill from you, you don't care what form of cash I use to pay you back so long as you get $20 in return. This is what it means to be fungible. In the same way, blood is fungible. If you get into an accident and need a blood transfusion, they don't have to track down the bag of blood you donated to the blood bank last month; any blood of the same blood type will do no matter whom it came from. (By comparison, organs are nonfungible, which is why transplantation is so difficult. The body will reject replacement organs without a very complex transplant and acclimation process.) Money is like blood, not like organs, in that you can receive money from millions of people and the source doesn't matter.

All of this points us to a profound connection between money and blood. This is because money is our economic lifeblood. Money is not just one part of your life; money is integrated into all aspects of your life. Money is absolutely essential to everything we do. I am not saying money is the only thing of value in your life, not at all. But money is *always* of value in your life and therefore holds a valuable place. You may really like playing golf and so it is very important to you to always play golf on Wednesdays, but on the other days of the week golf is probably not a major part of your life or thoughts. Golf is not a lifeblood, but money is because it is always important. You have probably never said: "Wednesday, I think I will play tennis and Thursday, devote to my interest in money." Tennis, stamp collecting, watching movies, reading books, or whatever your hobbies are will only be important when engaging in them. But money is always important even when it is not at the forefront of your mind. Just as with blood, money needs to be a concern every day of the week. It lubricates and fuels the economy and is also a primary measure of our professional and personal success.

In Genesis (2:12), God says, "The gold of that land is good." Which land does He speak of? Any land upon which there is regular economic interaction and transactions, because that is how gold is produced. Gold is a metaphor for all money in Scripture, because it was the currency of Biblical times, which is why gold has always been the most monetized metal. There are few practical reasons why we don't use some other metal, such as platinum. The reason we use gold to store value is because God chose gold to be the symbol of wealth when He said: "The gold of that land is good." And so what He is saying there is that money is good.

You need to internalize that lesson: money is good. Do not be ashamed of owning or earning money. When you take money from a customer, you do so in exchange for serving them. You are doing them a favor for which you are being rewarded. There is nothing shameful or immoral about this—on the contrary, it is the most basic way in which you can and must serve your fellow man. Someone who has acquired much wealth is someone who has done much good in the world. Once you internalize this lesson, once you really feel it, your whole relationship with the world, customers, and other business professionals will change for the better.

You Can Best Attract That Which
You Best Understand

N ow you have a fairly firm understanding of what money is and what its role in creation and the economy is. A firm understanding of money will benefit us as business profes-sionals because it is imperative that we understand that which we seek. This is true of all things, not just money.

I should not offer fishing advice. During our family's boating in British Columbia I have spent considerably more time fishing than catching. Finally, the breakthrough discovery in my frustrating quest for the elusive Chinook salmon was the miracle of fishing guides.

I had spent several week's earnings on fishing gear. It seemed so satisfyingly primitive to feed my family by rowing away from the mother-ship before dawn and return in a few hours laden with my catch of beautiful fresh salmon. Except it never worked out that way. Fine fishing rods, gleaming Penn reels, electronic fishfinders, colorful lures whose effectiveness had been solemnly testified to by the fishing store clerk. I even had a small library of books promising to persuade salmon to leap from the waters of Georgia Strait onto my dinner plate. I caught nothing.

Then I discovered Bill, the fishing guide. He had simple rods, nothing fancy. But he knew salmon and whenever Bill guided me, I returned with fish. It was satisfying. But more importantly, it taught me that knowledge of your quarry is more important than fancy equipment.

Similarly, a solid understanding of money will facilitate the accumulation of wealth. As business professionals, we must fully understand money. By reading this far, you now understand that money is good and that it is your lifeblood. But what all constitutes money?

Your instinctive response may be that money comprises those metal discs in your pocket and the green strips of paper in your wallet. Or maybe you think of money as that strip on the back of your credit card or sum in your bank account statement. How about if somebody writes you a check? Is that money? Or what happens if someone promises to pay you $100 the next Friday? Is that I.O.U. also money? Does the promise of an I.O.U. such as this constitute the same creation of money as if someone prints a hundred-dollar bill or buys $100 in Treasury bonds?

The answer is that all of these things can be money.

Money is a means of facilitating transactions because it is a token showing that you are someone who has served God's other children and so they should serve you in turn. When a roofer fixes a roof and receives a handful of twenty-dollar bills for his service—certificates of performance, if you will—he may take those with him to the local Surf and Turf restaurant to buy his family dinner. The restaurant owner is unlikely to want to serve him without these certificates because a man who has not earned money is a man who has not served others. People may not think of this in these terms explicitly, but they definitely do so subconsciously. Think of earning money as your ticket to an elite club to which only those who understand the value of subservience belong. When you participate in the economy, you get to take part in this incredibly wonderful club of human beings who are happy to serve each other. Dollar bills, credit cards, checks—these are simply tokens to keep track of who has served whom. The more you serve, the more tokens you collect, and the more people want to serve you. Money is a representation. It is a proof of performance. It shows others that you care to serve other people.

The only stipulation is that these tokens must have been transferred in good faith for a service or product provided. Otherwise, you have served no one and your wallet is not full of real money. No, then it is full of ill-begotten gains that God and your fellow man will punish you for eventually.

But that's not what we are talking about here: We are talking about money you have earned legitimately. If you have a dollar in your pocket or bank account that was not obtained by theft, extortion, fraud, unlawful coercion, or any other immoral or unlawful way, then you earned that money by pleasing one of God's children. Any dollar given to you voluntarily, no matter the physical form, is a certificate of performance and validation of a job well done. Usually this will be from a customer, but even if it was from a family member giving you your allowance for staying out of trouble, you still earned that dollar. That it was given to you voluntarily says that you did something that somebody else greatly valued. Maybe you sold them the latest gadget. Or perhaps you fixed their latest gadget for them. Or maybe you just got straight As in school and stayed out of trouble and collected an allowance from your parents. Whatever the case, I know you earned that dollar by pleasing someone or they would not have voluntarily given it to you. You provided a service to one of God's children and God rewarded you with money.

Part of understanding money means understanding how it is created, the process by which money is brought into existence. To illustrate this point, I want to tell you the story of Grandpa Lapin. He is a real person, but the story I'm going to tell here is a fictionalized version of his life, though the spirit of the story remains true to the actual details of his life. I am simply distilling the story of his career down to a hypothetical business day for dramatic and educational purposes.

Grandpa Lapin had a career as a peddler, which, once upon a time, was a very noble occupation. Peddling was the way that many Jews who immigrated to the United States made their living in the 1800s and early 1900s, practicing the trade they had learned in the Old World. Peddlers were basically mobile traders. They went from house to house and town to town and bartered and sold items for a profit.

So Grandpa Lapin knocks on the door of a house and asks the lady who comes to the door if she has any items she no longer needs. She says that she was about to put a wobbly old table out in the alley. It's worth nothing, but the city is going to charge her $5 to cart it away. Grandpa Lapin says he has a better idea. He offers to pay *her* $5 to take the table off her hands. She happily agrees!

Pause here to do some math. How much better off is the lady now that Grandpa Lapin came to her house? She does not have to pay $5 to the city and she is getting $5 in cash out of Grandpa's pocket. So she is $10 better off because Grandpa Lapin knocked on her door. Keep that in mind.

Grandpa Lapin takes the wobbly old table. He goes over to the hardware store and spends a dollar to get some screws and a brace for the leg and some new varnish. Once he is done fixing up and varnishing the table, he takes it to another house down the road and asks if anybody needs a table. As it turns out, the man who lives there has a son getting married next week, and he will need furniture to furnish the apartment he will live in with his new bride. The son says that he was going to go down to the furniture store to get a new kitchen table for $20. Grandpa Lapin says he has a perfectly good table out on the truck that he just fixed up good as new. He says they could have it for just $10. The newlyweds take a look at the table and decide it makes a pretty good starter table. They buy it.

So how much better off are the newlyweds? There were going to pay $20 for a table but got a perfectly good one for only $10. So they are also $10 in the black. Add this to the $10 the lady who originally owned the table is up. Now the community is up $20 because of Grandpa Lapin's wheeling and dealing. But wait, don't forget that the till of the hardware store has another dollar, too, in sold hardware supplies. So far the village has benefited $21. And this is before you factor in the money Grandpa Lapin spends for the hotel where he will spend the night and for the food he will eat. And he's going to knock on other doors today and make more deals. His presence echoes through the economy!

And, of course, let's not forget that there's an arbitrage, which is the profit made by buying and selling products. There's now extra money in Grandpa Lapin's pocket, too. He paid $5 for a table, spent $1 fixing it up, and sold it for $10 for a cool $4 worth of profit! Even after creating $21 of wealth for the community, Grandpa Lapin has also created $4 for himself—all of this out of thin air! Where does this money come from? This is not some Rabbinic smoke and mirrors trickery I am selling you here. This is how the economy creates and distributes wealth. It is both mundane and miraculous, simple and perfect. This is the way God has designed the economy to work. Money is created when human beings serve one another. Economic transactions create money. We literally will money into being by serving one another.

Still skeptical? Think this doesn't apply to the complex modern economy? Think again.

One of the few Internet companies to ever make money from day one was eBay, an online auction site. They turned a profit from the first day they went into business, unlike Amazon, which lost money for years before turning a (now very tidy) profit. Why was eBay so successful? Because it was basically thousands and thousands of Grandpa Lapins working simultaneously. Thousands of peddlers and merchants making deals with each other and the general public. The vendors on eBay buy things that people don't need and sell them for a profit to people who do need them. The people who are selling these items to the vendors want the money more than the object. The people who are buying want the object more than money. And the vendors, the middlemen, the "peddlers," are also able to make a profit by brokering the deals. Even eBay and its shareholders are able to pocket a little bit of the money off each exchange as well.

The reason eBay is so successful is because it functions as a microcosm for the larger economy. When we do things for one another, we all benefit because we are doing exactly what God wants us to be doing. God never promised me I would be rich. But he did create a world where we would all be obsessively preoccupied with filling one another's desires and needs. He wants us to be totally focused on serving his other children. When we engage in this kind of economic activity, getting together to collaborate and serve one another as God planned for the entire schematic of human economic interaction, we are also carrying out his will of rewarding one another for doing his will. Being a good and loving God, He rewards us for doing this by bestowing on all participants the incredible blessing of bountiful prosperity.

Secret #31

You Must Know Your Money, Which You Must Be Able to Measure and Count

L osing weight is difficult enough; imagine trying to do it without a scale. How would you keep track of how much you lost? How would you even be sure you had lost, and not gained, weight? You need a system for keeping track of all of this. Most personal trainers and nutritionists recommend that you weigh yourself at the same time every day and record the measurement so that you can track your progress and assess your methods. No cheating, either. You have to write down the truth, even if it horrifies you! Especially if it horrifies you! The truth will help motivate you.

And then you work hard to lose the weight every day. You cut back on high-fat and high-carb foods. You do cardio and lift weights. And if all goes well, you weigh a little bit less every day. Wonderful! But you would be lost without a way to keep track of your progress. Seeing that you have lost a pound is encouraging and so you keep at it. And a day later, you are down another pound. And by the end of the week, you have lost four pounds. And so on and so forth. The numbers are encouraging whereas the gradual improvements are imperceptible on a day-to-day basis. The numbers provide substantiated proof that you are making progress.

Creating wealth is much easier than losing weight, but both endeavors take considerable sustained effort. Saving money is another gradual process that requires the same kind of long-term commitment to see substantial results. You put away a little more each day. It's not much on a daily basis, but it adds up. How do you know? By looking at your monthly and yearly statements and watching your savings grow over time.

Saving money is hard because people would rather spend than save. When you spend money, you get instant positive feedback. You put down $200 and you get a nice new pair of leather shoes that you can wear and feel comfortable and luxurious. You put the same $200 in the bank and you get, well, $200 in the bank. Of course, you also get security and the accumulation of capital with which you can later launch a business. However, as important as those are, you cannot put them in your hand and so our tendency is to not save enough.

While the idea of $200 locked away in the bank isn't so exciting, you can make it exciting by tracking your savings. Count exactly how much money is there. Watch your interest payments and add that in. Track how your wealth grows over time. The actual counting, tabulating, and tracking gives us encouragement to keep saving because it keeps us involved with our money. You don't need to save it and forget it; save it and invest it. Put the money to work for you. And by working with your savings, you will increase your desire to save because you will no longer see savings as an abstract thing.

As humans, we love order and enumeration, which is why we love lists. Comedians like David Letterman exploit this love of lists for the sake of humor all of the time. Books are structured as lists, even the one you hold in your hands now. The "listicle" is a new form of journalism that combines the traditional article with the list. Online media outlets are full of listicles with titles like "The Top 10 Reasons to Do So-and-So," "The Top 100 Most Influential People in Business," and "The Top 10 Things You Must Know about X and Y." We like things to be enumerated because it brings order and efficiency to information. What do you want to read more, an article called "A Marital Mistake Made by Men" or a listicle called "The 10 Worst Mistakes that

Husbands Make"? Clearly the latter—the list and title tell you that here are 10 things you need to know and you can see that the author has taken the time to organize them for you.

In Hebrew, there are five words that all mean "counting." Each word has subtle nuances that distinguish them, but they all mean some form of counting. That we need so many words for counting in the Lord's language, each one with such subtle nuance, tells us that the concept of counting is very important.

Let's discuss these Hebrew words for counting. *Pokaid* means counting in the most traditional sense of counting numbers—tabulation. But *pokaid* also means "a powerful official." *Nosay* translates to counting and is the word used in the Book of Numbers (1:2) when God says to Moses, "Count the heads of the tribes." But *nosay* has another meaning, which is "prince" or "president." The word *sophair* means to count but can also refer to "a distinguished scholar or teacher." The fourth word for counting, *moneh*, also means "an important appointed official." The last Hebrew word for counting, *hoshave*, is also still used in modern Israeli Hebrew to refer to accountants. *Hoshave* also means "prominent person of importance" in ancient Hebrew.

Are you seeing a pattern here?

The Lord's language repeatedly reinforces the connection between counting and importance. You cannot separate the idea of counting from importance because counting something indicates its importance. Why would you take stock of something unless it was important? No one wastes time counting the individual grains of sand on a beach because no one cares how many grains of sand are on a beach. You may want to swim in the water or even relax on the sands, but you do not spend time thinking about the grains because they aren't important to life.

But money, as we have established, is our lifeblood, and so we spend a great deal of time counting and taking stock of our finances. My weight is something I also take seriously, which is why I measure it regularly. My counting of pounds signifies the importance of my weight. Moreover, the importance of my weight is why I spend so much time counting pounds. Given that money, that certificate of subservience we discussed earlier, is even more important, you should spend even more time counting and keeping tabs on your money. And just as you would not try to lose weight without a scale, you should not try to count money without the right tools and know-how. This is why I urge you to take the time to learn how to read and interpret your financial statements.

Maybe you are saying to yourself that you are not really a numbers person. Well, to that I say: choose to be. You can be any "type" of person you want. When I was 16, I had enough pimples for 10 teenage boys. So what did I do? Did I say, "Well, I guess Daniel Lapin is a pimply type of guy"? No, sir. I washed my face regularly. I spent a good chunk of my high school income and allowance on pharmaceuticals to rid myself of my accursed acne. So you may not be a "numbers person" today, but that doesn't mean you can't be tomorrow. It's just a matter of learning simple math, good monitoring habits, and a little knowledge of financial statements and instruments. Although it may take you a little while to become familiar with accounting methods, the knowledge will pay great dividends to you as a business professional, and you will also experience the thrill of knowing how to read financial statements.

Trust me: You will find it thrilling to become financially literate. Make it a point of pride. Know what a balance sheet is. Know what a cash flow statement is. Understand basic financial documents and those that are relevant to your profession and business. Everyone should be able to read and fully understand their bank statements, credit card statements, and investment account statements. These things are important and valuable, and you will feel better in your heart knowing that you are taking your money seriously. And it really isn't as hard as you may think. Learning to read financial statements is a little more complicated than just knowing how to add and subtract, as financial statements can involve more complicated calculations and financial concepts, but this isn't rocket science and anyone can master these concepts and principles by putting in a modest amount of effort. There are great books and websites that can explain these things to you. Your own bank is also a valuable resource; your local banking associates will be happy to sit down and explain some of these things to you for free. You can be an expert in basic finances in no time and you will feel and be much more in control of your money and business affairs once you have committed to understanding how to count your money properly.

Secret #32

Money Is Spiritual

So far, I have referred to the spiritual nature of money several times in this book. You already know about the difference between the spiritual and physical elements of the world. We looked at the difference between physical and spiritual needs and the ways in which the world meets those needs spiritually or physically. We placed money squarely in the spiritual realm because money represents a token of participation in the economy. We learned that money is both God's way of rewarding us for serving his other children and of motivating us to do so. Now I want to delve deeper into what it means for you as a business professional to realize that money is a spiritual matter. Let's look at what is at stake, what you have to gain and lose here. We are going to take all of these earlier concepts and biblical business secrets and meld them into a unified theory of money.

The first thing that I want to establish is that when we speak of money, we are talking about money as a concept—money as wealth. We are not speaking of physical dollar bills and coinage. A characteristic of physical objects is that they can only be in one place at a time. A dollar bill is this way. So are coins. So is this book in your hands. These things can only be in one place at a time because they are clearly physical objects. But we are not talking about money here as a physical object; we are talking about the spiritual construct that legal tender is meant to represent. There is no spiritual underpinning to a pen or a book, but that is not true of legal tender. While this dollar bill can only be in one place at a time, the value that it represents flows through the economy as its lifeblood. The spiritual aspect of money—wealth—is infinite. Think back to Grandpa Lapin who rode into town with his $5, which, through the magic of exchange and transaction, he turned into $30, $9 of which he kept and $21 of which went to the community.

The distinction between physical legal tender and money, which is spiritual, is not mere semantics or some kind of chicanery. This distinction matters. If you view money as only a physical object, then you have to believe that it is finite. And if money is finite, then you can only accumulate more money by taking it away from someone else. No decent human being wants to do that, but, as Grandpa Lapin and the market economy show us, you do not have to rob anyone to make yourself richer. In fact, by making yourself richer, you will usually benefit everyone. But if you operate under the misguided belief that money is physical and thus finite, you can logically buy into closed-system economic theories in which earning wealth means taking it from others. If money were physical, socialism would make a lot of sense, and indeed, early socialist theorists believed that the world was like a pie that needed to be divided equitably because there was only so much to go around. They didn't appreciate what both free-market capitalists and ancient Jewish wisdom understand to be the fact: that there is no reason to quibble about dividing up the pie when you can simply grow the pie and make more for everyone. But for this to be true, you must believe that money is spiritual and thus infinite and capable of being in many places at once, like God.

Believing that money is physical is a terrible, fatal handicap to any decent person or society. Such a belief robs you of the ability to participate in business ethically. Thankfully, you need not believe this. Money is not finite.

Money is not interchangeable with products and services. They can be exchanged but they are not interchangeable. This is because cost and value are not the same thing. Let me give you an example. Suppose I buy a pair of shoes from a local shop for $25. I have been looking for these shoes for weeks and I finally have them. A friend compliments them and wants to know how much they cost. I tell him and he offers me $25 for them. I say no, I want to keep them. That's why I bought them. But is this logical? Aren't they *worth* $25? No, they *cost* me $25. But they are worth more than that to me. He offers me $30, but I say no because I don't want to have to go to the trouble of tracking down another pair. Now suppose my friend offers me $50 for the shoes. Now that is an offer I might take him up on. I would be $25 better off than I was before I bought the shoes and I could still go look for some new, fancier shoes. If I were drafting a balance sheet I could post a $25 profit. And how about my friend? He paid $50, so clearly the shoes were worth more to him than me, and so he too is happy. And the shopkeeper, he has posted a profit as well; he collects his margin on the shoes, which is the profit of the shoes after subtracting their cost and his costs of doing business from the net take of his sales. Everyone wins. The economic pie is larger and we are all better off for the transaction. This may seem mundane because we never stop to think about the miracle of such transactions, but such win–win economic transactions are miraculous. They literally create wealth from thin air.

The Hebrew word for a store, the quintessential place where transactions take place, is *Chanut*, which is based on the Hebrew word *chen*, which translates to "God's grace." This shows us that God smiles on human economic interactions and business enterprises. As long as an economic interaction isn't coercive, we can be certain that it will make all parties to the transaction happier and richer than they were before the exchange. Engaging in economic transactions literally creates money.

This is why the stock market can continue to go up and up and up. Yes, there are market corrections, but the trend is endless economic growth. It is also the reason that a central bank must mint new physical money. Because wealth is spiritual and endless, the physical markers of money must be created in an amount that matches the growth of wealth that occurs from these spiritual transactions. Governments everywhere struggle to mint a physical amount of legal tender that is equal to this growth in wealth. Too much physical money leads to inflation. Too little causes deflation. Striking a balance between inflation and deflation is difficult because physical money is just a marker for the creation of spiritual wealth, which grows at fluctuating rates. The spiritual growth of money is perfect and absolute and represents all of the good created by all economic interactions. But physical things, including bills and coinage, don't work that way, only spiritual things. So, inflation and deflation are observable proof of the difference between the physical and the spiritual aspects of money. They are proof that the creation of money is spiritual, even though its markers are not. You can literally observe the tension between the physical and spiritual in quantifiable terms.

Let me give you an analogy. A musical tune is also a spiritual creation. A saxophone is an instrument, which is tangible and physical. If you take my saxophone, I am down one saxophone and very sad. But take a tune from me and we can both enjoy it. You haven't hurt me. You're not taking anything away from me. This is why a good tune is so valuable to the creator. It can be rebought and resold infinitely. Money can also be re-traded infinitely. You have to divorce the physical markers of money from the spiritual concept it represents. Think of money as a certificate of performance to prove that one human being benefited another human being. Such benefits are infinite and exponential in their effects. So we have to print more and more markers to keep track of this growth, but the markers are just markers to facilitate transaction. The creation of wealth is the true miracle.

One Hebrew word for money is spelled *Ke—Se—F*. The structure of a word in ancient Hebrew is always based upon the meaning of the letters. The spiritual meaning of a word can be understood by analyzing the meaning and order of the letters. The first and last letters of this word, when combined, spells *kuff*, which is Hebrew for both the palm of the hand and/or the sole of the foot. What does this tell us? Well, the back of the hand is primarily used for punching and hitting, for defense and offensive combat, but the palms of the hand are different. The fingers curve and bend toward the palm so that we may use them to do work and to create things. The palms are therefore related to creation. The sole of the foot is used for movement and for transporting things. When we use our palms to create something and our soles to carry our creation to market, we are able to create value. A bucket of sand is not worth much. But if we use our hands to turn that same sand into glass or silicon chips and our feet to carry it to market, we can create value and thus money.

Creation and transport are the two primary ways of making money in this world. Like a bucket of sand, an iceberg in Alaska isn't worth much. But, prior to the creation of freezers, humans made icebergs valuable by breaking them into small cubes and transporting them to warmer locales where the ice could be used in iceboxes. Leave an iceberg where it is and you have an iceberg. Float an iceberg down to the desert and you have valuable fresh drinking water. By transport and creation, we are able to create value from the natural world.

The middle letter of *KeSeF*, the Hebrew word for money, is notable for its circular shape. This letter first appears in Scripture in Genesis (2:11), a verse describing a river that encircles a land of gold where God declares that "the gold of that land is good." This first mention of that circular letter appears in a mention of a waterway encircling a land of money, the whole land of Havilah, which is the land of which God spoke. A circle here indicates movement that goes around with no end, and we can see that movement must circle money through the economy. Gold, money—it must move through the economy to be of value. Money must be kept circulating. Saving money is good, but an economy requires spending too so that money may circulate and multiply. If everybody in a society decided to put all of their money under their mattress, the economy would collapse. There would be no more business transactions and no wealth would be created. The whole economic system depends upon the circulation of money.

You can do your part to keep money circulating by allowing other people to serve you. I could mow my own lawn if I wanted, but doing so would be hours of tedious, backbreaking drudgery. But I can pay $20 to an in-shape teenager who can have the whole thing done in an hour. Have I lost $20? No, I have gained three hours and I have employed someone. By allowing someone to serve me, I have bettered my condition and theirs. We must keep money circulating by looking for opportunities such as this to let other people serve us. This increases the time that we ourselves can spend serving others in our own specialized profession. This allows each person to do the most serving and the most good and will grow both the economy and your own personal wealth faster than anything else. Do not waste time doing that which you can better employ someone else to do. This is an important secret to good business sense: pay others with specialized skills and occupations to serve you so that you can better specialize and focus on serving others.

In Genesis (32:23–35), Jacob transports his family over a river and then goes back to the other side alone to check in on a few minor possessions. A strange man confronts Jacob on the other side and they wrestle all night. You may wonder whether or not this return trip was really worth the effort. The possessions may be minor, but they were Jacob's. Our possessions represent our money, and we must protect our money. Someone stealing your car radio or wallet is a very serious matter because they are actually stealing part of your life. Accumulating wealth takes time. The time you put into earning a car stereo are moments from your life that could have been put toward something else. When somebody steals that radio, they are effectively stealing some of your life, and the legal system should treat an act of theft as such. No more slaps on the wrist, I say! Theft is seen as a minor offense because we do not, as a society, respect money and property as we should. People would revere money more if they understood its important role in our lives and the economy. Money is our lifeblood. Steal someone's money or possessions and you are stealing a part of their life.

Let me solicit your legal opinion on a hypothetical scenario. Imagine a man sees someone falling from a skyscraper. Now this first man likes going shooting and he loves target practice—shooting skeet is his hobby. When he sees this falling man, the first man thinks it is safe to say he is a goner and so he decides to shoot him for target practice. What should the legal system do? The man who gets shot was planning on taking his own life and had maybe a second more of life at most. It's true: he was a goner. But this does not change the fact that, before he hits the ground, somebody murdered him. What do we as a society do? We take him to court, charge him with murder, and put him in jail like any other murderer. Every legal system in the world would imprison or execute someone for such an act. Murder is murder, whether it robs the victim of years, decades, minutes, or, in this case, a mere second.

Why then do we punish theft so lightly? If I spend a year worth of my waking hours saving up to buy a luxury car that someone then steals from me, the perpetrator has stolen far more of my time than was stolen from our hypothetical jumper. And yet, we punish the man who steals a second from someone far more harshly than we punish the man who steals a year from me. This makes no sense. It's a miscarriage of justice. I'm not saying we should throw people in jail forever on a small theft, but we should recognize it as the heinous crime it is. Theft is akin to murder. The difference is a matter of degree, not type.

Exodus (22:1) reads: "There's a thief who's stealing your possessions and while he's stealing your possessions you discover him and you hit him and you kill him." Is this murder? No. God says: "If the thief be discovered breaking in and he is struck and dies there is no blood guilt." (Exodus 22:2). Killing a thief in the act of committing a crime is an act of self-defense. Both theft and murder involve the stealing of life. If you shoot someone for trying to steal your stereo, you are not just trying to save your stereo. You are actually trying to save part of your life. That's how important money is to us. Our money is our life force. Our money is part of who we are. Money represents everything we create. Your money represents the entire aggregate of your time, experience, effort, diligence, dedication, and persistence. We must respect money as this holy, spiritual thing that it is. Understanding and respecting money also has the salutary effect of making us better able to attract and create it.

One of the greatest secrets of ancient Jewish wisdom is the power of charity to return money to the giver. This is quite counterintuitive and thus one of the most valuable biblical business secrets I can share with you. The best way to obtain more revenue, more profits, more earning potential, and more gross wealth is to reach deep into your pockets, take out some of that hard-earned money, and let it out of your own orbit and control. Note that I am not necessarily talking about giving money away to charity in a traditional sense. Investing money is another way of giving money and receiving a dividend for the good you are doing.

I am not recommending that you never give to charity. In fact, I recommend just the opposite and much of the rest of this book will be devoted to discussing exactly why you should give charity. But you need to understand that even if you never write a check to a charity, never drop any money into a donation box, and never engage in any other philanthropic activity ever again, you are still doing good for society simply by working and creating wealth. Do that and you are already giving services and creating wealth that will be distributed throughout the economy. Even if you never give a penny away, you have still done good for society by making the money in the first place.

Your economic transactions have created money from thin air, which is spread around the economy and circulated to others through further economic transactions. You have served your fellow man and each dollar is proof of that, whether you keep it or not. You do not need to give to charity just to justify having made money. You have nothing to justify; making money is noble and pleases God. Do not think me stingy—I give a great deal of money to charity. But I don't do it to justify having made the money. Creating wealth is a good in and of itself. Giving it to a worthy cause is just the icing on the cake. Additionally I like to point out that 10 percent of what I earn never belonged to me. Or, in another way of putting it, God is that rare boss who allows me to work on a 90 percent commission.

Many companies and corporations attempt to persuade the public of their virtue by making charitable donations. I actually think this is wrong. The board of directors is taking shareholder money and giving it away to a charity or cause they happen to believe in. That may sound good, but as a shareholder, I would prefer to have my entire share of the profits so that I can decide what portion of my profits I will give away and to whom, thank you very much. I will give to charity, and probably in a far greater proportion of my wealth than any corporation would, and it should be my choice, not the directors', where the charity is given. Each and every one of us should be free to adopt our own approach to charity. I don't want the government giving my money away for me and I don't want a private enterprise doing so, either. I am of the firm belief that an individual best knows what charities his or her own money should go to.

While we are on the topic, you should know how to pick a worthy charity. There are many causes out there of varying worth and many claims on your charitable dollar. How do you establish some means of assessing the inherent worthiness of a charity? There is a way. Ancient Jewish wisdom gives us a very useful principle that you can apply in almost all cases. Deuteronomy (22:4) reads: "You shall not see your brother's donkey or his ox fallen down by the way and ignore them. You shall help him to lift them up again." The Scripture is telling us that we must act when we see a person in need. We are not allowed to pretend we did not see what happened. We must stop and render aid. However, notice the phrasing. The Scripture instructs us to help this person to lift the donkey or ox back onto the road. Note that nowhere in Scripture does it say that we must do it for him. The phrasing is very specific. We are ordered to help them with their task. We are in no way obligated to do it for them.

Imagine that you driving home from work and you see a car on the side of the road with a flat tire. You stop to render aid, as the Bible says you should, but when you pull over, the driver tosses you the keys. "The spare and the jack are in the trunk!" he says, settling into the back seat of the car for some shade. He says just let him know when the flat is fixed. That is not a legitimate use of your time. What you should do in such a situation is toss him the keys right back and drive off. The Scripture is very specific: You must offer help, but you need not do it for him. Worthy charity helps people. Unworthy charity that completely takes over a task makes recipients of such charity dependent. Such charity robs people of their independence and erodes their dignity as a human being.

This principle can be applied to all charitable causes to determine their validity. A charity should help people help themselves. When a charity simply takes care of everything, it creates more problems than it solves and is probably not a worthy recipient of your charity. If a charity is regularly handing out free money, it is probably not doing much good for the recipients. They become dependent upon and feel entitled to the money. It is better to give to a charity that teaches people how to make money.

Whatever charity you pick to give to, the most important thing is that you are free to make this choice for yourself. No one, not the government nor a private enterprise, should get to make this choice and judgment for you. It's your money. You earned it by serving somebody. You get to decide what to do with it.

Society is being corrupted by the notion that the masses can best decide what the individuals should do with their money. This is false and immoral. Telling someone what to do with their money is equivalent to stealing it, which, as we discussed, is equal to stealing a piece of their life. As long as you made the money without robbing, coercing, or defrauding anyone, you get to decide where it goes. Why? Because you earned the money yourself by serving someone. It is your certificate of performance and you get to spend it or give it away as you see fit, so long as the money was truly earned and you didn't take it from anyone.

Now, what do I mean by take?

Bill Gates is one of the richest men in the world. Did he take any money from you? No. Nobody had a gun to your head when you purchased your Microsoft software. You could have bought Apple products. Or installed a Linux operating system. If you purchased Microsoft Windows, you must have done so because you believed it would somehow improve your life. Therefore, Bill Gates has already improved your life and he didn't have to give you charity to do so. I'm not saying you have to send him a postcard every week thanking him. You don't have to do that because you already paid him and the other Microsoft shareholders. Should Bill Gates give to charity? Probably, and as it turns out, he has given a lot through the Bill and Melinda Gates Foundation, but this is only a small fraction of the benefit he has given the world. Bill Gates has already benefited you and millions of other people at an amount equal to at least his entire net worth. He earned every last dollar by serving other people. He could not have earned the money without doing good in the world. Whether or not he gives the money away, he has already given back. That is a key principle of economic transaction: We give before we get. Always. He gave you Microsoft Windows and only then did you give him your hard-earned cash.

To quote the great British man of letters, Samuel Johnson, "Seldom is any man more innocently engaged than when he's trying to increase his own income." Somebody who is trying to increase his own income is not hurting anybody. If he did, they would not be his customers. Such a person is going to be racking his brains trying to figure out a way to make my life better so that I will pay him for his troubles. This is why I don't get worried when people tell me their goal in life is to make money. On the other hand, I get very nervous when somebody tells me they want to go into public service. That concerns me because I know that this means another pair of hands reaching for my wallet. But when somebody just wants to make money, I can rest assured they will be doing something to help other people. Otherwise, they aren't going to get very far with making money.

Helping and earning necessarily go hand in hand, as we have discussed. This fact is, at the end of the day, the source of money's spiritual nature. And it is a wonderful thing that makes the world go around.

Don't Live Beyond Your Means—Give Beyond Your Means

R ead that heading again. Does it seem to fly in the face of everything that I just said? Are you surprised? It does not and you
shouldn't be.

I may have just spent the last few pages telling you that anyone
earning money is doing good in the world whether or not they give
away a portion of their money to charity. It does not necessarily follow that they should not give to charity anyway. We absolutely should.
Giving charity is healthy. In a study conducted by the University of
Buffalo, researchers found that volunteering significantly lowers the
association between stressful life events and death. We are better able to
cope with pain and stress when we give of ourselves.

And what is more, giving charity is one of the primary tools we
have for making money. I have a friend named David, a well-known
entrepreneur in the medical industry who also helped fund the construction of a major megachurch in his native Southern California.
David gave the initial commitment of $2 million to have the church
built. It might surprise you to learn that he made this commitment
before he had ever earned the money. His pastor told him he needed

the money to build the church. David said he would help if he could but that he didn't have that kind of money. The pastor told him to go ahead and make the commitment anyway. Why? Because he understood this: We must give before we get. That is how you make money in this world—you put out money and it comes back to you with dividends.

David promised the money to the pastor. He didn't think there was any way he could ever meet such an obligation, but it was money he didn't have anyway so he conceded. He promised to pay the donation within two years, since he didn't have the money now. No sooner than he made this promise, his business began to take off. From that moment, everything seemed to turn around for him financially. He was able to pay the full $2 million donation within the two years and he still came out with a huge profit. He was so thankful. He was convinced the pastor had changed his life. This may seem farfetched, but it makes perfect sense if you understand ancient Jewish wisdom. This story doesn't surprise me in the least. You must give before you get. It is one of the great paradoxes of ancient Jewish wisdom, but you can count on it every time.

The Hebrew word for "tithing," for giving charity, is *ashar*, which, as you may remember from earlier, is also the word for "wealth." The Lord's language is once again trying to tell us that these two concepts are inextricably linked. This particular connection may seem counterintuitive. Wealth is all about making money and charity is all about giving money away. You may have assumed that the most surefire way not to get wealthy is to keep giving your money away, but that's not how it works. We give first and then we get. This is why charity is one of the greatest tools you have for making money.

I am telling you this so that you may, like David, change your thinking about giving charity. My concern right now is not for the poor, although I am concerned for the poor. My concern is not that the poverty stricken get your money—that is for you to decide. I'm not concerned, at the moment, with whether or not good causes get funded. What constitutes a good cause is up to the giver, and that is a discussion for another time and place. This book is all about exposing the biblical business secrets that can help you unlock the potential to wealth. Right now, I'm concerned about enhancing your moneymaking capacity. It is on this basis that you need to change your thinking on giving. We don't give once we've got. We get once we give. This vitally important principle is why you should work as hard as you can to earn money, but you need not spend that money. You may be better served by giving it away.

Spending money makes us feel good. This is why people engage in what is known as shopping therapy or retail therapy. There's no question about it: you do feel good when you spend money. But only until the credit card bill arrives at the end of the month. Then, it may not always feel so good if you spent beyond your means. But that doesn't totally invalidate the feeling of goodness and bigness that buying something brings. That is valuable. But you have the capacity to achieve exactly the same good feelings you get from spending money by giving away money.

Charity is a wonderful act that will make you feel better about yourself. It is also an act that will make other people view you more favorably, which is always good for business. Every act of making money involves human interaction. As we have seen, these interactions inevitably create wealth. These interactions can make you come across as generous and high-minded, selfish and venal, or, for most of us, somewhere on the continuum between these two extremes. Human beings are sensitive and finely tuned creatures when it comes to evaluating other people. We are good at intuiting each other's motivations and intentions because we get constant practice. We interact with other people all day long and, as such, we get very good at reading each other. In fact, we get so good that we tend to become confident in our ability to make snap judgments about others.

This is why first impressions are so important. Perhaps you used to roll your eyes when your mother or a schoolteacher repeated this axiom to you: No one gets a second chance to make a first impression. It may be a cliché, but it is absolutely true. People form rapid assessments of you within moments of meeting you. These assessments are based on many things, but one of the most important is your countenance and demeanor. People who are selfish and possessive and who care only about their own welfare tend to project this negativity wherever they go.

On the other hand, if you walk around with a beaming smile and sense of generosity for your fellow man, others will detect your positivity and view you positively. As customers and business professionals, we tend to make our choices about where to patronize and whom to do business with based on these intuitions about other people's personalities. If you come across as a good and generous person who is concerned about others, then people will want to do business with you. All of that goodwill tends to flow from the very first impression you make. That maybe isn't always fair, but the truth is, we are good at intuiting things about each other, so it is hard to blame someone for not wanting to work with you if you seem like a negative person.

You cannot blame people for judging you like this. If you seem like a negative person, you probably are one. There are sociopathic con men who are good at fooling others, but for the most part, the overwhelming majority of people project their true inner selves loudly enough that others can tell what a person is thinking and feeling immediately. People read us very, very quickly. It's not hard to spot a whiner or a miserable individual. They are usually whining and they look miserable! Likewise, spotting a positive and generous person is also fairly easy. They are probably trying to serve you from the get-go.

Living beyond our means causes us to radiate subtle signals of selfishness. But when we give beyond our means, we tend to beam with confidence, courage, and compassion. If you have an important interview, one of the best ways to build up your self-confidence and pep yourself up beforehand is to write a check to a good charity and drop it in the mail on your way to the interview. You will walk into that interview feeling like you are the kind of person who knows how to serve. And this will radiate from you.

The opposite is also true: we can radiate negative feelings, as well. I'm sure we have all had the unpleasant experience of working with a desperate salesperson. The experience is uncomfortable and unpleasant. The salesperson comes off as greedy and needy because you can tell they absolutely have to make the sale. In fact, they seem more concerned with making the sale than serving you. This is putting the cart before the horse—making money is the result of subservience, not the other way around. Such a salesperson has only his or her own interests in mind and you can tell. That doesn't mean they are a bad person necessarily, but it is off-putting. They seem like they need to make the sale in order to make rent and buy food, they're so desperate. It's uncomfortable. I don't like that kind of emotional pressure when I am trying to conduct business. Most people, myself included, would rather do business with someone who radiates confidence. A confident salesperson seems less desperate and makes customers feel like they have the customer's interest at heart, not just their own. The customer doesn't care if you make a sale; they just want to be served.

All of this is to your benefit if you put in the effort to be helpful and subservient. Do so and you will come off that way to others in all of your business dealings. The way to develop this quality and appearance, which you really cannot fake, is by training yourself to offer service to others and give charity.

Giving Money Away Makes You Feel Wealthy

Having money to spare is a great feeling. It makes us feel confident, useful, and good to willingly share our hard-earned money to support others down on their luck or a good cause. It makes us feel wealthy to spread money around in a noble and charitable way. But you may ask yourself: What's so great about feeling wealthy? Because money is an inherently good thing, this question is almost too fundamental to answer. It's almost like asking: what's so purple about being purple?

For one, your fellow man will respect and listen to you if you are and feel wealthy. In the Book of Proverbs, King Solomon said: "Wealth is a crown upon the heads of the wise." It may seem cynical, but we tend to listen carefully to people who are financially successful. We tend to give more deference to the opinion of a wealthy person, because, deep in our hearts, we know that the only way people make money is by successfully interacting with others. Successful people tend to be good communicators and good people. So when we meet someone we know is successful, we tend to be interested in getting to know that person. For someone to have made substantial money, a large number of other people must have trusted and liked this person. We recognize this and want to be their friend. We also correctly assume that there must be something we can learn from such a person. After all, everyone else can't be wrong—there must be something great about this person if everyone thinks so. So we want to get to know them, too. This doesn't mean we act smarmy. We don't have to approach them in a fawning, obsequious way. It just means we are generally interested in a person who is successful, a person who is good at serving God's other children. This is only natural and to be expected.

You want people to view you in this way, too. If you are successful, which should be your goal, you want to project that to others because it will attract them to you. And the best way to project your own wealth is to be generous with your money. Philanthropy and investment are the surest ways to successfully project the impression of success. You don't need to spend money on overpriced cars, suits, or jewelry. You don't need the gold Rolex or the biggest flashiest house. You don't need any of the trappings of conspicuous spending. You just have to be charitable and generous. Knowing this will give you a whole new outlook on life and boosted confidence. You will appear more positive to people, who are, as we have discussed, very astute in reading other people. By being charitable you can feel wealthy, rather than merely acting as if you were.

How we appear to others has a great impact on our business dealings. Have you ever noticed the number of things for which we all employ agents? We use real estate agents or realtors to help us buy or sell homes. You may think to yourself, "Why do I have to waste the money on a commission?" Typical commission for a real estate agent is 6 percent. If you are a buyer, you may be tempted to deal directly with a seller to save that money. And why not? They are selling. You are buying. Who needs a middleman? You could both save 3 percent each! And yet real estate agents are very popular.

The reason real estate agents are so popular is because many sales fall through without an agent to broker the deal. When the buyer and seller deal directly with one another, there is often too much emotion involved and the deal is likely to sour. Neither the buyer nor the seller wants to get a bad deal, and they are both too worried about getting the short end of the stick to come together and make a deal.

They both have too much at stake to negotiate properly. Emotions can run high. This is why we need realtors—to act as arbitrators. They earn their commission every single time because they serve as an emotional buffer between buyer and seller. A good realtor acts as a go-between and is able to camouflage both the concerns of the buyer and the desperation of the seller. This keeps emotions out of the deal. The realtor does have skin in the game, though. They want to close a deal and earn their commission. They do this by getting a fair offer on the table that both the buyer and the seller can be happy with and commit to.

The buyer and the seller can usually not get to this point on their own because they are too invested in the deal—they begin to come off as self-interested and neither can do business with the other. If they could appear to be more generous, they would fare far better in the real estate market. Now, luckily we have realtors to help act as a buffer, but you don't have a buffer between you and your customers. It is important that you come off as generous and truly interested in your customers.

Deuteronomy (15:4) tells us that a society that follows all of God's rules will have no poor people. Immediately after this, Deuteronomy (15:7) tells us that we "must always give money to the poor." This is interesting because Scripture both tells us we need not have poor people but also tells us that we need to always give money to the poor. That's not an outright contradiction, but why waste time and resources giving to the poor when we can instead focus on eliminating poverty totally? This is followed by Deuteronomy (15:11), which reads: "The poor shall never cease out of the land." This seems like a direct contradiction of what came before. First, the Bible tells us that there will be no poor people if we always follow the rule. Then it tells must that we must always give to the poor. And then the Bible says there will always be poor.

So what is going on here? Ancient Jewish wisdom tells us that nobody should ever think of themselves as poor. We have no right to think of ourselves as poor. And so, if we followed that rule and all other rules, there would be no poor people. Think of it this way. If you went into a crowd of 50,000 people and asked everyone who is poor to put up their hand and no one did, you could conclude that there are no poor people here. Why? Because poor is subjective. Except in the most extreme of cases, you cannot decide that you are poor.

But just because you should not think of yourself as poor does not mean you may not think of others as less fortunate than you, less wealthy, more poor, more deserving of charity. A person has no right to think of themselves as poor, but someone else may see that they could use a hand. If I notice that someone needs help and I can stop and render aid, I should. With respect to me, such a person may be poor and I should be charitable to him. This is why there will always be poor people *with us*.

You cannot be a poor person, you are not allowed to, but there will always be poor people with us. Do you see the difference? What this implies is that no one is entitled to charity but it is still incumbent on all of us to be charitable to the less fortunate. This is because wealth, and thus poverty, is a relative condition. There are no "poor people" because no one is poor in absolute terms. But this does not at all preclude any individual from giving charity to the poor. Finding someone who is financially worse off than you are in *relative* terms is easy.

So what we originally see as a contradiction in Deuteronomy, chapter 15 is not a contradiction at all. It is merely a paradox—one of the many paradoxes that speak to God's mysterious, but magnificent plan for our economic interaction.

Do not ever think of yourself as poor. To do so would be animalistic. A dog needs to get its daily scoops of food. If a dog doesn't get the four scoops of kibbles it needs, the dog could be called poor because it's not getting its daily sustenance. Human beings are different because they have more complex wants, needs, and obligations. Consider two people, one of whom uses his discretionary income on sending his children to private school and another who spends his discretionary income on eating out at expensive restaurants. There is no way to say how much money they need each month to be rich or poor. It's impossible because all human beings have their own dreams, aspirations, and desires. It doesn't make sense for society to label any one person as poor because wealth is relative. But an individual can very easily find someone who needs help. And if we are in the position to volunteer help, we should. This is what Deuteronomy, chapter 15 means by, "No matter what you do there will always be poor." It means that there is always a person I can find to help with charity, even though that person does not and should not think of themselves as poor.

So do give charity to those in need that you have the power to help. But do not believe that there is some well-defined class of poor whom you are obligated to support. And when you do help in this way, you help not only the recipient of the charity, but you help yourself as well by bolstering your own morals and sense of self-worth, which will, in turn, improve the way others see you.

Secret #35

How You Feel About Yourself Is How Others Will See You

Because other people can so naturally intuit your feelings, how you feel about other people is one of the main influences on how other people view you. How you feel about others also dictates how they feel about you. This is kind of an extension of the Golden Rule: Do unto others as you would have them do unto you. Except you can replace "do unto" with "feel about" because, generally speaking, people can read your face and actions well enough to know what you are feeling about them and about yourself. And others will see you the way you see yourself.

In the musical *West Side Story*, there is a scene in which the character Maria sings a song that goes like this: "I feel pretty, oh so pretty. I feel pretty and witty and bright. And I pity any girl who isn't me tonight." I rather like these lyrics because Maria highlights the principle behind this biblical business secret. She knows that she looks great because she feels pretty. Most people can relate to feeling this way at times. Maybe you have had the experience of your spouse telling you that you look beautiful or handsome, only you don't really feel that way at the time. Maybe you are self-conscious about the outfit you are wearing. Or maybe you feel like your stylist or barber gave you a bad haircut the last time you went in. When we don't feel attractive, there is nothing our spouse or significant other can say to change the way we feel. The thing of note here is that this feeling is not entirely delusional—it is not necessarily just poor self-esteem. We may, in fact, be right. This is because thinking you look bad is a self-fulfilling prophecy. Maria looks pretty in *West Side Story* because she feels pretty. If she felt unattractive, others would see that she was glum or unconfident and would probably find her less attractive, too.

We can see this same phenomenon at work in the Book of Numbers, chapter 13, in which the Israelites have just listened to the report of the spies that Moses sent to scout out the Promised Land. The spies have come back with this terrifying report: The inhabitants of the Promised Land are frightening, warlike giants. The spies lament that there is no hope of displacing the giants. They despair that Israelites are going to be stuck in the desert forever. The spies report that, when they looked upon the giants, they "felt like grasshoppers next to them and that's how they viewed us" (Book of Numbers 13:33). Note that the spies did not even speak with the giants. So how could they possibly know how the giants thought of them? Are the spies being presumptuous? Not at all. Because the spies felt small, they knew that this was how the giants would view them. This is why Moses did not ask how they knew how the giants felt—he understood this principle.

And so too should you. This biblical business secret is directly applicable to your professional life. The way you feel about yourself dictates how others are going to see you and this includes customers and business partners. Subtle spiritual emanations that betray how you feel about yourself will radiate from you and others will pick up on them. If you feel unworthy of wealth or undeserving of good, people will think these things are true. And these will become self-fulfilling prophecies because creating money depends upon human interaction. You do not want to be alienating potential customers and partners.

If your children are anything like mine were when they were young, they are always asking for cookies. They're not very naturally persuasive, in my opinion, even with those big innocent eyes. A young child may look at you and say, "Daddy, don't you feel like giving me a cookie?" The answer just rolls off your tongue—no way. Saying no to such a self-interested request is the easiest thing in the world. But a child who has grown a little older and is a little more responsible might remind you that he has done a terrific job looking after his baby sister and keeping his room clean, and then look at you and ask, "Could I please have a cookie?" Such a request is much harder to turn down. He really feels as if he deserves a cookie. The parent perceives this and is wont to agree, even if the child has had way too many cookies already.

When you really feel you deserve something, you will be far more confident in your pursuit of it. Knowing you deserve a raise because you worked hard for it gives you the confidence you need to look your boss in the eye and make your case. Contrast that with someone who harbors feelings of moral unworthiness. They will barely even be able to meet their boss's eyes. Don't think that your boss doesn't pick up on this—he will.

To succeed in business, you must not only be a good and moral person, you must also hold a strong and confident conviction that you are. You don't need to be pompous, smug, or self-righteous. And I'm certainly not trying to encourage a sense of entitlement. I merely hope to engender in you a deep conviction that you are not a selfish and loathsome human being. I want you to understand that making money is not shameful—it speaks to the highest of morals and is something to be proud of. The power of such an understanding is incalculable. Be confident in your successes. Don't brag, though. Your own strong character and self-esteem will naturally radiate from you. If you feel a sense of harmony with yourself, with God, with the world, and with your money, people will see and feel this. And they will judge you favorably.

Secret #36

Giving Money Away Automatically Connects Us with Other People

I

f you have read this far, you understand that making connections with other people is crucial to your career and the health of the overall economy. Charity is an incredibly good tool for connecting with others, perhaps the best.

In the Book of Leviticus, chapter 4, there are five separate places in a span of 27 verses where Scripture informs us what happens when someone sins. Leviticus (4:2) is about what happens when a person sins. In Leviticus (4:3) we are told what happens when a priest sins. In the third case, Leviticus (4:13), we see what happens when an entire congregation sins. Leviticus (4:22) tells us what happens if a ruler or king sins. The fifth and final mention, Leviticus (4:27), tells us what happens if "one among the people" sins. This last one may catch your eye: how is the fifth mention any different from the first? What distinction is the Scripture drawing between "a person" who sins and "one among the people" who sins? They sound similar, but they are not. The distinction is lost in translation from the Hebrew.

The three Hebrew words for "if" are: *KeY, IM,* and *ASHeR.* We use the word *KeY* (pronounced *key*) when the conditional is likely to occur.

The word *IM* (pronounced *em*) is used when the conditional is possible, but unlikely to occur. The final word, *ASHeR* (pronounced *osher*), is reserved for when the conditional is a certainty. *ASHeR* is a powerful word because you know that the result will always happen because the conditional is a certainty. *ASHeR* almost translates to "when."

Returning to Leviticus, chapter 4, we see that the word *KeY* is used to tell us what will happen "if" a person sins. This makes sense because we know that, whenever we do anything in life, we are likely to sin. It isn't a certainty that we will sin at any one moment, but pursuing a career, family, and life invariably ends in sin sooner or later. Contrast that to the use of *IM* when talking about whether a priest or congregation will sin—this word indicates that the sinning is unlikely. The priests, who are part of a tight knit league, spend most of their time in one another's company and in temple service can of course sin themselves, but are less likely to do so. Likewise, a congregation is unlikely to sin because a large body of people, especially pious people, is unlikely to sin in unison or with consensus. The Scripture employs the word *ASHeR* in the case of whether a ruler will sin. This tells us that a ruler will always sin. This is because authority brings power and the temptations of power are almost irresistible. Almost all rulers sin. We all know this. When we go to the polls, we are happy to vote for rulers and representatives who sin as little as possible. I see this every year when I head to the polls—the lesser of two evils is always my guy! This is because I know that a ruler or leader will not be able to totally avoid some level of sin. Power corrupts.

In the fifth and final mention of sinning, in which the Scripture tells us what will happen to a sinner who is "one person among the congregation," the word used here is *IM*, which indicates that one among the congregation will probably not sin. Contrast this to a single person, which uses *KeY*. What this tells us is that by being part of the congregation, you move from being likely to sin to being unlikely to do so. This makes logical sense: if a person is alone and disconnected from other people, he will find it easier to sin. He does not have the accountability and sense of connectedness that being among a congregation brings. When left to our own devices, we will often do the wrong thing. But as a group, we can all lift each other up and hold one another accountable.

Our connections to others are important because belonging to a group is a powerful thing. It need not be a religious congregation. You may choose to belong to a church, but you may also choose to belong to business groups, political groups, professional organizations, and more. Individuals in a group—almost any group—are connected to one another and thus less likely to sin than they would be on their own. Being in a group means you are being held accountable by the most virtuous people in the group. And this is why giving charity is so important. Giving charity links us to a group of highly virtuous people—those who give charity. Joining a charitable group allows you to self-select virtuous peers.

There are many charitable groups to which you may belong and it always connects you to others. Of course, giving charity connects you to those you give money to. But giving charity also connects you to the wider philanthropic, social, and business communities, all of which engage in charity. Give to several charities and you can count on being invited to formals, galas, fundraisers, and other events. Giving money makes you a desirable person and others will want to be around you. They will want to form communities with you, making this effect exponential.

This is extremely important in business, because your professional network is the lifeblood upon which your career depends. Now, I understand that saying this may sound vulgar. There are obviously great reasons to give charity that involve how others will benefit and the morality of charity. Those are all very important reasons to give charity, but this book is about biblical business secrets and using ancient Jewish wisdom to increase your earning potential, and so for our purposes here, I am focusing on the consequences of giving charity that flow towards the giver. And there is much that will flow to you when you engage in such charity. First and foremost, when you associate with other givers, you connect with these people and form groups.

There are other ways to do this, of course. You could join business development clubs. But most working professionals have limited time, and if this describes you, consider passing on joining a business development club. In case you are not familiar with them, business development clubs are groups formed by people from different professions who get together regularly to meet and exchange business cards.

The idea is to network with people in other professions with whom you would not normally spend much time. This way you benefit from a diverse community of working professionals you already know personally. In theory, this sounds like a great idea, and I want to be clear that these kinds of groups can definitely be helpful, but they are not ideal and you have better options at your disposal.

Business development clubs have no real advantage over networking through charitable organizations and groups, but the former does have one significant disadvantage over the latter. People join business development groups primarily to further their own interests. People at these groups are there to hand out business cards because they want people to call them for work. There's nothing wrong with this, but your motives are perfectly clear and obvious—you are in it for you. This can make you come across as a somewhat venal person. This is why such business and networking is more commonly done at churches, synagogues, and other religious and charitable institutions rather than at these artificial business development clubs.

Some pastors and rabbis may be sad to hear that their congregations are motivated in part to attend services for the networking advantage, but not this particular rabbi. I think it is a wonderful thing that people come to synagogue to meet other virtuous and charitable people who genuinely care about other people. This extends beyond religious congregations. Rotary Clubs are another great vehicle for this type of networking. Lots of business is conducted at Rotary Clubs, too. You know that anyone you meet at a Rotary Club is someone who is there to do good for the community just as you are. It is natural for two virtuous people in close proximity to conduct business with one another. That's the sort of thing you don't always get at a business development club, which creates an artificial community of people who are only in it for themselves. Those kinds of groups aren't self-sorting the way a charitable group is.

Giving charity connects you to the best possible people in the best possible way. And the connection is vital. Genuine connections are vital. Charitable groups and spiritual congregations are not just about exchanging business cards once a month. You attend a rotary club, or church, or synagogue often enough and you are going to really get to know people. Genuine connections are formed, and you will make friends, not just acquaintances.

Giving charity shows others that you understand this fundamental truth: You have to give before you get. This is an essential principle of both business and credit. In business, you have to give something before you take. At the most basic level, a shopkeeper puts your purchase in your hands and only then does he take your payment. When it comes to credit, you see this same principle amplified. Once you have proven yourself responsible and trustworthy, people will be happy to give you whatever you want, confident that they will get your payment later. This takes earning the trust of lenders by working on your credit score and establishing a track record as a dependable person who gives as well as takes.

Internet and e-commerce gurus will stress the importance of giving stuff away for free. Giving out freebies encourages customers to return for more. And it's not just products. Many businesses today, even small businesses, run blogs in order to dole out insider knowledge for free. By giving out this valuable information, they know that many customers will return later to purchase products and services. A customer will see that a business is giving them all of this information out of the goodness of their hearts, so they return to patronize the business. As you can see, giving before you get is a fundamental principle in business. You need to train your mind and soul to be comfortable with doing this. This is what charity is and how it works. You freely give of yourself, knowing that it will return dividends down the line.

There is a marked similarity between making investments and giving charity. Both activities involve a strong faith that you will get something back after putting something in. Charity and wealth are part of the same circle. You give and then you get back. And then you give back more and you get more. Investments are the same: When you invest, you (usually) receive back more than you put in, which can then be reinvested. Investments and charity create cycles that generate great wealth by paying dividends on what you put in up front.

Now, of course, not all financial investments work out and there is no guarantee that the return you get from charity will be one for one. But generally, in both cases, the return is greater than the investment and you simply need to have faith in the system and spread your money widely across charities and investments. Financial investments and charity will, on average, both pay dividends and give returns.

The two processes also reinforce one another. Giving charity develops our "giving" muscle. Charitable people find it easier to make investments because they are conditioned to give before they get. People who don't give charity tend to be stingier with their money. They are too afraid of parting with even a single penny to make proper investments. You need to develop the mindset of the giver if you want to do well in investing or business. The old adage that "It takes money to make money" is true, and this is why. Because you have to give before you can get.

On the surface, this principle is counterintuitive, which is why so many people have a problem grasping it. What I am asking of you here is to take something valuable out of your pocket and kiss it good-bye, in the form of either charity or investment. Either way, that money is out of your pocket and beyond your absolute control. This can be scary and uncomfortable if you are not accustomed to making such an act of faith. And that is what it is, an act of faith in the system. Deep down inside you know that the money is going to come back. And generally, it will. Maybe not on each expenditure. Not every investment succeeds and not every charitable donation can be traced to a return. You don't always know why a certain client came to you. Sometimes it will be because they have heard of your generous spirit, sometimes not. You cannot know for sure when talking about any one client. But, on average, you will get back more than you put in—this you can have faith in. But you have to play the game. You have to give of yourself first.

It is crucial that you understand that the economic system is intentionally structured this way and you do yourself no favors by ignoring these truths. God works with us in the vast divine system of economic interaction. He encourages a largeness of spirit and welcomes our ability to be high-minded, generous people. Rewards for this kind of charitable behavior are built into the economic system.

Do you know why the origin of the handshake is a universal symbol of friendship? The reason might surprise you. The Hebrew word for hand is *yad*, spelled Y—D. The Hebrew word for friend is spelled Y-D-Y-D. Friend is spelled by spelling hand out twice. In the Lord's language, two hands together means friend. This is the reason that clasped hands are the universal sign of friendship.

An outreached hand with the palm up signals that the person needs or is taking something. We put out our hands when we are asking for help. When I put out my hand, I'm asking for something. And, in contrast, when I put out my hand with the palm forward, this means that I do not need something, that I already have enough. It might interest you to know that the Hebrew word for "enough" is "hand" spelled backwards.

So an outreached hand in one direction indicates taking and an outreached hand in the opposite orientation means giving. And two hands clasping is a symbol for people giving and taking from one another. Another word for this is, of course, a transaction. What is a transaction other than two parties giving each other things? One gives a good or a service. The other gives money in return. The clasped hands of a handshake are a symbol for coming together to make a transaction. This is why we shake to seal business deals, too.

There's an old Hebrew adage that states that people who are trading don't fight. This is true of individuals as well as whole nations. The globalized market that emerged after World War II is one reason why we have seen so much less global conflict in the past 70 years. It's not only nuclear deterrence that has cut back on warfare. It is worldwide economic interconnectedness and our global economic ties that have reduced the incidence and severity of major warfare so dramatically in the past half-century or so.

In the same way that nations engaged in trading don't fight, individuals that engage in trade care for one another. Shopkeepers take care of their loyal customers. Regular patrons of dining establishments care deeply for their proprietors. This is no surprise: These people regularly do business that benefits one another and that leads to the formation of spiritual bonds between customer and business professional. But there are other surprising ways in which people who do business together help each other.

A number of years ago, a friend of mine from Los Angeles owned a factory that burned to the ground one night. He was devastated and distraught because his customers depended upon him to refurbish their goods. He would be unable to fill their orders in the morning. Trucks would start dropping off electronics for servicing in the morning and he would be unequipped to take them. He didn't know what to do.

Then, he started getting phone calls from his competitors. They offered to take care of his customers until he got the factory up and running again. Keep in mind: These are his *competitors*. But they are also people that do business together from time to time. They let him divert his customers' trucks to their factories where they did the work and then returned the merchandise to their competitor's customers. These competitors took care of him and helped him back on his feet. And when he had his factory up and running again, they went back to being competitors. That's what business is really all about. Shaking hands. Clasping hands. Real friends giving and taking, exchanging and trading. This is the most reliable form of friendship that there is because it is reciprocal. And it starts with two clasped hands, giving and taking from one another.

If There Is No Hebrew Word for Something, Then That Thing Does Not Exist

A few years ago, I had the fortunate experience of sailing across the Pacific, a lifelong ambition of mine. My wife and I loaded the sailboat up with our children and provisions and we set sail from the West Coast to Hawaii. It was a 22-day voyage. One of the most trying parts was standing watch at night. You have to stand watch to make sure you don't hit other ships or cargo containers that have been washed overboard; I was reminded of this by what happened to the character played by Robert Redford in the 2013 movie *All Is Lost*. Nighttime watches can really strain your eyes, so we take shifts. About halfway into the trip, I was exhausted and my eyes were tired and I was getting worried about water. Having little kids onboard, I wanted to be sure our water tanks were okay. Normally I check the water tanks every day or so to be sure we aren't using too much. I measure the water with a dipstick.

On this particular night, I found that there was nothing left. It was all gone. My first instinct was to panic. I wasn't sure if we had sprung a leak or if a pump had gone haywire and pumped all our water up out of a pipe. I started laughing hysterically.

What was I laughing about at this inopportune time? The United States Declaration of Independence, which states that everybody has a right to life, liberty, and the pursuit of happiness. My dire situation exposed this promise for the absurdity that it is. It was the middle of the night, everyone else was asleep, and here I was sitting on the floor of the boat laughing manically about the absurdity of this guarantee. The Declaration of Independence guarantees me life? Well, great. I'm a thousand miles out in the Pacific Ocean. I would like to draw on that right at this very moment, if you please. Send the Navy if you guarantee me the right to life. I'm laughing because I am thinking, How would they find us? And why should they? Nobody told us to go out into the ocean on a sailboat. So what is this all about, this "right" to life?

I realized then and there that this word "right" is completely meaningless. And who, pray tell, has the obligation to fulfill this right? Anytime somebody tells you that you have a right to anything, be very suspect. Ask them who you can call to make sure that this right gets fulfilled. Because if there isn't anybody who accepts the obligation to deliver on that right, you don't have that right. That right is absolutely worthless if you cannot collect on it. And so the word "right" is, on its face, nonsensical. It just doesn't mean anything. How can something be guaranteed to you if there is no guarantee that someone can and will deliver it to you?

It wasn't until later that I thought to recheck the water supply. To my amazement and relief, there was plenty of water. In my exhaustion I had somehow misread the dipstick we use to gauge how much water is left. Embarrassing, yes, but what a relief to know we were going to live! Everything was going to be fine, but the ordeal had taught me a lesson. It had reminded me that the English language is full of words that are pure nonsense. These words define concepts that do not exist.

There is no word for rights in the Lord's language. There is no Hebrew word that translates to even roughly the same thing. And you can be sure that, if a word doesn't exist in the Lord's language, that thing does not exist at all. It is not real. Otherwise, God would have named it.

Now, this doesn't apply to words describing modern technology. There's no word in biblical Hebrew for helicopter or telephone, of course. I assure you helicopters and telephones are real. There is a word in Modern Hebrew for telephone—it is *telefon*—but there is no such word in biblical Hebrew. But this is not what we are talking about. Helicopters and telephones fall into the realm of things that do change, which we discussed earlier, which includes technology, medicine, and science. We are speaking here strictly of those things that do not change—man, God, the spiritual, the Earth. With all of these things, if there is no ancient Hebrew word for a thing or concept, that thing or concept does not exist.

So forget the word "rights." The word doesn't exist and neither does the thing. Now you may say, "But Rabbi Lapin, what do you mean? I have so many rights! Why, just look at the Bill of Rights! There they are, enumerated and everything!" There is something of an epidemic of so-called rights in the modern world, especially in the United States of America. We are promised so many rights. But where are the obligations? Who guarantees these rights? Without guarantors, rights are utterly meaningless. The government had made it its mission to fulfill these so-called rights, but the government only does this to the best of its ability and at its own whim. If a right can be discontinued, is it really a right? This idea of an inalienable right is completely bogus. It's a nice idea, but specious.

Nowhere in the whole Torah does it ever mention a right to anything. Not once is a right mentioned anywhere among the 613 commandments. There are only obligations. Do poor people have a right to charity? Absolutely not. I have an obligation to give charity, but I do not have to give it to someone just because they are poor. I don't give charity to loathsome, disgusting persons, even if they are poorer than I am. I give my charity to whom I choose and if no one gives charity to you, well, that's tough, but it's not my problem. God doesn't like people being miserable human beings, and so you will get no rewards for being one, not from Him and not from me. The system is set up this way so as not to reward bad behavior.

There's no such thing as an entitlement because no one is entitled to anything. If you plan to live off of the generosity of your neighbors, it would behoove you to endear yourself to them so that they actually want to help you, because you do not have a right to anybody else's money. Nobody does. There isn't such a thing. We all have obligations but nobody in the Bible has a right to anything. The word doesn't exist in Hebrew because it doesn't exist in the world. When anyone coerces you to provide such a right, it is not charity by the very definition of charity, which is voluntary giving. If you are being coerced to give your money to someone, this is theft.

There is also no word in Hebrew for coincidence. The concept of a coincidence is contrary to God's plan. Calling something a coincidence is a fallacy because it conceals God's involvement in the world. There are no accidents or coincidences, only purpose that you fail to see. Just because you fail to take notice when God is conveying something to you does not make His message a coincidence. What we think of as coincidence is usually nothing more than God camouflaging His purpose. There is a reason for every single thing that has and ever will happen. Do yourself a favor and spend a few minutes trying to figure out what the reason could be rather than chalking one up for coincidence, a thing that does not exist.

There is also no Hebrew word for "fair," another nonsense word that the Lord's language does not recognize. Some people invoke fairness when they see inequality. They see you with two of something when they have none and they call it unfair. But why should we all have the same amount of something, especially when you might have worked for something that I have not? Children internalize this nonsensical notion of fairness from a very young age. The parents reading this will know what I mean. How many times have you heard your children say, "But, Mommy, Daddy, it's not *fair*." Perhaps you feel the same way sometime when things aren't going your way or you find yourself coveting what someone else has. Well, I'll tell you the same thing I told my kids: You're right, it's not fair, because life isn't fair from a human perspective.

Life isn't the only thing that isn't fair. Nothing is fair. Because *fair* doesn't exist. There are obligations. There are rules. There are systems. There is equitable distribution of goods and wages and services, but they are not distributed by any system of fairness. Goods and services are bought with money, and money must be earned. You don't have any right to money. You must earn it.

Another modern word for which there is no ancient Hebrew equivalent is "vacation," which again tells us that the thing does not exist in the eyes of the Lord. This should be obvious: The Lord wants us to serve each other, which requires that we work, and a vacation precludes working.

Why on earth would you stop working? Now in this modern day, where we don't always take off one real day a week for a Sabbath and we don't observe and regularly celebrate the biblical festivals, I can see how life can be a little monotonous without vacations. Modern life can be a little tiring, and I, for one, admit that I love vacations. But I also recognize that there is something intrinsically unhealthy about feeling the need to get away from everything for an extended period of time. I realize that the contemporary notion that vacations are healthy is fallacious. Personally, I find it hard to return to work after a vacation, which is an indication that the vacation probably wasn't a great idea, even if I enjoyed it. God put us here to serve each other, and when we go on vacation and stop serving each other, we begin to feel spiritually unhealthy.

Knowing that, it probably won't surprise you to know that there is no ancient Hebrew word for retirement. The concept is a relatively new development. People did not retire in the Stone Age. They did not retire in medieval times or even during the Renaissance or Victorian times. The first mention of retirement came in 1883, when Otto von Bismarck, the chancellor of Germany, instituted a retirement age of 65. This was a fairly safe age for a society to pick back then, as most people didn't live this long—infant mortality was high and penicillin didn't exist yet—but the precedent was a bad one. People are living well past that age now, but the precedent took and now societies all across the Western world observe this cutoff. But before 1883, it was unheard of. This was the first time a society had instituted the strange notion that the government would pay people not for working, but for simply growing old. We got by just fine without retirement before then, but now we see it causing many problems. Entitlement programs for retirees, such as Social Security in the United States, are bankrupting whole nations. And for what? So we can stop working? We are bankrupting society so that we can help people stop serving each other? This makes no sense. These programs are unaffordable because the system was designed by God not to support them.

Sometimes the case is made that retirement is a social obligation. Retirement is framed as a way for the elderly to make room for the next generation entering the workforce. This argument is fallacious. Think about it: If it is such a good idea to retire people at 65 so that younger people can easily find jobs, then why not retire people at age 50? Why not retire everyone at 30 so all of the 21-year-olds can find work? This makes no sense because there are no hard limits on human wealth. When people stop working, they stop producing, and often become less healthy as a result.

Everyone who works produces vastly more than they consume. You can verify this fact by looking around your own neighborhood. Sewage does not run down the street because someone put in sewer lines. You live in a house and not a field. You eat food from the supermarket, not food from the woods. All of these things required a surplus of production for you to be able to enjoy them through trade. Your modern conveniences and your discretionary income are proof that we produce far more than we actually consume. This is true for almost all people around the developed world.

Why then should we put productive people out of work? How does this help anything? There is no point at which somebody automatically becomes useless. Everyone has something to contribute—yes, some more than others. But everyone can contribute. We are never too old to contribute. Our ability to contribute may change or morph, but every person has something to give, some way to serve.

In the Book of Numbers, we are introduced to a set of priests with less than desirable job duties. They must drag animal carcasses, perform sacrifices, and deal with recalcitrant customers or worshippers. In Numbers (8:24), God tells Moses that these priests "shall withdraw from the legion of those who do this work and no longer do that work." Is this a biblical reference to retirement? No. Toward the end of Numbers, chapter 8, God declares that these older priests "shall minister with his brethren in the tent of meeting." They are still doing a very important job and getting paid for it. It's just a different job.

God recognizes that the physical labor of dragging around heavy carcasses is no longer suitable for a priest at the age of fifty. The work is beyond them physically and beneath their dignity. These older priests are moved into an elevated advisory position. They become the boss priests. But they are still working. There is no point in the Bible that espouses the notion that we quit working altogether at any age. This

notion of retirement is relatively new and tremendously problem-
atic. Retirement should not be a core principle of the working life.
We must get away from the notion that the point of working is so that
one day we can retire and do whatever we want to do and never serve
anyone ever again. If God had planned this, He would have named
such a thing. There's no Hebrew word for retirement and so we know
He did not.

Retirement Is Unhealthy

I have known many people who could not wait to retire. They worked their whole lives and were at the peak of their physical and mental health. Then they hit age 65 and retired immediately. They got their gold watch and enjoyed their retirement party and quit working. Then, they received Social Security and drew down their savings, if they had any. Almost instantly, their health began to decline. Sometimes, to combat a deep depression, a few retirees will go back to work just to have something to do, to have a way to meet and connect with people as they did when they were working. Suddenly, they feel good again.

The bottom line is this: Retirement is unhealthy, physically, emotionally, and spiritually.

The *New England Journal of Medicine* has published many articles over the years that correlate faith and prayer with good health. There is an observable connection. This does not bode well for retirees because it is a tough thing to ask for God's help in maintaining your health when you are not even working. On what basis do you ask God for help and good health when you are not out there every day helping His other children? You can't. This is one reason why so many people's lives deteriorate when they quit working and they no longer have the structure and discipline that working provides. People stop working and they lose their drive and the thrill that comes from producing and being helpful. They begin to decline not only physically, but spiritually, too.

Many people replace work by volunteering, which is better than doing nothing, but less healthy than actually working in a paid career. There are many very worthy organizations that depend on volunteer work, and everybody should do some volunteer work. It is noble and good. But you should do it in addition to actual paid work, not as a replacement for work. The problem with volunteering is that it is something we do only when we feel like it. There is no accountability and thus no discipline involved. Say you promised the Red Cross, where you volunteer, that you will come in on a Sunday, but then when Sunday morning rolls around, you notice that the weather looks perfect for a long day of fishing. What is to stop you from calling in your regrets and going to the lake instead? It's not as though the place where you volunteer can fire you. You can come and go as you please. For most people, volunteering is really just doing what you feel like doing. I will grant that there are a very few who are able to treat volunteering like a job and show up day in and day out whether they feel like it or not. These rare few show up even when they feel bad, just like people who have a job for which they get paid. But this is the tiny minority, a small fraction of a fraction of all people.

Most of us need the economic incentive and administrative oversight. We do much better in situations that force us to overcome our personal wants and desires. When we retire, all of the sudden we can do whatever we want whenever we want. You lie in bed all day when you feel like lying in bed. You go fishing on days you want. Other days you want to play golf and so you do. These are all very nice and fine pursuits, but it is not healthy to pursue them, or any personal pleasures, to exclusion. Without a job, you have no accountability or discipline. Human beings thrive when they are growing and developing and this requires discipline. Discipline and accountability keep us alive. Working engenders a growing, strengthening willpower that ensures that you go into work to serve your fellow man each and every day. If you do that, you can stand up and proudly say you have been working decades without ever missing a day and you will do decades more if you can. And you know this is a good thing because working means you are serving. Do that and you will find that you are more likely to stay in good shape, physically and spiritually. It's not that you haven't missed a day of work because you're in good shape. It's the other way around. You are in good shape precisely because you haven't missed a day of work.

Another problem with volunteering in lieu of doing paid work is that you can never be totally sure you are actually doing something that is necessary. Organizations want to keep their volunteers. Volunteers are important when an organization is busy. But they aren't always busy, and often they will give volunteers pointless work to occupy them just to keep them around for later. One of the great things about being paid, aside from the paycheck, is that you know you are doing some good for somebody. This must be true or no one would pay you. Being paid ensures that you are delivering value to at least one other human being, and probably more. This is, ultimately, why you must keep working. Retirement is so unhealthy precisely because it leads to a sense of worthlessness. If we don't think we are serving, if we don't think we are adding value, we feel worthless. When people only do what they feel like and do not have the opportunity and luxury of serving others, they begin to feel as if their life force is being eroded. Our spirits will feel damaged and defective, which translates into mental and physical health problems.

When the prophet Samuel is still a young boy, his mother takes him to the temple so that his life may be devoted to God. Early in the first Book of Samuel, we are told that: "The boy served God before Eli the priest" (1 Samuel 2:11). Note that Samuel is not even named here. This is a man who will one day grow up to be a prophet, but right now he holds a lowly status. He is at the beginning of his career at the temple. It is not until later that we are told that: "The lad Samuel served God before Eli" (1 Samuel 3:1). Here we see that he is named. He is still referred to as a mere lad, but he is named because Samuel is beginning to take over and advance in his career.

I want to show you how these verses are linguistically marked in the Hebrew text in a way that is necessarily lost in all of the translations. The Hebrew word *ET* is made up of the first and last letters in the Hebrew alphabet, which suggests an embrace and parentheses. *ET* is often used before a name to signify tremendous emphasis and importance. In the Hebrew text, Samuel (2:11) reads: "And the lad served *ET*, the Lord and *ET* the face of Eli the priest." The word *ET* here indicates that Samuel is splitting his focus between God and his master, Eli, both of whom he is serving. But in 1 Samuel (3:1), the text reads: "The lad Samuel was serving, *ET* God." Here there is no priest and no second *ET*, so we know that the focus has now shifted away from serving his master to serving his God. This is a normal and natural shift for Samuel. It is the natural development of a career at the temple—first you serve your master, then later you move to serving God. Now what if the temple had found that, once Samuel was too old to serve his master, it was time to put him out to pasture? This is a ridiculous idea! Samuel still has so much to give and so many ways in which to serve, just perhaps not in his former role.

A person's skills, abilities, and experience develop and change over the course of a lifetime, but that does not mean that they are put out to pasture when they are no longer well suited to a particular job. You are still useful, just in different ways. The idea that older people are no longer useful is a terrible and destructive modern idea that hurts both individuals and the larger economy. Forced retirement is a strange and unnatural thing. Many companies have policies of forced retirement age and this is a total mistake. Older people have so much to give still. If you want to make room for young people, you should just expand the company. Expansion is what leads to growth and economic growth is good for everybody. Forcing people to retire is good for no one. The business suffers, the retiree suffers, and society suffers. Everyone suffers a loss of potential wealth and fulfillment.

You Can Ruin Today by Planning Bad Things for Tomorrow

Nothing throws the brakes on success like worrying about the future. You might be going about your day, meeting all of your obligations with aplomb, diligently serving other people and God, doing everything right, and you feel great, when suddenly this niggling feeling about tomorrow descends over you. This kind of nagging worry is a terrible form of spiritual gravity because it is so pernicious. Everything may not fall apart at once, but we can feel ourselves slowly coming apart at the seams. We start planning and fretting over what must be done the next day, or the next week, and we worry about what the following year holds, and suddenly we are not living fully in the present. Worry about the future is troubling for humans. Bad thoughts about tomorrow can infect our spirits and performance today in noticeable and measurable ways.

The end result of your life is a direct result of what came before. You do not get to the end of anything without having come from the beginning and having traveled along the way. If we find that we have ended up somewhere bad, we can assume that we got there by traveling the wrong path. We didn't just have a "bad ending," we also got off to a bad start or, at the very least, took a wrong turn somewhere along the way.

This is an extreme example, but have you ever seen those prime-time crime documentaries about husbands who murder their wives? Usually there is life insurance or inheritance money involved. These are grisly tales I bring up only to make a point. Whenever I see one of these documentaries, I always wonder what kinds of warning signs the wife and her family missed. Were things good right up until the murder? I cannot imagine that they were. One of documentaries that I found particularly haunting is about a husband who murdered his wife on their honeymoon. Is there any possibility that the first day or week of marriage or their entire courtship was really great and then it was only after the marriage that he decided to kill her for the insurance money? There is not. We can say with near certainty that he was planning to do this evil act before he actually did so. Even if he had no conscious plans to kill her, there was obviously something seriously wrong with him and their relationship. Good people do not, by definition, kill each other, especially their spouses. There is no way their marriage was good all the way up until this tragic event. That's not how things work. Good people in good situations also don't just suddenly decide to divorce. In such a case, you have to ask yourself what was wrong in the marriage before it all went wrong.

The plan to do wrong in the future inherently negates the situation you are in today. You cannot have a good marriage while planning to murder or divorce your spouse down the line. A good marriage and plans to wrong your spouse are mutually exclusive. This is also true of making other bad plans, such as retirement. If we know that retirement is an unhealthy condition and a bad choice, then we should realize that planning for retirement, no matter how far down the road it is, negatively impacts us in the present. You simply cannot thrive today while planning to be slothful and idle tomorrow.

If you have ever played golf, you know that the swing is the most important part of the game. In fact, it is the entirety of the game. Before you take a swing, you walk up to the ball, plan your swing, maybe wiggle yourself a bit like they do on TV, and then you bring the club back and crack the ball. What happens next? The ball either goes the right way or it doesn't. Once the club has connected with the ball and sent it soaring down the fairway, what you do on the green is irrelevant. You cannot sway its path by moving the club, or by dancing, or leaning in hopefully. The swing and the motion of the ball in the air are part of the same continuous movement. If you don't properly plan the swing the entire way through to the end, the ball won't go onto the green. Pro golfers focus on the swing and the follow-through movement, that one continuous movement, because they know they have no control over the end except at the beginning of the ball's travel. What this also tells us is that, if the ball didn't go where it was supposed to go in the end, then the beginning wasn't good, either. The swing was off or the follow-through was wrong. The beginning and the follow-through and the end are inextricable from one another. They are one smooth motion.

And so it is with life. When we plan our lives and careers with a bad ending such as total retirement, we can be sure that our present will be as wrong and bad as the end result we are likely to see. You cannot disconnect the future from the present and you cannot disconnect the present from the past. That's not how time works. Time moves in a continuous motion.

So why is retirement such a bad ending? Well, there are the health issues we mentioned earlier, but that's not all. Retirement presents us with a moral problem as well—retirement requires that we stop working, which means we are no longer serving God's other children. That moral problem manifests itself not only in retirement, but in the lead-up to it as well. These problems will manifest not only in retirement, but in your current working life today.

Planning for retirement corrupts your entire career. As I have stressed repeatedly in this book, we work in order to serve other people. The joy of work is serving God's other children. Money is the inevitable consequence of that. I don't chase money. I don't love money. I love the opportunity of serving other human beings. The fact that God has set up a world in which serving others results in earning money is just icing on the cake. Don't get me wrong: Bountiful prosperity is a huge blessing. But I try never to lose sight of the goal, serving others, and I try to view money as mere testimony to the fact that I have served many of God's children. But money is not the end goal.

And that is the problem with retirement. Retirement is the idea that, once you have earned enough money, you drop out of the system.

You can see that, if you focus only on the monetary rewards of working, you lose sight of the true goal, which is to help other people. If we are willing to retire, clearly we are only working for the money, not for the serving. No one retires when they have "served enough."

This is not God's plan for us. Working isn't about what you get; it's about what you give. Working is about asking: "What can I do for you?" There is no reason you should stop asking that when you turn 65. The obsession, the preoccupation, the joy, and the exhilaration of work arise from serving other people. The more you serve, the more the money flows toward you. But do not get this backwards. Your focus is the serving, not the money. The more you focus on the money, the less it flows toward you. This is the paradox of work and it works with utter reliability. This is what I mean when I say you give before you get.

Just because I advise you never to retire does not mean you should not have savings. It is nice to have the capacity to not need to work out of desperation for the money. It's nice to already have enough. That's wonderful even. You should absolutely save and invest for the future. But to quit work? When you say you are going to quit working as soon as you have the means to do so, what you are really saying is that you are working for money and not to serve. You are saying that you are only doing what you should be doing now so that you can plan to do whatever you feel like later.

That's a terrible idea. It means that all along you have been working only to make money. This will not work out for you. Your focus must be on serving other people and then, and only then, will you see money flow toward you. You must be obsessively preoccupied with the needs and desires of other human beings, not on money. Making retirement your main goal undermines the real goal of subservience. Focusing on retirement corrupts your entire career because it means you are only in it for the money.

In the same way that spending much of your professional career dreaming of retirement can be harmful, focusing on the positive can be quite helpful. Let me give you an example. While dining at a kosher restaurant in Dallas recently, I was eavesdropping on a conversation between a waitress and another customer. The customer asked the waitress what she did when she wasn't waiting tables. She responded that she was a recent immigrant and hadn't found any other work yet.

The customer smiled and said, "You give great service. How would you like to help people enjoy healthier skin and better looks?" Her eyes lit up when he offered to hire her to do sales from a cosmetics kiosk in one of the largest malls in Texas.

Never mind hiring the waitress—I would have liked to hire that man! He knew not to ask his prospect, "How would you like to make money persuading passersby to try a hand cream?" Instead, he motivated her by appealing to a slightly higher purpose. He asked her how would she like to serve her fellow man.

One thing I learned as a parent was that igniting a contagious enthusiasm for chores among my young daughters was easy, provided that I first spoke about how much we all owed my wife, their mother, before assigning tasks. Rather than lecturing on why clean dishes and swept floors are so important, I appealed to a higher purpose. This is a common tactic. You have probably seen those U.S. Army commercials imploring you to "be the best you can be." The marketers who created these commercials understood that most of the brave men and women who enlist in the military do so to defend freedom and protect their loved ones. Army recruiters rightly emphasize these attributes rather than the pay or the working conditions. Such tactics can light a fire in the hearts of humans.

Needless to say, just as fire can cook delicious food, heat our homes, and provide mechanized transport, it can also burn and destroy. The more powerful a tool, the more powerfully it can be used for both good and evil. Similarly, the ability to tap into the worthy human desire to strive for a greater purpose than merely our physical existence can also be used for both good and evil. Politicians win support for unpopular policies by explaining, for instance, that confiscatory rates of taxation are necessary to "give every citizen free medicine," to "help the children," or "to end poverty." They know better than to justify higher taxes by explaining that they wish to hire more of their cronies and provide them with lavish retirement benefits.

Nimrod, who enslaved the populace to build the Tower of Babel, knew, as all tyrants know, that you cannot subdue people by telling them, "I want to enslave you. I want you to work for my aggrandizement." You have to find a way to appeal to their desire for a higher purpose. When, in Genesis (11:4), Nimrod said, "Come; let us build a city and a tower whose top will reach heaven," he was speaking to a spiritual need. The tower was a metaphor for appealing to a higher purpose.

In the Lord's language, Hebrew, the word for tower, *MiGDaL*, is closely related to the word for great, *GaDoL*. Not only is a tower a great building, a tower is also the physical depiction of our own human yearning to find transcendent purpose in our lives. Often companies build enormous headquarters, not because they need the space but because they want a symbol of their vision. Every one of us yearns to reach for the sky. Similarly, by orating about his stairway to Heaven, Nimrod is saying, "Come with me, I will help you reach for your highest aspirations."

Knowing that on the deepest level most people are motivated best by a call to higher purpose is a practical and indispensable tool for managing a military, a business, or a family. A good leader takes the time to share his or her vision and the idea and passion behind it rather than simply relaying the task that needs to be accomplished. Mundane and often boring jobs lay the groundwork for majestic missions. Being able to envision the goal in grand terms makes even difficult tasks achievable. This is true for organizations and for individuals.

Retirement Tends to Isolate You

I t is an unfortunate truth about our society that many older people are very isolated and alone. The majority of these people are retired. They may no longer have surviving family near them. Having retired, they have no coworkers and no professional network to fall back on. They don't even see customers every day. Do not underestimate the value of companionship that customers provide. Some of my closest relationships in life are with valued regular customers and others with whom I conduct regular business. Because I serve these people regularly, I have grown to love them very dearly and we remain very close even years and decades later. That's a testimony to the power of mutual service to bind us together.

Some people are able to maintain contact with other people during retirement, but these connections tend to be far weaker and transient than those you can forge in the working world. Perhaps you have already retired and you spend several days a week playing golf. You love golf, but what you are really craving is human contact. So three times a week you go down to the local green and meet up with three other guys to play a few rounds of golf. The same few guys show up every day and you have gotten to know each other fairly well. You get along well enough and have fun together.

But ask yourself this: Would they really miss you if you stopped showing up? They would be a little put out, maybe, if you missed a game because they need a fourth body on the green to compete against. But you are really just a warm body. You are completely replaceable. If you don't show up to play your 18 holes, they'll just find someone else who will. You are very replaceable and thus your communication with others is tenuous and superficial. Contrast that to the relationships you forge in your working life. Because coworkers, professionals, customers, vendors, and the like depend on each other for their needs, the bonds they form are deeper. Golf may be fun, but it ultimately doesn't matter. Work is how we earn money, our lifeblood, and so the relationships we form there take on a deep significance in our lives.

If you are a good worker, you are probably indispensable to your boss. He needs you showing up every day, providing your unique knowhow, skillset, and character. Chances are that you are very difficult to replace as a worker or colleague.

Unfortunately, some business management experts have adopted the modern notion that all workers are dispensable. These so-called experts believe that businesses run like machines and that workers are merely interchangeable cogs that can be swapped in and out at will. This is patently untrue. Anybody who has ever run a business knows enough to reject this notion. Nobody is dispensable. Every compensated associate plays a vital role.

This is not to say that losing an employee causes the system to grind to a halt. People quit sometimes. People make lateral moves or take promotions to other divisions or employers. Layoffs and firings happen. People retire, although they shouldn't, and people switch fields. None of this means that a business must grind to a halt. Businesses find a way to carry on. But there is a cost associated with losing personnel. This is why companies strive for maximum retention rates. Having a high incidence of employee turnover is expensive and disruptive to workflow and customer satisfaction. High turnover of staff also makes it difficult for companies to build a brand. While companies like Google and Microsoft technically could fire and replace all of their employees overnight, the resulting companies would not be the same even if they hired all of the same positions and retained the same corporate structure. People make all of the difference in any company. Why do you think companies continue to pay high salaries to senior and upper-level employees when they could easily just hire a newly minted graduate into the position for a third of the payroll expense? The answer is that seasoned employees add value, far more than the sticker price of their higher salaries. Continuity of personnel leads to a continuity of business, which is good for the bottom line and brand building.

This is why researchers and employers the world over have devoted so much time and resources into figuring out how to retain staff. They understand that good personnel are not easily replaced. This only applies to good personnel, of course. Staff members that do not function efficiently and effectively and do not add value to the company or increase the bottom line are quite dispensable.

Not working makes it very easy to become isolated because no one has an economic incentive to stay in contact with you, nor do you have an incentive to communicate with others. Think about how much of your daily interaction and human connections flow directly from your professional life. You have coworkers and customers. You may be part of a work association with fellow workers, professional groups, and self-improvement and development programs. One of the keys to this equation is that you see these people regularly. Scientific studies have proven that forging human connections requires proximity and repeated unplanned social interactions—these are hard to replicate in a nonworking life. As a worker, you are an indispensable part of a larger operation. You are in regular contact with others. And you are serving people, which creates bonds of love that idle play cannot.

The people with whom you work really care about you, provided you are a good coworker. If you have ever had the unpleasant experience of working with somebody who regularly slacks off at work, if they show up at all, you will know what I mean. Showing up matters. Showing up ready to work matters even more. Good workers are missed when they miss a day, change jobs, or retire. Their absence causes real problems and hardships for the company. Therefore, your connection with others at work is inherently significant. And no one wants to work with someone who doesn't show up and put in the effort. By filling your needed position as a hardworking, moral, enthusiastic, service-oriented worker, you ensure that your bosses, coworkers, and customers will appreciate you and recognize you as the valuable asset that you are.

Earlier we looked at several Hebrew words for "friend," of which there are many because friendship and connection is so important in ancient Jewish wisdom. I now want to introduce one more Hebrew word for friend: *haver*. If you divide this word down the middle, you get *hav*, which is another word that forms the essence of friendship. *Hav* is Hebrew for "obligation." This tells us that a friend is somebody to whom we have obligations.

Relationships are intensified by a sense of obligation. On a practical level, you can use this principle to help make new friends and establish new connections. Doing favors for someone is the best way to make friends, and not just because people like favors. Doing someone a favor is a subtle but powerful way of entering into an obligation with another person. When you do someone a favor, they feel obligated to return the favor. Doing favors creates bonds and reoccurring interaction between those who do business together.

Treat this as a tool for making friends and business contacts, but do not approach this cynically or in a self-interested fashion. I am not saying we should grant favors or request them in order to manipulate people into liking us. Do favors because you have a genuine interest in making connections. Though you must not be cynical about this, you may be pragmatic. Favors establish and reinforce business connections and you do yourself no justice by ignoring this truth. Doing favors for someone obligates them to do the same in kind. You don't want to go around doing this to collect on favors. That would be self-interested. You do this so that you can establish a "conversation" of favors. You do it to establish communication and lasting connections. There is a joy in doing other people favors and it is something both parties can and should engage in. It's a wonderful thing that brings people closer together and binds them. That is your goal. The side benefit is that the person you do a favor for feels an obligation to reciprocate the favor, and this establishes a cycle that intensifies the relationship. This is what friendship is: a set of reoccurring obligations that people fill. Two people that have and feel no obligations to one another are not friends. They aren't in any kind of relationship at all.

What is friendship but a relationship between people who do each other favors and incur obligations to one another? Often people express happiness that they are married to their best friend. They may consider themselves lucky. But is it luck? Or is it a self-fulfilling prophecy? I contend it is always the latter. Friendship is based on having shared obligations. Is there anyone in the world you share more obligations with than your spouse? Of course not. And so it is only natural that married people identify their spouses as their best friends. Marriage is one of the greatest obligations you can enter into with another person. And obligation produces friendship. Therefore marriage begets deep and lasting friendship.

But obligation and friendship are not confined to marriage. Serving each other in the "favor economy" is another way we develop such deep connections.

Doing a person a favor in order to make friends is not the only way to apply this principle. That is a highly effective way of making friends, but occasionally you will meet a person for whom you simply cannot do a favor. You may want to become friendly with this individual for personal and professional reasons and you know that friendship is based on obligation. So you are doing your best to engender a sense of obligation in him by doing favors, but due to circumstance, or your lack of ability to actually help them, you simply cannot find a way to do them a real favor. There's absolutely nothing you can do for this person.

So what do you do in a situation like this? When you cannot offer someone a favor, you do the reverse: you ask a favor of them, instead. This is the same principle working in the reverse direction. You might be astonished how often they will say yes, but you shouldn't be. Good people like being asked for favors, so long as they are reasonable favors. Most people will go out of their way to do a favor that is within their reach, provided the request is reasonable and doesn't require them to compromise their reputation or relationships. Most people jump at the chance to fulfill reasonable favors. And once someone does you a favor, the lines of communication are now open. And now you are obligated to them and will more easily be able to do them a favor. From there, the relationship strengthens as favors and goodwill are passed back and forth.

Remember that these relationships are everything in your personal and professional life. They are the lifeblood of your career and, by extension, your personal life. This is the main reason to shy away from retirement. Retirement severs, mutes, and precludes these deep professional connections. In doing so, retirement tends to isolate us, both while in retirement and during the course of our careers. Planning for retirement signals that you are only in it for the money and this turns off business associates, whether they realize it or not. They will be lukewarm to you even if they can't say exactly why you engender negative feelings in them.

More than anything else, isolation destroys our ability to create money and build prosperity. Recognize that this is about more than making money. Your salary or wage is not just a measure of purchasing power. Money is a quantifiable analog for your entire life force. Money is the aggregate of your time, skills, persistence, morality, and ability to build and maintain relationships. People with many strong relationships tend to be people with lots of money. People who hold themselves to a high moral standard tend to be wealthier than those who fail to live virtuously. Those who have lived dissolute lives in which they failed to make and keep commitments and accept discipline do not tend to do well financially. If you live in such a way, you simply will not prosper. Only those who live by God's laws will truly prosper, spiritually, mentally, physically, and financially.

Money plays a central role in God's plan for creation and human economic interaction by forcing us to live a deliberate, purposeful, calculated life. This is the beauty of money and the economy. The particular placement of money at the center of all economic and social interaction gives us a vested interest in committing to mutual subservience. It keeps us from floating along, happy-go-lucky, doing what we want just because we feel like it. Money is not the goal and you will not thrive on ill-gotten funds and goods. The result of this way of thinking has led many people to lead miserable lives of poverty. It has led them to lead lives in which they do very little to help those around them.

A purposeful, examined, deliberate life naturally follows from having the right perspective on money and its role within creation. Remember Samuel Johnson's sentiment: People are never more innocently occupied than when they are trying to make money. How could anybody be hurting you by trying to make more money? They cannot. A business professional must serve you and serve you well in order to make money. Anyone who goes into business pursuing an idea that doesn't serve people is going to go out of business. It was a dud idea from the start if it failed to serve anyone. If he is smart, he will try something else. He will keep trying until he succeeds.

Earning money is a good and healthy activity for everybody because it forces us to build and maintain relationships. It forces us to be good to one another. Earning money forces us to find ways, often new and ingenious ways, to serve one another. Earning money allows us to live a measured and reasonable life without excess as long as we are focused on earning money in the right ways—by serving people. This may sound counterintuitive to you if you have been indoctrinated to view the pursuit of wealth as a self-interested, immoral act. You have probably been told that money is the root of all evil, when in fact it is the foundation of all good. Money is one of the driving forces behind human interaction. You have probably been told again and again that money is not the most important thing in life. No, it is not the most important thing in life, but neither is it the least important.

Sometimes people accuse me of holding the belief that life is all about money. They accuse me of thinking about nothing other than money. This is far from the truth. Money is not all I think about. But I will freely admit that I do spend much time thinking about money, because money is more important than my hobbies. When we are earning money, we know that we are serving at least one other person. So, yes, guilty as charged—I think about money every single day! I love sailing and I love a good meal. But I do not engage in these activities every day, nor do I think about them every day. But other than on the Sabbath, not a day goes by in which I do not think about money. Am I doing my best to serve and earn? Am I finding the best opportunities to do so? I ask these questions of myself constantly. Doing so is as natural as breathing and just as necessary to life.

Making money and thinking about money makes not only for a better life, but also for a better society. The good that comes from wealth creation transcends the benefit of any one person. Making money isn't just about me and my bank account. It is about me actively helping to build a prosperous community, society, and nation. It is not about just me. Focusing on me, focusing on my own money, is just the best, most natural, and preordained mechanism by which I am best able to serve you, and us, and Him. I focus on my career, you focus on yours, and together we build a better, healthier economy.

As we draw to the close of this book, I want to tell you a story of my life. I consider myself very blessed. I live on a beautiful island in the Pacific Northwest. My family is happy and we want for very little. We are comfortable and happy as can be. I say a prayer of gratitude every morning, honestly, for being able to live where and how I do. I live on the middle of the island, though. Around the perimeter of the island there are about 300 waterfront homes. To be perfectly honest, I would very much like one of these waterfront homes. I really would. Being right on the water must be splendid. You get to have a private dock and you can park your boat right outside your front door. That is something this seafaring rabbi could get used to!

But I am not the only one who wants one of these waterfront houses. Millions of people in America would like a waterfront home too, but there are only about 300 here to be had. So how do we decide who gets one and who doesn't? How do we make that decision? There are really only five ways to do so, some better and some worse than others.

The first way is to hold a lottery. The outcome is totally random. Three hundred lucky people get a free home and everyone else is out of luck. You might think this is a terrible idea, and it is, but let's not forget that almost every state in the United States holds government lotteries. And, yes, they are terrible ideas, every last one of them. The lottery is like a tax on the naïve and desperate people. Sometimes, the government will try to gussy the scheme up by painting it as a good cause. Often lotteries are used to pay for education, for example. Education is great, but there are more equitable and moral ways to raise money for schools. The lottery cultivates a terrible culture of winning, not earning. Gambling fools people into thinking they can receive the benefit of serving others without having to put in the work.

If a lottery turns you off too, consider the second option: brute force and survival of the fittest. We could reward the houses to whoever could take them by force. I could recruit and arm a hundred thugs to do it for me. Now you might laugh at that system, but unfortunately there are many parts of the world today where this is the economic system. Property is divided based upon the use of force. Dictators do this. Tribes do this. Criminal thugs around the world do this. It is the system of tyranny and anarchy.

But maybe you are a strong person and this sounds like a good way for you to take one of the waterfront houses for yourself. Just don't forget, once you get the house, you have to keep it under your control. You have to keep your army of thugs around to keep someone else from coming in to evict or even kill you. This scenario invariably leads to a brutish and unpleasant existence, even for those on top. Dictators, mobsters, and cartel owners operate in this world and even those on top are at constant risk of being dethroned and dispatched. I, for one, would rather keep my quiet life and little house in the middle of the island than risk my neck for a waterfront home. So this method has drawbacks, but it is certainly a way to assign ownership of the houses.

What some might consider a more civilized way to decide who gets the houses is to set up a committee to assign ownership. We get a few politicians, a couple of academics, and some bureaucrats all into the same room and we form a think tank. They are tasked with the job of deciding who should receive the houses. But do they pick who is most worthy? On what basis would they make these decisions?

As it turns out they have no problem assigning ownership of the homes. What might come as a surprise is that all of the most worthy and deserving people in the world just happen to be closely related to the people sitting on the committee. What a coincidence! Also, some of the people on this committee seem to suddenly be very rich, as if someone had just sent them large sums of money. But as we all know, bureaucrats and politicians are not venal people. Surely not! You may be laughing at my cynicism, but this is again how property has been distributed in many parts of the world. Such cronyism and nepotism exists all around the world, even here in the United States. The problem with this system is that people are venal. Power corrupts. Absolute power corrupts absolutely.

So none of these ideas sound too great, huh? The problem is that there always seem to be winners and losers, right? What if there were a way we could all enjoy the waterfront? This brings us to the fourth option: give the waterfront houses not to a few people, but to everybody. How is this possible? By pulling down all the houses on the waterfront and turning the whole ring into a beautiful public beach that wraps all the way around the island. This way everyone gets to be on the waterfront. Isn't that great? Even setting aside the destruction of wealth that pulling down the houses causes, this doesn't really solve the initial problem. The waterfront houses are gone and the land has been socialized and made public, but what about the ring of houses behind the waterfront houses? These are now the best on the island. Not only do they have closest access to the water, they also have beach access, too! So how do we decide who gets these houses? Unless we are prepared to tear down all of civilization, we are back to square one.

Clearly none of these methods are workable or desirable. There is only one other option I know of. If you think of another, please feel free to write me about it and I will add it to my next book. But I really don't think there's anything else. There are only five, and here is the fifth: We invent something called money. Money allows each and every one of us to decide how badly we want that waterfront house. We have a limited number of these tokens, and the person willing and able to part with the most tokens gets the waterfront house of their choice. We each have to decide if we want the waterfront house more than we want a vacation, a nice car, or a good education for our children. Do you want the house more than you want your current career? Because to get it, you might have to give up your current career and pursue more education and enter a more lucrative career field to get one of the waterfront houses. You are welcome to bid as much of your money as you can spare. You get to decide how much to bid and everybody else does the same.

Do you think this is a perfect system? Is this system without any drawbacks? No, I don't think so. I can see there are obvious problems. But it is clearly a better way of assigning ownership of the houses, a very scarce resource, than any of the other four options. There's no brute force involved, no random chance, no opportunity for corruption, no wanton destruction of the very thing you were trying to divvy up. It's a straightforward direct system.

The best part of the system, of course, is that achieving a waterfront house, or anything else you want to buy, impels you to serve your fellow human beings with enthusiasm, passion, zeal, and dedication in an attempt to earn enough money to make a high bid for a waterfront house. And what's wrong with that? We've all been conditioned to

think that there's something crass about earning money. We are indoctrinated to believe that money is a tainted object. We are taught to turn
our noses up at money in order to put on airs of a higher sensibility.
This is folly, though.

Money is a miracle of God. Money is something that helps us live
good, healthy, productive lives. Money is something that generates a
deep desire in each and every one of us to serve our fellow human
beings without ever stopping, without ever staring longingly at a clock
or calendar, waiting for the hour and day on which we can go home
and never have to help someone again.

Money is not evil. It does great good in the world. We live in a
world where the greatest thrills, the deepest passions, and the most profound joy come from serving God's other children. Doing that from
the moment we start working and not stopping until the day that the
good Lord invites us home is the best way to live a fulfilling and meaningful life. And what a glorious and magnificent ride it is. We get to
spend each day building our lives around the magnificence of making
money, building not only lives in which we each do well, but also lives
in which we do good for one another.

Final Thoughts

Now that you have come to the end of this book, I have one last lesson to impart. Taking in all of the knowledge contained within this book has probably felt like a long journey. But there is one more journey that this material must make. It is not a journey from my mouth to your ears—that has already happened. It is not the journey from your ears to your brain. Again, that has already happened. You now know what you need to do. The final journey is for the information and wisdom contained in this book to move from your head to your heart.

You have to now transition from knowing what to do to actually willfully doing it. And you have to want that. It is easier for us to do what our heart wants than what our heads tell us we should do. You must therefore move everything you learned from this book from your head to your heart so that you will actually *want* to employ the tips, tools, techniques, and principles previously discussed.

Do this, and these biblical business secrets will become not only a part of what you think and what you know, but also a part of who you are and how you live. Do this and making money will no longer be an unpleasantness to be endured for 40 to 50 hours a week. Making money will become your calling. You will integrate your soul and your body, unite your values with your work, and be filled with the delight of serving God's children each minute of your working day. You will know that each and every dollar that flows into your bank account is yet another eloquent witness to the effectiveness with which you have served others.

May God bless your efforts and your diligence in following this Biblical blueprint and may bountiful abundance be your lot for all your days.

About the Author

Rabbi Daniel Lapin

Rabbi Daniel Lapin, noted rabbinic scholar, best-selling author, and host of *The Rabbi Daniel Lapin Radio Show* on San Francisco's KSFO, is one of America's most eloquent speakers. He is famous for his ability to extract life principles from ancient Jewish wisdom and make them accessible to people of every background. He is credited with encouraging vast numbers of Christians and Jews to re-embrace their respective faiths. *Newsweek* magazine included him in its first list of America's fifty most influential rabbis. With his wife Susan, he hosts the daily television show *Ancient Jewish Wisdom* on the TCT Television Network.

He is president of the American Alliance of Jews and Christians, (www.aajc.org), the national organization promoting Biblically-based Judeo-Christian values and is one of America's most compelling voices in defense of what he calls Ethical Capitalism.

Before immigrating to the United States in 1973, Rabbi Lapin studied Torah, physics, economics, and mathematics in Johannesburg, London, and Jerusalem. Rabbi Lapin was the founding rabbi of Pacific Jewish Center, a now legendary Orthodox synagogue in Los Angeles.

Rabbi Lapin is a frequent speaker for trade groups, political, social, and civic institutions, financial conferences, organizations, and companies. He also speaks regularly at synagogues and churches around the world.

An enthusiastic boater who has sailed his family across the Pacific on their own boat, Rabbi Lapin lives with his wife Susan, who home-schooled their seven children on Mercer Island, Washington.

Index

Did you enjoy this book?

OTHER TEACHINGS
FROM RABBI DANIEL LAPIN

www.RabbiDanielLapin.com

Books

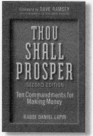

Hardcover Book

Thou Shall Prosper (2nd Edition): Ten Commandments for Making Money

Thou Shall Prosper explains:
- Why Jews throughout the ages flourish economically
- How you can benefit from this Jewish wisdom
- What "being in business" means, whether you are a professional, a CEO or flipping burgers
- Why you should never retire

Softcover Book

Thought Tools: Fifty Timeless Truths to Uplift and Inspire

Vol. 1, Vol. 2

- Reprogram the software of your soul with these popular bite-sized message.
- Each page provides a launching pad for thoughtful conversation and growth
- Travel with Rabbi Lapin through the pages of the Bible, the Jewish year and the Hebrew language

Softcover Book

Buried Treasure

Secrets for Living from the Lord's Language
(2nd edition – hardcover book)

Discover God's understanding of
- Love
- Happiness
- Faith
- Wealth

Two audio CD set plus
a 16-page study guide

Genesis Journeys:
Clash of Destiny

Decoding the Secrets of Israel and Islam

- What Muslims know about prayer that most people, even those who pray regularly, don't
- The dark side of laughter
- Why recruits in Arab terrorist training camps say "Heil Hitler"
- How to rise above our cultural and genetic legacy

Two audio CD set plus
a 16-page study guide

Genesis Journeys:
Tower of Power

Decoding the Secrets of Babel

- How every Hebrew Biblical name has a meaning that sheds light on the person's true character
- The seductive lure of socialism and how it affects you
- What both Abraham and Pharaoh have to do with the Tower of Babel
- Why companies often fail after constructing huge buildings

Two audio CD set plus
a 16-page study guide

Genesis Journeys:
The Gathering Storm

Decoding the Secrets of Noah

- What parenting technique Noah used that resulted in his children being saved
- Why the dimensions given for the ark are vital for your life
- The hidden meaning of the entire "begat" section of Genesis
- Similarities between our own days and the days preceding the Flood

Continued on next page

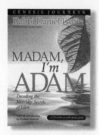

Genesis Journeys: Madam, I'm Adam

Decoding the Marriage Secrets of Eden

- Why understanding the Hebrew words for man and woman can improve your marriage
- Can "being in the mood" destroy your marriage
- What is the difference between a physically mature male and a Man?
- Who is more responsible when a couple divorces – the husband or the wife?

Two audio CD set plus a 16-page study guide

Biblical Blueprint Audio Series

One Audio CD

Day for Atonement

Heavenly Gift of Spiritual Serenity

Day for Atonement answers these questions:
- Are you handicapped by yesterday's mistakes
- The truth behind astrology and horoscopes
- Why the Bible mentions the Day of Atonement three separate times
- Jonah's lesson for your life

One Audio CD

The Ten Commandments

How Two Tablets Can Transform Your Life and Direct Our Nation

- Why the Ten Commandments must be displayed in public
- How positive human interaction is based on these vital verses
- Why they had to be on two tablets, not just one
- How crucial differences between America and the old Soviet Union are dictated by each country's attitude toward these phrases

Continued on next page

Continued from previous page

One Audio CD

Let Me Go

How to Overcome Life's Challenges and Escape Your Own Egypt

- What three Bible secrets can help everyone escape difficult times
- Did Moses really say, "Let My People Go"
- How to recognize your angels in disguise
- Why the Jews needed to leave Egypt in broad daylight

One Audio CD

Festival of Lights

Transform Your 24/7 Existence Into a 25/8 Life

- Are you handicapped by how you think of time
- What do the numbers 8 and 25 mean in ancient Jewish wisdom
- What lessons of Chanuka are embedded in Scripture

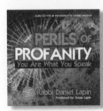

One Audio CD

Perils of Profanity

You Are What You Speak

- How vulgar speech damages your chances for success in both business and personal relationships
- Why Joseph recounted his dreams to his brothers, knowing that they would be angered
- What damage to the soul comes from using or hearing profanity
- Why everyone, even those who don't curse, should be concerned about the prevalence of foul language in our culture

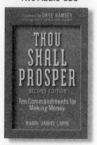